To the incomparable Elizabeth R. Peck...I had no idea how much my life would change when you answered that posting so long ago...thank you.

To Karen...nothing quite like selling a house, packing your goodies and editing a book. All in the same day.

Welcome to Charlotte: The Queen City photography from the UNC-Charlotte archives.

A special Thank you to Visit Charlotte, the sales and marketing arm of the Charlotte Regional Visitors Authority.

To others unnamed, because my memory is as short as my hair.

You can find us at www.signaturetastes.com and on Facebook: Signature Tastes of Charlotte

Copyright ©2011 by Smoke Alarm Media

ALL RIGHTS RESERVED. No part of this book may be reproduced or transmitted in any form by any means, unless you have a note from your mother giving you permission. In lieu of a note, please contact Smoke Alarm Media at 2950 Newmarket Place, Bellingham, WA 98226.

Layout by Steven W. Siler

Photography by Steven W. Siler except where noted.

Library of Congress Control Number: 2011914982

Siler, Steven W.

 Signature Tastes of Charlotte: Favorite Recipes from our Local Kitchens

 ISBN 978-0-9867155-4-9

 1. Restaurants-North Carolina-Charlotte-Guidebooks. 2. Cookery-North Carolina-Charlotte

Printed in the United States of America

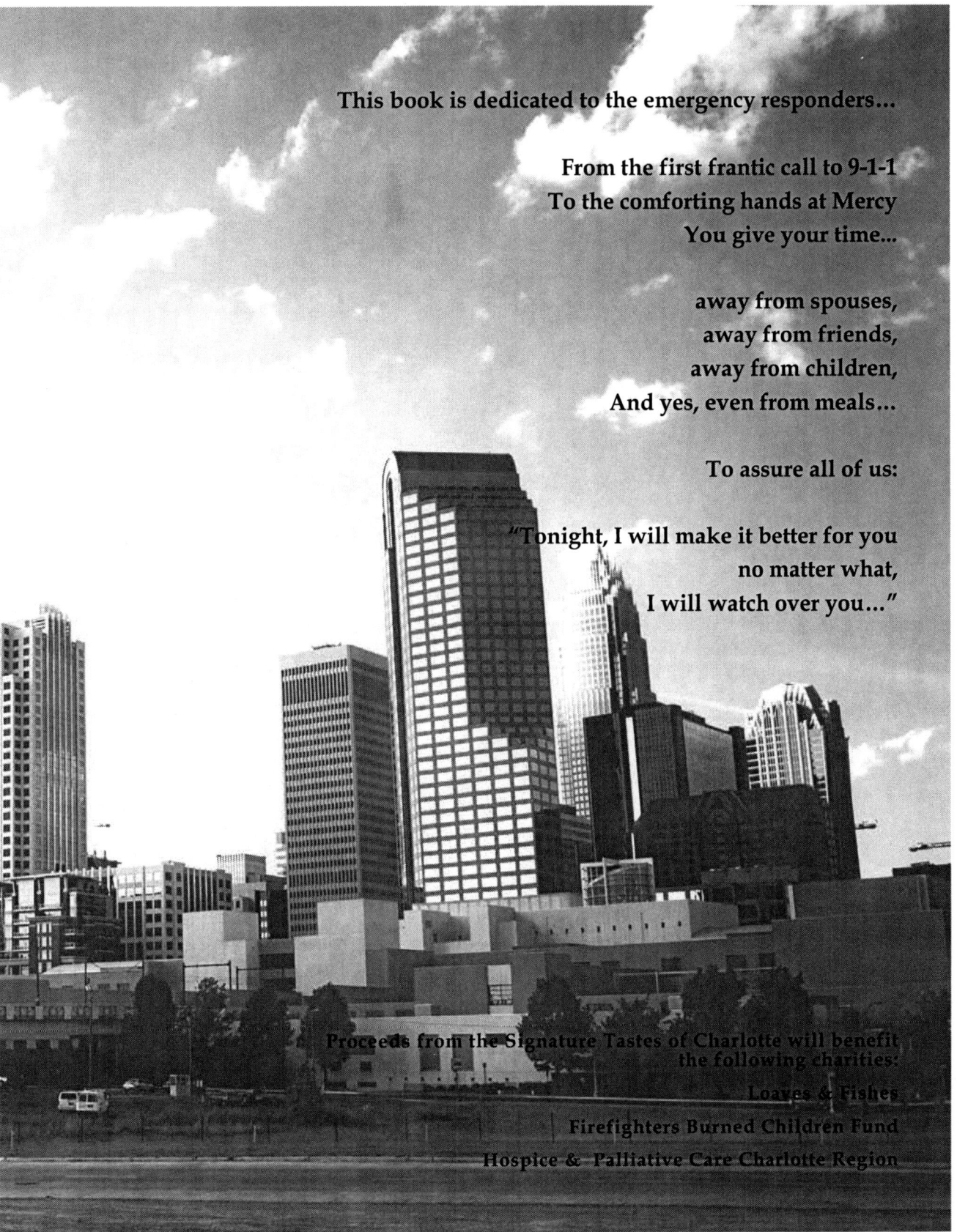

This book is dedicated to the emergency responders...

From the first frantic call to 9-1-1
To the comforting hands at Mercy
You give your time...

away from spouses,
away from friends,
away from children,
And yes, even from meals...

To assure all of us:

"Tonight, I will make it better for you
no matter what,
I will watch over you..."

Proceeds from the Signature Tastes of Charlotte will benefit
the following charities:
Loaves & Fishes
Firefighters Burned Children Fund
Hospice & Palliative Care Charlotte Region

I have always wondered if anyone really reads the Table of Contents. Now since this is a cookbook, I should have organized everything under its proper heading, like soups, pasta, desserts and the like. This is not just a cookbook as much as a Culinary Postcard; a celebration of the city itself...about the eateries, fine dining, casual dining, bars, drive -ins, and of course, the people.

Welcome to Charlotte: The Queen City............7

The Eateries...

15 North Roadside Kitchen 19	LaVecchia's Seafood Grille 119
Alexander Michael's Restaurant & Tavern 21	The Liberty 121
Amelie's … A French Bakery and Cafe 23	Lit'l Taste of Heaven 123
Aria Tuscan Grille 25	Lulu 125
Ballantyne Country Club 27	Mac's Speed Shop 127
Big Daddy's Burger Bar 29	Mama Ricotta's 129
Heidi Billotto-Food Editor 31	Robin Marshall 131
Barrington's 33	Shane McDevitt 133
Beef & Bottle 37	McNinch House Restaurant 135
Bistro La Bon 39	Mez 137
Blue Restaurant 41	Midwood Smokehouse 139
Bonterra - Dining and Wine Room 43	Mimosa Grill 141
Cafe Monte French Bakery and Bistro 45	Mike Minter 143
Cajun Queen 47	Moe's Original Bar B Que 145
Canine Cafe 49	Morton's The Steakhouse 147
Cantina Fifteen Eleven 51	New South Kitchen 149
Carpe Diem 53	NIX Burger and Brew 151
Charlotte City Club 55	The Not Just Coffee Shop 153
Charlotte Fire Department 57	The Olde Mecklenburg Brewery 155
Charlotte Regional Visitors Authority 61	Paco's Tacos and Tequila 157
The Charlotte Symphony 63	Park Lanes 159
Char Bar No. 7 65	The Penguin Drive-In 161
The Chef's Wife-Bonnie Jones 67	Pewter Rose Bistro 163
Clean Catch Fish Market 73	Petit Philippe/Twenty Degrees Chocolate ..165
Common Market 75	Providence Cafe 167
Compass Group 77	Queen City Exclusive 169
Cowfish Sushi - Burger - Bar 81	Queen's Sweets 171
Crave Dessert Bar 83	Red Rocks Cafe 173
Cuisine Malaya 85	Roots Farm Food - Good Local Food 175
Customshop 87	Roosters Wood-Fired Grill 177
The Diamond Restaurant 89	The Secret Chocolatier 179
Dressler's Restaurant 91	The Speedway Club 181
The Fig Tree Restaurant 93	Soul Gastrolounge 183
Firebirds Wood Fired Grill 95	Stool Pigeons Restaurant 185
FireWater 97	Table 274 187
Shiela H. Fletcher 99	Terrace Cafe 189
Fran's Filling Station 101	The Tiny Chef 191
Global Restaurant 103	Tom Condron 193
Greater Charlotte HTA 105	Upstream 195
The Hickory Tavern 109	Vida Mexican Kitchen y Cantina 197
Beverly Howard 111	Village Tavern 199
Johnson & Wales University 113	Vivace 201
Kennedy's Premium Bar and Grill 115	Wolfman Pizza 203
King's Kitchen 117	Zada Jane's Corner Cafe 205
	Zebra Restaurant and Fine Catering 207

TABLE OF CONTENTS

TENNESSEE
470 MILES
CHARLOTTE MAINE
1164 MILES
TEXAS
1275 MILES
CHARLOTTE VERMONT
893 MILES
CHARLOTTE IOWA
940 MILES
CHARLOTTE WATERS, AUSTRALIA
9,975 MILES
CHARLOTTE HALL, MARYLAND
390 MILES
CHARLOTTE NORTH CAROLINA
THE CENTER OF THE KNOWN WORLD!

The Queen City

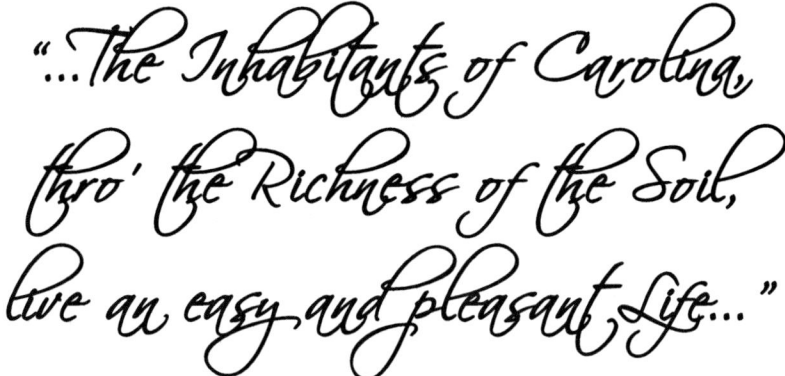

"...The Inhabitants of Carolina, thro' the Richness of the Soil, live an easy and pleasant Life..."

John Lawson, British explorer and author

And while these were the observations of some of the first visitors to the city at the foothills of the Appalachian mountains, they had no way of knowing that this small farming community would rise in national and international prominence to become one of the financial titans of the United States.

The recorded history of Charlotte, as well as that of North Carolina, goes back well over two hundred years. The nickname of "The Queen City" refers to good Queen Charlotte, seen in statuary around the city. "Charlotte Town" is incorporated in 1768, which means the new town will have a courthouse and a prison. Even though the residents disagree with laws set forth by Britain, they hope that naming the town for Queen Charlotte will win favor with her husband, England's King George III.

A flattering portrait of Queen Charlotte

However, the desire to please the King was short-lived. In 1775, The Mecklenburgers announce their freedom with a proclamation called the "Mecklenburg Declaration of Independence." The document forever dissolves the colonists' bonds with Britain. The day is nicknamed Meck Dec Day and will be celebrated annually. The colonists in Charlotte would fight the English until the end of the Revolution in 1783.

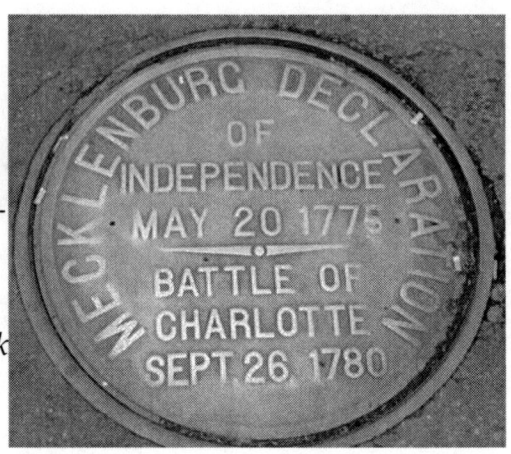

The community would continue to flourish, aided in part by twelve-year-old Conrad Reed, who finds a glittery rock in a stream 25 miles northeast of Charlotte. His father, John, asks a silversmith to identify the 17-pound stone, but no one knows what it is. Once identified, a gold rush boom in Charlotte follows shortly thereafter, one of the first to occur in the nation.

Leading up to the Civil War, Charlotte grows as a tobacco and cotton leader. The fertile soil and temperate climate is ideal for farming, and the business interests grow also as these goods find regional and national customers.

Gold miners digging by hand

THE QUEEN CITY

In 1861, the Civil War begins, and with North Carolina joining the Confederacy, the wages of war are indeed extreme. Upon seceding and joining the other southern states, North Carolina sends and loses more troops than any other state in the Confederacy. As a historical foonote, Confederate President Jefferson Davis meets with his complete Cabinet in Charlotte for the last time at the war's end.

President Jefferson Davis and his cabinet

The years after the war were a rebuilding time. The city's first boom occurred in 1880 as a result of cotton brokerage and the city's terminal for the railroad, doubling the population to over 7,000.

Until now, firefighters in Charlotte have been volunteers. Two companies are white, one is black. Now, in 1887 local elected lawmakers, called the City Council, create the town's first professional fire department. The four firemen who are hired each earn $25 per month.

Charlotte attracts captains of industry and begins to emerge as a model city of the "New South." Belk department store founder W.H. Belk, *Duke Energy visionary James B. Duke, and Southern States Trust president George Stephens (decades later transformed into Bank of America), all plant roots in Charlotte.*

James B. Duke

The Queen City

In 1913, a culinary event would occur that can still be felt today. From Charlotte's street corners, Philip L. Lance sells peanut butter and crackers. By 1926, the Lance Company will occupy a three-story building on South Boulevard. The company that began by selling its products "door-to-door" will offer its snacks from thousands of grocery store shelves for generations to come. The eponymous "Toast-Chee" with its distinctive orange crackers are still found, and popular, today.

Philip L. Lance, taking a break!

Welcome To Charlotte
Charlotte Regional Visitors Authority - 500 S. College Street, Ste 300

11

In 1924, not long after the invention of the automobile, racing has already taken hold in Charlotte. The old dirt track has been replaced, and the first race is run on Charlotte Speedway's new wooden track south of town. The 250-mile race draws nearly 50,000 fans. The track will operate until 1927, then close. The new Charlotte Motor Speedway will not open until 1960.

Wood Brothers Racing, 1960's. Can you imagine racing in a convertible?

THE QUEEN CITY

Although the nation suffers from economic depression, in 1936, North Carolina's first art museum opens - The Mint Museum. The old Charlotte Mint building was dismantled and moved brick by brick from West Trade Street to suburban Randolph Road. Mary Myers Dwelle encouraged donations from Charlotteans to make the project possible.

Original Mint Museum

The onset of war pulls the nation out of the depression, and Charlotte is proud to have more than 20,000 men and women from Mecklenburg County serve in the U.S. military during WWII. After the war, Charlotte remembers its veterans by collecting donations, which fund the construction of Freedom Park, now one of the city's most beloved green spaces.

In 1991, NationsBank, now the present day Bank of America, is announced as a new institution, created by merging two powerful Charlotte and Atlanta-based banks. The new bank is headed by powerful civic leader Hugh McColl, Jr. Now the nation's second leading financial center, the city was fittingly built upon the crossroads of two affluent Native American trading paths. The intersection of these two paths, now major streets, is known as the heart of Charlotte -- "Trade & Tryon."

Portrait of 1920's Trade Street

THE QUEEN CITY

WELCOME TO CHARLOTTE

CHARLOTTE REGIONAL VISITORS AUTHORITY - 500 S. COLLEGE STREET, STE 300

15

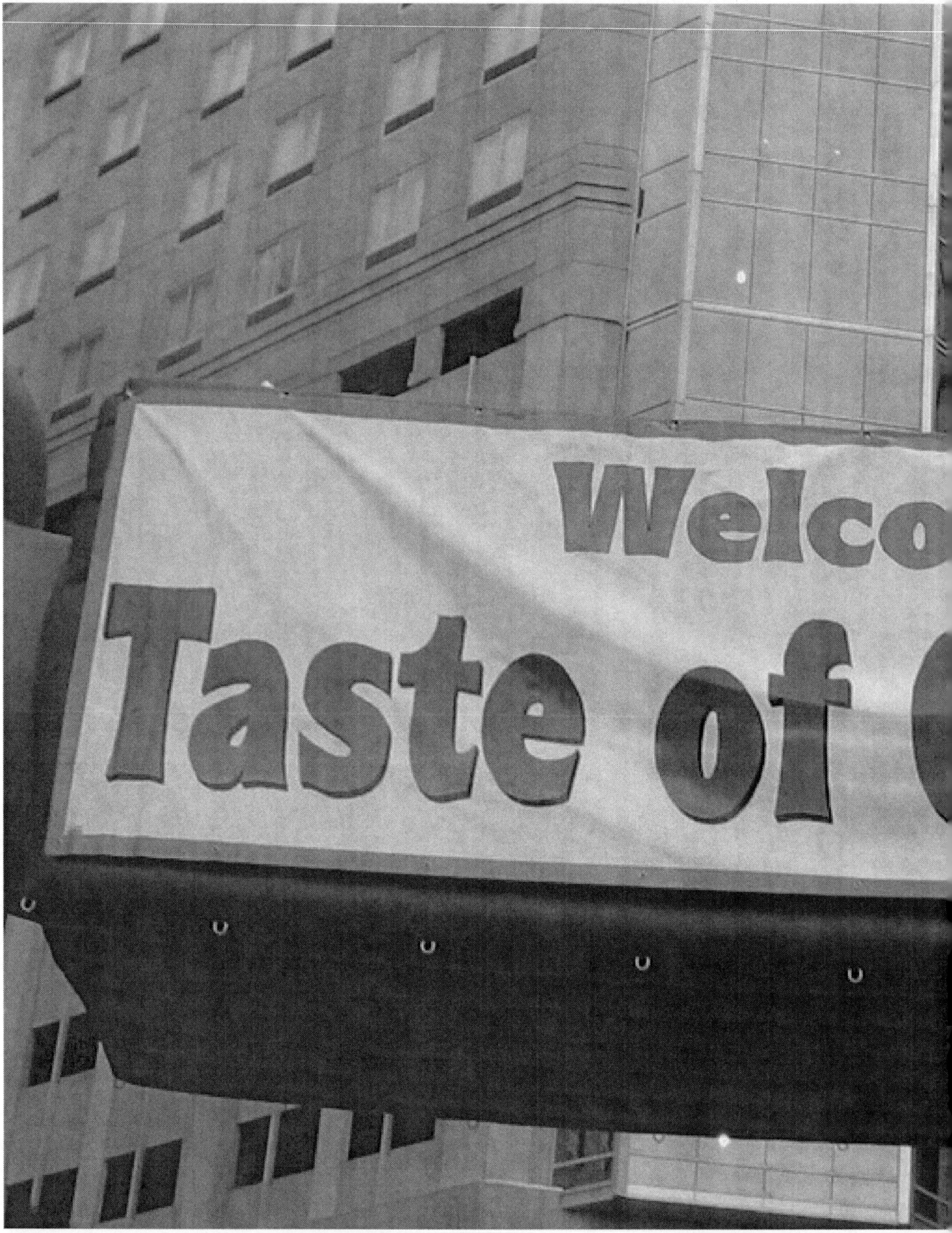
Taste of

Recipes & Restaurants

Chef Michael Bowling in his best "Iron Chef" pose.

Vanilla Braised Short Ribs with Cheddar Grits & Swiss Chard

Signature Tastes of Charlotte

Roadside Kitchens features classic comfort food and some elevated new takes on traditional favorites, built around the area's demographics with fresh and local ingredients. Our chefs, staff, and restaurants provide the best dining experiences through upscale service and food in a casual, relaxed and welcoming environment.

15 North Roadside Kitchen
1513 Montford Drive

4 short ribs
1 vanilla bean, split or
2 Tbsp vanilla extract
6 C. fresh brewed coffee
4 C. beef stock
2 C. red wine
1 carrot, roughly chopped
1 large white onion, large dice
2 stalks celery, roughly chopped
4 cloves garlic, smashed
1 bay leaf
4 Tbsp canola oil
Salt and pepper
1 Tbsp butter
Pinch of sugar
Grits:
1 C. stone ground grits
1 qt. whole milk
⅓ C. sharp cheddar cheese (shredded)
1 Tbsp butter
Salt and pepper to taste
Chard:
1 large bunch Swiss chard, washed
1 clove garlic
4 oz. beef stock
2 Tbsp canola oil
Salt and pepper

1. Pre-heat oven to 275°F. Heavily season the short ribs with salt and pepper. Heat a cast iron skillet with canola oil to the smoking point. Hard sear the ribs in the skillet until caramelized brown on both sides. Remove from the pan and place in the bottom of a casserole. Saute onions, carrots, celery, garlic and bay leaf in the same pan. When the vegetables are tender, deglaze with the red wine and reduce by half. Add all the remaining ingredients to the casserole, and cover tightly with plastic wrap, then with foil. Place in the oven and bake for 3-3½ hours.

2. In a saucepan, bring the milk to a boil. Whisk in the grits and seasoning, and reduce heat to simmer. When the grits are nearly cooked, add the cheddar cheese and butter, and adjust the seasoning if necessary.

3. Get out a large saute pan and heat with canola oil. When hot, saute the chard, adding the garlic about 90 seconds into the cooking. Once most of the greens have wilted down deglaze the pan with the beef stock and add the butter and salt and pepper.

4. Remove casserole from oven when ready, and remove the short ribs from the pan. Strain the liquid into a sauce pan and reduce by a third. Add 1 Tbsp of butter, and season with salt and sugar. Plate the short ribs on top of the grits and greens, and drizzle over top.

"To me heaven would be a big bull ring with me holding two barrera seats and a trout stream outside that no one else was allowed to fish in and two lovely houses in the town; one where I would have my wife and children and be monogamous and love them."
Ernest Hemingway

4TH WARD STROGANOFF

Signature Tastes of CHARLOTTE

ALEXANDER MICHAEL'S RESTAURANT & TAVERN
401 W. 9TH STREET

Al Mike's as it is known, has been a place that has endured and in some instances resisted the many changes that have taken place in our progressive city. We know that we are not for everyone and frankly...some people are just wound too tight to come here. Alexander Michael's is a place you can count on and owes its' success in no small way to the unique individuals that work here now and the people that preceded them.

6 oz. marinated flank steak (cubed)
1 Tbsp finely diced shallots
1 tsp chopped garlic
1 Tbsp butter
1 C. thinly sliced mushrooms
3 Tbsp sour cream
½ C. red wine
1½ C. cooked rotini
¾ C. heavy cream
Salt and pepper (to taste)

1. In a large sauté pan melt butter.

2. Add shallots and garlic and caramelize.

3. Add meat and mushrooms.

4. Sauté until meat is browned.

5. Deglaze the pan with red wine and reduce by half.

6. Stir in sour cream, salt and pepper.

7. Simmer on medium heat for 2 minutes.

8. Add rotini and cream, then toss all ingredients in pan. Let simmer on low heat for 1-2 minutes or until desired consistency is reached.

Makes 1 or 2 servings, depending on how hungry you are.

"Count Pavel Stroganov, a celebrity in turn-of-the-century St. Petersburg, was a noted gourmet as well as a friend of Alexander III. He is frequently credited with creating Beef Stroganoff, but in fact a recipe by that name appears in a cookbook published in 1871, well ahead of the heyday of the genial count... "
Rare Bits: Unusual Origins of Popular Recipes, Patricia Bunning Stevens

Amelie's Signature Spinach Asparagus Leek Soup

Amelie's is a funky French bakery and cafe in the historic NoDa arts district, just five minutes north of Uptown Charlotte. Along with hand-crafted, award-winning pastries and confections, the bakery offers soups, tartines, sandwiches and salads, all make from time-honored family traditions, as well as locally roasted European style coffee. Additionally, the cafe now offers their delicious creations for special events and catering. Open 24/7/365

3 large leeks, sliced into ¼ inch pieces
1 large onion, chopped
3 Tbsp butter
4 medium carrots, sliced into ¼" pieces
1 tsp salt
2½ qts. chicken broth
½ C. long grain rice
1 lb. fresh asparagus, sliced into 1 inch pieces
½ lb. fresh spinach, rinsed
Pepper to taste (and then some!)
1 C. heavy cream

1. In a large pot, sauté leeks and onion in butter until tender.

2. Add salt, broth and rice. Cover and boil for 10 minutes.

3. Add the carrots and boil covered for an additional 10 minutes.

4. Add the potatoes, cover and boil for another 10 minutes.

5. Add the asparagus, cover, and boil for 5 minutes, or until tender. Remove from heat.

6. Add cream, spinach and pepper. Cover and allow spinach to wilt slightly.

Yield: Approximately 15 servings

Signature Tastes of CHARLOTTE

Amelie's ... A French Bakery and Cafe
2424 North Davidson St #102

"Anyone who tells a lie has not a pure heart, and cannot make a good soup."
Ludwig van Beethoven

Ricotta Gnocchi with Sausage and Fennel

Signature Tastes of CHARLOTTE

Bringing the best of Italy to Charlotte, Aria Tuscan Grill & our Bubble Lounge, are Charlotte's newest urban neighborhood restaurant and champagne lounge in the heart of center city. Serving mouthwatering old world comfort food in a modern Italian setting, Aria brings the flavors and colors of Tuscany to Charlotte. From the House Roasted Suckling Pig prepared based upon market availability & seasonal ingredients, to "Grandma B's" Lasagna, Aria features simple, classic Italian with a modern edge in a contemporary atmosphere that is both warm and ultra hip!

Gnocchi:
1½ lb. fresh ricotta
1 C. unbleached all-purpose flour
2 large eggs, beaten
1 tsp salt
¼ tsp black pepper
olive oil
Parsley (garnish)

2 lb. of your favorite Italian sausage, crumbled
1 Tbsp red pepper flakes
1 sweet onion, finely chopped
1 bulb fennel, cored and thinly sliced
1 medium carrot, diced
4 cloves garlic, sliced

2 C. of your favorite tomato sauce
Freshly grated Parmesan cheese

1. Drain the ricotta in a sieve overnight in the refrigerator. Cheese will become firmer.

2. Combine the ricotta, flour, eggs, salt, pepper, and stir together until dough forms.

3. Dust your hands with flour, and shape dough into little balls, and set on a nonstick sheet pan.

4. Bring 5 quarts water to a boil, and set up an ice bath nearby. Drop gnocchi balls in boiling water, stir gently with a wooden spoon. Gnocchi will float when cooked through (about 8 minutes.)

5. Scoop gnocchi with a wire skimmer and transfer to ice bath. When gnocchi are cooled, drain and toss them in olive oil.

6. Cook sausage in a pan until brown; transfer to a plate.

7. Using the same pan, add red pepper flakes, onion, fennel, carrot and garlic, and cook until browned.

8. Add sausage, gnocchi, and tomato sauce to vegetables and simmer over medium heat.

9. Transfer to plate, top with parmesan and parsley garnish. Serve immediately.

ARIA TUSCAN GRILLE
100 NORTH TRYON STREET

"Nothing would be more tiresome than eating and drinking if God had not made them a pleasure as well as a necessity."
Voltaire

Grilled Marinated Skirt Steak

Chef Anthony Sorriano holds a BS degree in Biological Science from Florida State University and a BS degree in Culinary Arts from Johnson & Wales in Rhode Island. After moving to Charlotte to be closer to family, he worked at Upstream Restaurant. He was Executive Chef at Stratos Group's Nolen Kitchen, an upscale 160-seat restaurant. While with Stratos Group, Anthony was responsible for opening the group's brand new Big View Diner, also as the Executive Chef. Anthony and his wife have two young sons.

2 lb. skirt steak, cleaned, and cut into 8 oz. portions

Marinade:
1 C. olive oil
1 oz. Worcestershire sauce
2 oz. garlic, chopped
2 Tbsp fresh oregano, chopped
1 Tbsp black pepper

Salt and pepper to taste

1. Whisk all the marinade ingredients together.

2. Pour over the steaks and marinate overnight. Preheat the grill.

3. Remove the steaks from the marinade and allow excess marinade to drip off. Season with salt and pepper and place on grill.

4. Cook to desired doneness (about 2 minutes a side for medium rare.) Remove from grill to cutting board.

5. Allow to rest several minutes, and slice across the grain for serving.

"Red meat is not bad for you. Now blue-green meat, that's bad for you!"
Tommy Smothers

16

DILWORTH

Big Daddy's

BURGER BAR

EST. ★ 2007

FRENCHIE

Welcome to Big Daddy's Burger Bar. We do exactly what our name suggests - we have amazing burgers, a killer bar, and it's all very, very good. Tucked perfectly into Charlotte's Dilworth and Ballantyne neighborhoods, we love serving you amazing food in a lively, laid-back atmosphere. Big Daddy's is a part of the FS Food Group (Owner Frank Scibelli), including the restaurants Big Daddy's Burger Bar, Cantina Fifteen Eleven, Mama Ricotta's, and Paco's Tacos and Tequila ... Special thanks to Corey Laton for this recipe!

2 lb. ground turkey
¾ C. panko bread crumbs
1 Granny Smith apple, sliced in ⅛ inch slices, seeds removed
8 slices applewood smoked bacon, cooked
1 C. Duke's mayonnaise
6 oz. Brie cheese, sliced in quarter inch slices
¼ C. seasoned salt
¼ kosher salt
4 hamburger buns
1 C. vegetable oil

Turkey Burger:
1. In a large bowl, mix ground turkey and panko together thoroughly. Divide into 6 equal patty portions.

Garlic Mayo:
1. In a small saucepan over medium heat, roast 4 cloves garlic in 1 C. vegetable oil until brown (should acquire a light brown peanut butter color).

2. Remove garlic from pot, and strain as much oil as possible.

3. Puree the garlic while still hot. Allow puree to cool and then whisk into mayonnaise.

Frenchie Seasoning:
1. Mix ¼ C. seasoned salt with ¼ C. kosher salt.

Assembly:
1. Generously season turkey burgers with Frenchie seasoning on both sides.
2. Cook burgers over medium to high heat on grill, until well done.
3. Melt 3 slices of Brie on each burger.
4. While burgers are still cooking, grill apples on a flat portion of the grill.
5. Place burger, with melted Brie, on top of bottom bun.
6. Top with 2 slices of bacon and grilled apples.
7. Spread 1 Tbsp garlic mayo on top bun.
8. ENJOY!

Signature Tastes of CHARLOTTE

BIG DADDY'S BURGER BAR
1626 East Blvd. & 15102sA John J. Delaney Drive

"You can find your way across this country using burger joints the way a navigator uses stars."
Charles Kuralt

Chicken with Savory Blueberry Sauce

Charlotte Culinary Expert, Heidi Louise Billotto has maintained the position of food editor, food and restaurant writer for Charlotte Living Magazine since the spring of 2008. For over a dozen years, prior to joining the staff at Charlotte Living, Heidi has written for local and regional publications about food, wine, chefs, and restaurants in and around Charlotte, North Carolina. Additionally, she hosts cooking classes in her home, offers a monthly culinary series called On the Farm, where she teaches at local farms in and around the Queen City.

For the local blueberry sauce:
3 Tbsp butter
3 Tbsp granulated sugar
1/3 C. dry white wine
1/3 C. orange juice concentrate, defrosted but not diluted
2 Tbsp raspberry vinegar
1 1/4 C. fresh, local blueberries and/or blackberries
1 1/4 C. beef broth
1/2 C. chicken groth
2 Tbsp orange cognac
1 whole local chicken, cut into bone-in serving pieces
Coarse grain sea salt and cracked black pepper
2 Tbsp extra virgin olive oil
Additional blueberries for garnish

1. Heat heavy large skillet over high heat until hot. Drizzle with olive oil.

2. Season chicken pieces with salt and pepper. Add chicken and sear until brown, about 8 minutes per side. Cover and keep warm until ready to serve.

3. Melt 2 Tbsp butter in heavy large skillet over medium-high heat. Add sugar; stir until sugar dissolves and mixture turns deep amber color, about 5 minutes. Remove from heat.

4. Add wine, orange juice and vinegar (mixture will bubble vigorously) and bring to boil, stirring to dissolve caramel.

5. Add berries and both broths; boil, stirring occasionally, until sauce thickens, and is reduced to about 1 C.

6. Strain through sieve into small, heavy saucepan pressing on berries with back of spoon. Mix in cognac. Set sauce aside until ready to serve.

"As far as we can understand when it comes to the blueberry, ... it comes to a harvesting of poop."
Paul Gallo

Barrington's Restaurant

ENTRANCE THROUGH IRON GATES

Apple Salad

Barrington's Restaurant opened in October of 2000 in the neighborhood setting of Fox Croft East in South Park. This cozy bistro style restaurant seats up to 45 people. The food is upscale American with a homey twist; in fact, Barrington's is named after Bruce Moffett's hometown in Rhode Island. The menu changes seasonally and features local and organic produce. In fact on any given Saturday, the entire kitchen staff can be found at the various local farmer's markets sourcing ingredients for nightly specials.

Cranberry Vinaigrette:
- ½ C. cranberries
- ½ C. port
- ½ C. sugar
- ½ C. oil

Salad:
- 1 red apple (Fuji), or one with good acidity
- 1 head belgian endive
- 1 C. baby arugula
- 2 tbsp toasted walnuts
- 2 tbsp crumbled blue cheese
- 2 tbsp lemon vinaigrette
- dash salt
- dash pepper

1. Place cranberries in saucepan with port and sugar and simmer until the cranberries burst.

2. Place mixture in a blender and slowly drizzle oil into the blender. The mixture should emulsify.

3. Strain vinaigrette through a fine strainer. Set aside.

4. Core the apple and then thinly slice apple in "half moons" on a Mandoline.

5. Cut endive in half lengthwise core and slice thinly. Mix endive, walnuts, blue cheese and arugula in a salad bowl.

6. Add vinaigrette and mix gently. Salt and pepper to taste.

7. Layer apple slices and salad on plate.

8. Drizzle with cranberry vinaigrette.

"Anyone can count the seeds in an apple, but only God can count the number of apples in a seed."
Robert H. Schuller

BARRINGTON'S
7822 FAIRVIEW ROAD

Signature Tastes of CHARLOTTE

Scallops over Butternut Squash Risotto with Fennel & Bacon

The word scallop comes from the Old French escalope meaning "shell," referring to the shell that houses the scallop. Scallops are mentioned in print as far back as 1280, when Marco Polo mentions scallops as being one of the seafoods sold in the marketplace in Hangchow, China. Paris restauranteur Gustave Chatagnier featured a special scallops dish on his menu in 1936.

12 or more large fresh pack sea scallops

Squash puree:
1 medium butternut squash
¼ C. honey
1 C. water
1 Tbsp kosher salt

Risotto:
1 small onion, finely diced
4 Tbsp butter
2 Tbsp olive oil
2 C. Arborio rice
½ white wine
1½ C. butternut puree
4 C. water

Garnish:
1 head shaved fennel
½ lb. bacon
juice of one lemon
1 Tbsp olive oil
several chives

1. Peel, halve, and seed the squash, reserving a small chunk to dice for garnish. Take the rest of the squash and cut into ½ inch slices. Transfer to a sealable baking pan with the water, honey and salt. Cover and place in 350°F oven for 45 minutes, or until very tender. Let cool and place in a blender, and puree until smooth, adding water if necessary.
2. Shave the fennel as finely as possible on a mandolin, and place in ice water for up to one day in advance. Drain well before using.
3. Render the bacon in a skillet that is large enough to also hold the scallops for roasting afterward without crowding.
4. To prepare the risotto, start the mixture of squash puree and water in a pot over medium heat, and bring to a light simmer, stirring occasionally.
5. Place the onion, butter and oil in a wide pot and cook on medium high heat until the onion is translucent; then add the rice and cook stirring constantly for a minute. Turn the heat down to medium, then add the white wine and reduce until almost dry. Add the squash liquid in ½ C. increments, stirring constantly throughout the entire cooking process. Just before serving, add the remaining butter, or more, if desired. Season with salt, stirring even more.
6. To prepare the scallops, pat the scallops dry, and season with salt and pepper. Heat the pan with the bacon grease on high heat, place the scallops very carefully into the pan. Let the scallops develop a golden brown crust, then turn off the pan, flip the scallops over, and move to one side. Add the bacon back to the pan to heat.

"The only kind of seafood I trust is the fish stick, a totally featureless fish that doesn't have eyeballs or fins..."
Dave Barry

BEEF 'N BOTTLE

RESTAURANT

Oysters Rockefeller

So many adjectives to describe Beef & Bottle, including cozy, comforting, unpretentious, and in the end, just really, good food. Tucked away in a non-descript building off South Boulevard, Beef and Bottle is the proverbial "more-than-meets the eye" type of restaurant. Under managing partner Rick Bouman, the menu is a straight forward cornucopia of steak and seafood, enough to tempt the palate of the most discriminating foodie.

16 to 18 oysters in shell
1 pt. of oysters (Extra Selects)
1 lb. rock salt
1 c. finely chopped parsley (or equivalent dried parsley)
2 pkg. frozen chopped spinach, thawed and drained
1 c. green onion tops
1 c. melted butter
10 drops Tabasco sauce
¼ tsp salt
½ tsp pepper
¼ tsp garlic powder
¼ C. parmesan cheese or Asiago
⅔ C. bread crumbs

1. Put parsley, onionsand spinach through food processor until finely chopped into a paste. Sprinkle Tabasco sauce on; then mix in bread crumbs, butter and seasoning. Mix well.

2. Open all oysters and use a sharp knife to loosen muscle. Place an oyster from the pint on each shell top. (Doubling the number of oysters).

3. Pour the rock salt on a rimmed cookie sheet (this provides a stable surface for the shells, and retains heat at the table).

4. Place shells on the salt. Put about 1 Tbsp of spinach mixture on each oyster and top with cheese.

5. Bake at 450°F for 5 to 8 minutes or until heated through. Serve with small forks and garnish with lemon.

"I had rather be an oyster than a man, the most stupid and senseless of animals."
George Berkeley

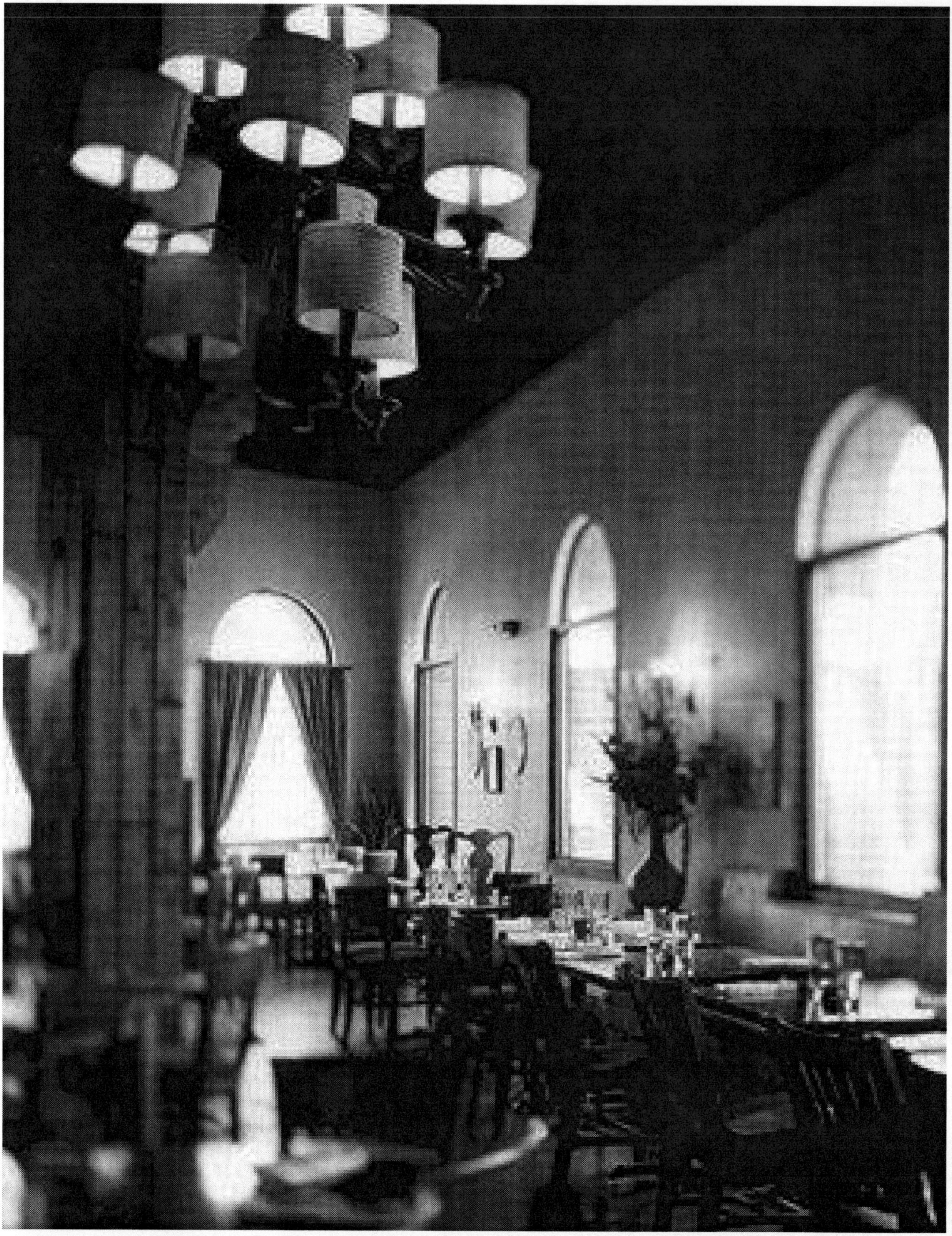

Prince Edward Island Mussels

Signature Tastes of Charlotte

Bistro La Bon is a restaurant that strives to create a unique culinary experience by utilizing the highest quality ingredients and a superior execution of traditional cooking techniques by the multi-talented kitchen staff for a very affordable price. We focus on small plates to illustrate gastronomic creativity to produce appealing cuisine in a way that stimulates the palate both visually and texturally while extracting the maximum amount of flavor through proper cooking. At Bistro La Bon, we shop local every chance we get and local farmers markets are the first destination for fresh produce throughout the week.

15-20 mussels
1 Tbsp olive oil
1 Tbsp shallots, finely chopped
1 Tbsp garlic, finely chopped
2 Tbsp leeks, finely chopped
1 pinch crushed red pepper
½ Tbsp fresh thyme
½ C. dry chardonnay
½ C. chicken stock
¾ C. heavy cream
Pinch of saffron
½ Roma tomato, grated

1. Heat sauce pan and add oive oil, garlic, shallots, and leeks.

2. Sauté 10-20 seconds.

3. Add mussels. Stir mussels to coat with olive oil.

4. Deglaze with white wine.

5. Add chicken stock, cream, saffron, thyme, and tomato. Cover for 1 minute.

6. Remove cover and continue to cook for 3 minutes.

7. Slowly rotate mussels. Salt to taste.

8. Serve with warm bread to dip in the broth.

Bistro La Bon
1322 Central Avenue

"So, have you heard about the oyster who went to a disco and pulled a mussel?"
Billy Connolly, actor and comedian

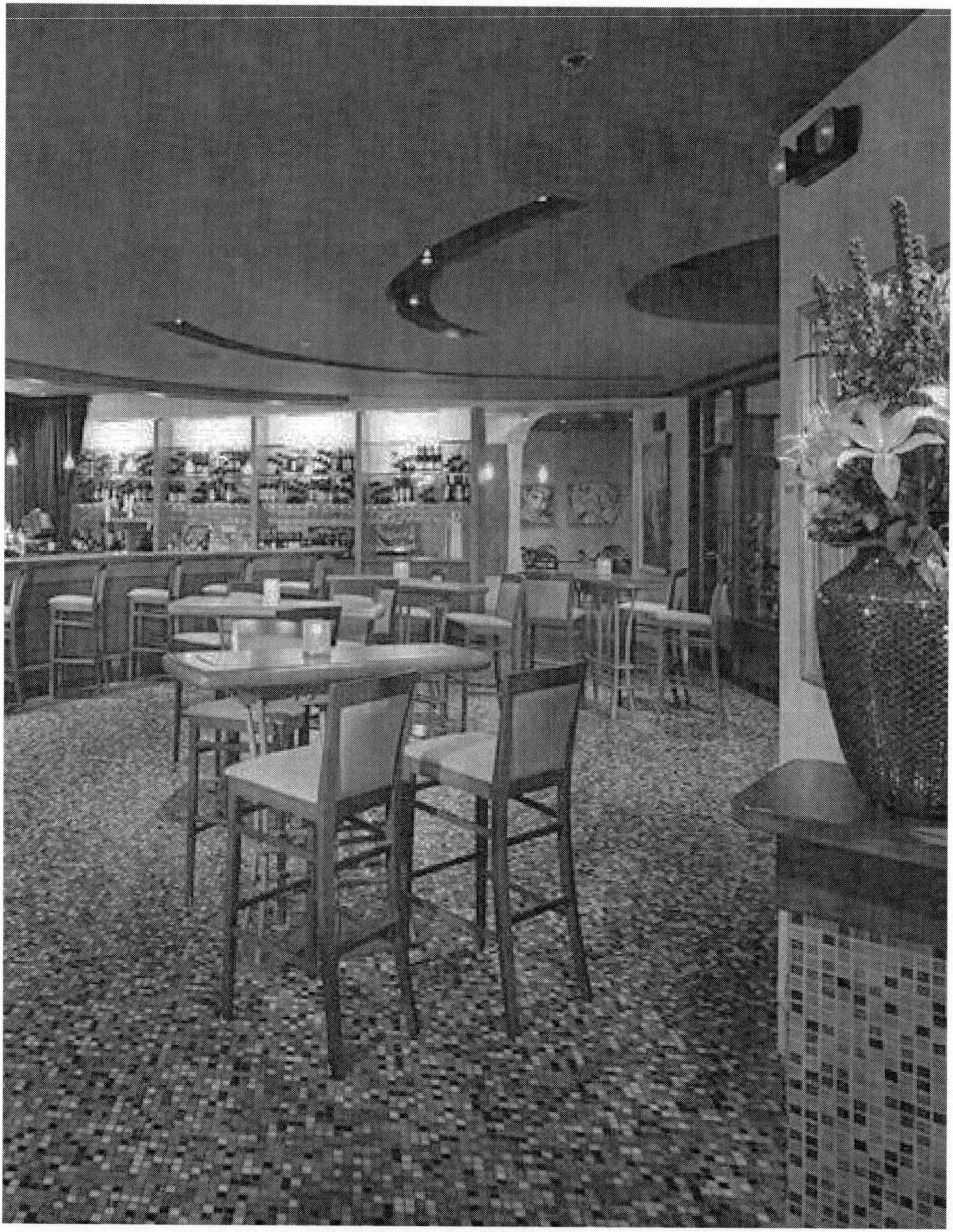

Lamb Tagine

Blue Restaurant & Bar is a sophisticated Charlotte uptown restaurant that offers flavors from around the Mediterranean region. Award-winning Executive Chef Gene Briggs has created a multi-cultural menu that takes fine dining in Charlotte to new heights, and your taste buds on a whirlwind tour. Prepare to experience a Moroccan Tagine, Whole Roasted Mediterranean Sea Bass, or Tenderloin a la Blue. As you travel around our award-winning Charlotte restaurant, the menu will delight you with familiar dishes and excite you by others you have yet to explore.

1 lamb shank
6 green olives
1 Tbsp sliced almonds
6 dried apricots
3 pitted dates
3 dried figs
4 quarters preserved lemons (recipe below)
½ onion, chopped
2 qt. chicken stock
1 Tbsp ras el hanout (recipe below)

Ras el Hanout:
1 tsp turmeric
1 tsp anise
1 tsp cloves
1 tsp allspice
2 tsp sumin
5 tsp cayenne
2 tsp nutmet
2 tsp coriander
1 tsp cinnamon
1 tsp dry mustard
1 tsp smoked paprika
1 tsp ground thyme
2 tsp salt

Preserved Lemons:
2 lemons
5 oz. kosher salt
1 Tbsp pickling spice

1. Heat a large skillet over a medium high heat.

2. Season the lamb shank with salt and brown on all sides.

3. Coat with ras el hanout and add half of all vegetables and fruits to the pan with the shank. Cover with stock.

4. Cover the pan, and place in a 325°F oven for 2½ - 3 hours.

5. Remove shank and strain sauce.

6. Add remaining ingredients, simmer until warm, and pour over shank.

Ras el Hanout:
Combine well and seal tightly.

Preserved Lemons:
Cut lemons into quarters, cover with salt and spice mixture. Seal tightly and store in a cool place for one month.

Signature Tastes of CHARLOTTE

BLUE RESTAURANT
214 NORTH TRYON STREET, #100

" I know the crew so well, so I forget I'm being filmed. It's like cooking with a friend in the kitchen - you're talking, as you do, and maybe you're telling her about this wonderful way to prepare lamb chops - it's more natural, more honest. "
Nigella Lawson

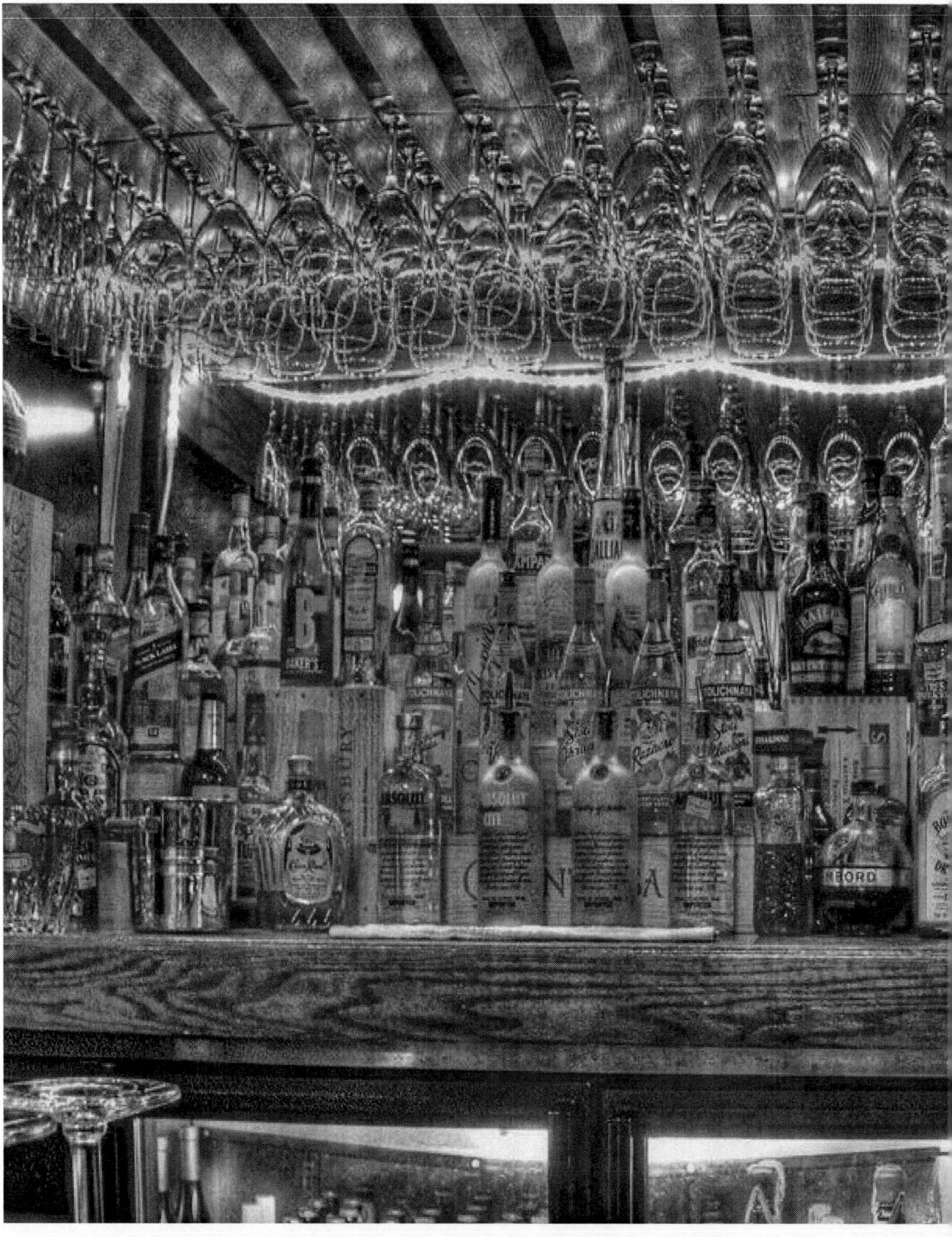

BBQ Duck Spring Roll

Bonterra Dining & Wine Room boasts an elegant, casual setting. Located in the heart of the historic Southend District near Uptown Charlotte, Bonterra is a unique establishment rich with ambiance and flavor. Housed in a renovated 110-year-old church, Bonterra's interior manages to blend the original architectural features of its historic building tastefully with modern additions.

Signature Tastes of Charlotte

1 pack spring roll wrappers
1 egg
1 carrot, grated
1 red onion, grated
6 duck legs
1 gallon duck fat

1. Cure the duck legs by fully submerging in a mixture of ⅓ part sugar and ⅔ parts salt for 24 hours. Rinse well.

2. Melt duck fat in pot. Submerge duck legs in duck fat, and bring to a boil. Simmer for 2 hours, or until meat is falling off the bone. Cool. Pull meat into medium sized pieces. Add salt and pepper, and toss in BBQ sauce to taste.

Assembly:
1. Brush 2 spring roll wrappers with egg wash.

2. Add about the width of a cigar of the BBQ duck mixture, grated carrots and onions.

3. Fold corners and roll tightly.

4. Place in deep fryer (350°F) for 2-3 minutes, or until golden brown.

Suggested plating with some chow chow in center of plate. Spring roll cut on a bias, and placed on the chow chow. Drizzle some BBQ sauce around and serve.

Bonterra - Dining and Wine Room
1829 Cleveland Avenue

"Be like a duck. Calm on the surface, but always paddling like the dickens underneath."
Michael Caine, actor

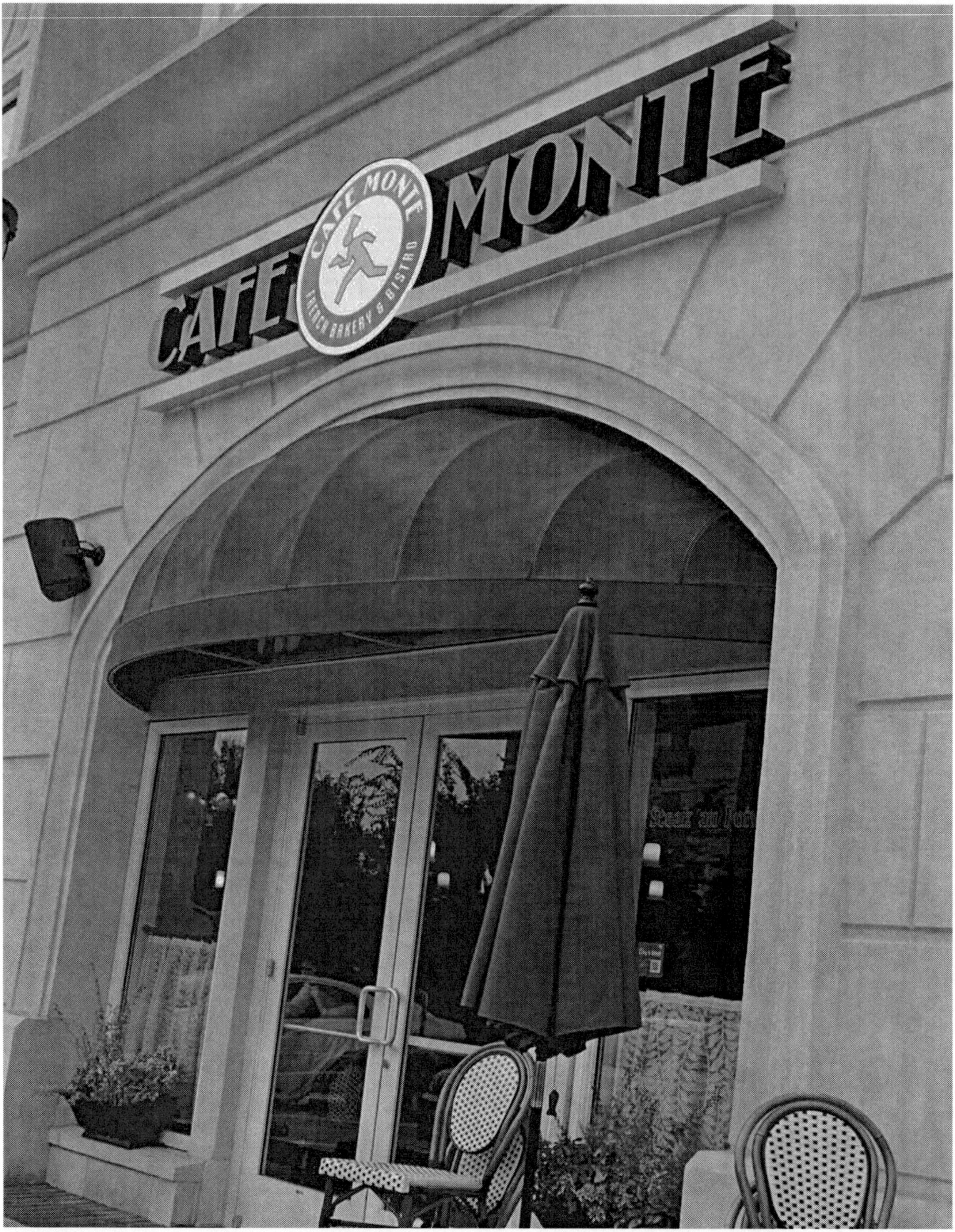
CAFE MONTE
CAFE MONTE
FRENCH BAKERY & BISTRO

Shrimp and Artichoke Crepes

Signature Tastes of CHARLOTTE

Cafe Monte French Bakery and Bistro is committed to using only the highest quality ingredients served fresh at an exceptional value for our customers. Offering breakfast, lunch and dinner seven days a week our goal is to be your neighborhood "Escape from the Everyday." With our value driven menu, farm-to-table specialties and gourmet approach, we make quality French food accessible to all.

⅔ C. lemon béchamel (recipe below)
½ C. quartered artichoke hearts
½ lb. small shrimp, peeled and deveined
¾ C. whipping cream
Pinch kosher salt
½ C. baby spinach
4 warm crepes
1 Tbsp chopped parsley

Lemon Béchamel:
Makes about 3 C.

1 Tbsp unsalted butter
¼ large sweet onion, sliced
4 C. whole milk
1 whole clove, or ¼ tsp ground cloves
Pinch ground nutmeg
½ bay leaf
Pinch kosher salt
1 lemon - juice and zest

1. In a large sauté pan, over medium heat, combine béchamel, artichokes, shrimp, and cream.
2. Add salt, and simmer until shrimp turns pink, indicating it is cooked through.
3. Fold in spinach and remove pan from heat.
4. Fill crepes with shrimp, artichokes, and spinach.
5. Spoon remaining béchamel on top of crepes, sprinkle with parsley.

Lemon Béchamel :
1. Melt butter in a sauté pan over medium heat. Add onions and sauté until translucent. 2-3 minutes.

2. Transfer onions to the top of a double boiler over medium-low heat, and add milk, clove, nutmeg, bay leaf, and salt. Add water to bottom of double boiler and simmer for one hour, stirring frequently, until béchamel coats the back of a metal spoon.

3. Pass béchamel through a mesh strainer to remove onion and whole spices. Add lemon zest and ½ tsp lemon juice. Taste and season with salt as desired.

Béchamel may be refrigerated for up to 4 days.

Cafe Monte French Bakery and Bistro
6700 Fairview Road

"We want to keep it simple. People can sit outside, have some crepes or Belgian chocolate and listen to World War II era music."
Maggie De Weirdt

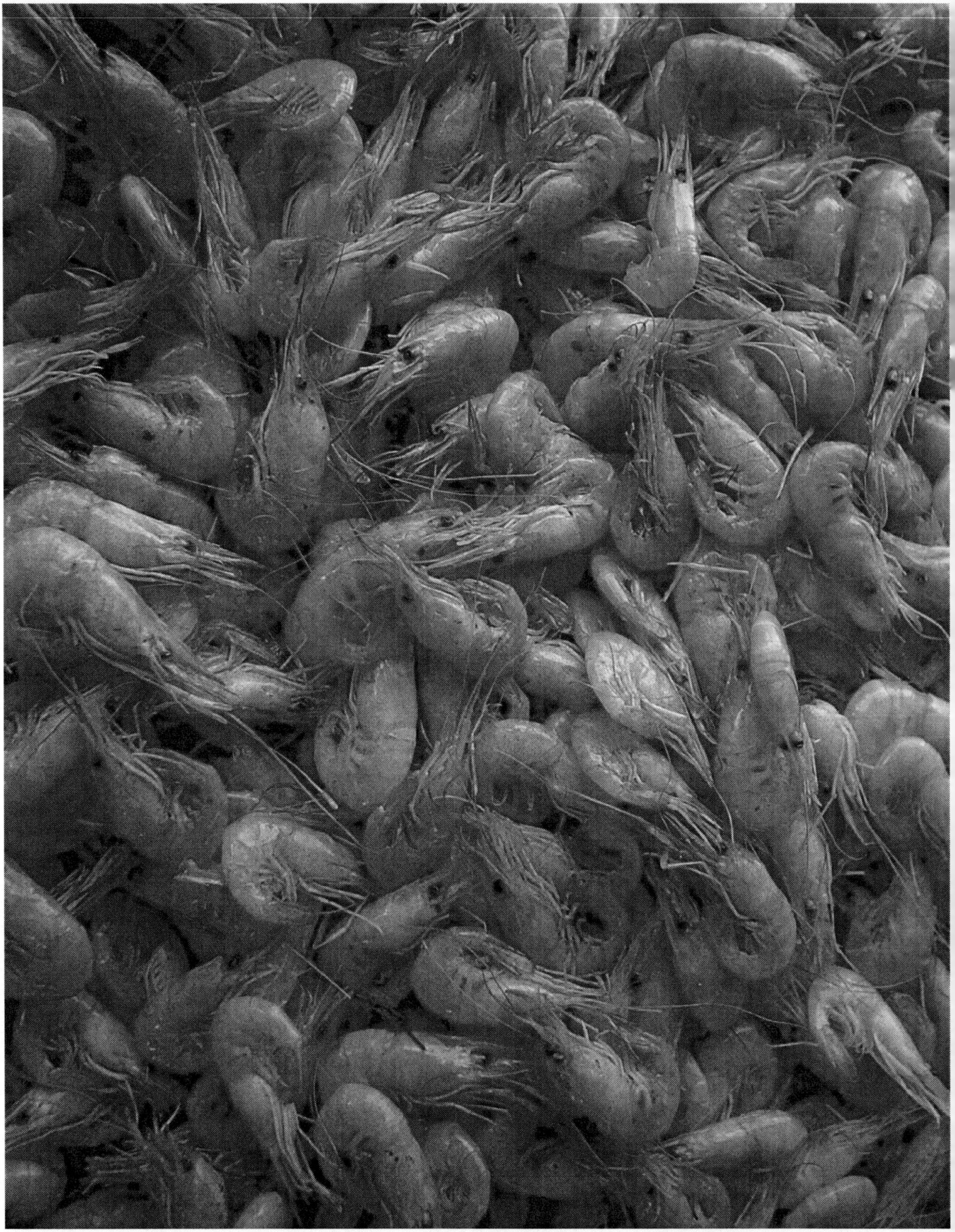

Creole BBQ Shrimp

Signature Tastes of CHARLOTTE

The Cajun Queen is the area's premier Cajun/Creole restaurant. In the Elizabeth Neighorhood, be transported to experience the flavors of 'Nawlins and the bayou, all while enjoying the ambiance of the restaurant itself, the upstairs bar, featuring Dixie Beer (the beer that made New Orleans famous) and drink specials, with live music regularly, or out on the porch to catch some breezes.

2 doz. shrimp, peeled and deveined
1 Tbsp Bayou Blend Seasoning blend (Available at the restaurant, or may be orderedl)
4 Tbsp butter
1 Tbsp fresh garlic, minced
1 tsp Worcestershire sauce
6-8 oz. beer (or non-alcoholic beer is fine)
¼ C. scallions, chopped

1. Melt butter in a skillet, add seasoning mix, garlic and Worcestershire.

2. When hot and bubbling, add shrimp and cook ¾ of the way (until just pink)

3. Add scallions and saute one minute more, or until shrimp are done.

4. Add beer and serve hot.

This version of this famous New Orleans dish may be served as an appetizer, without rice, and just French bread to sop up the sauce, or as a main course over white rice.

CAJUN QUEEN
1800 EAST 7TH STREET

"I shall be but a shrimp of an author."
Thomas Gray

Josephine, one of the CEOs (Chief Eating Officers) of the Canine Cafe.

Canine Carob Chip Mutt-fins

Signature Tastes of CHARLOTTE

All of our blends have NO sugar, salt, chemicals, preservatives, additives, fillers, dyes, or by-products and are low in fat. We add NO animal fat, and only a little oil for the dog's coat at the suggestion of the North Carolina State University Food Science Department. We only use wholesome grains, pureed USDA chicken, fresh fruits, vegetables and herbs. We developed these blends with the advice of veterinarians and the NCSU Food Science Department. Our crunchy formulas help in massaging the dogs' gums and cleaning their teeth which can promote fresher breath.

1½ C. plain, low-fat yogurt
3 eggs, slightly beaten
½ C. vegetable shortening
½ C. carob powder (can be found at health food stores)
4 C. unbleached flour
½ whole rolled oats
¼ C. unsweetened carob chips (can be found at health food stores)

1. Preheat oven to 300°F.

2. Lightly grease 9 muffin cups.

3. In a mixing bowl, combine the yogurt, eggs and shortening until well blended.

4. In another bowl, combine the carob powder, flour and oats until well blended.

5. Add the dry ingredients to the yogurt mixture and blend thoroughly.

6. Stir in carob chips.

7. Shape muffins with hands and place into muffin tins. (Wet hands with water to make this step easier).

8. Bake 25 minutes.

9. Cool and store in a sealed container in the refrigerator.

Yield: 9 muffins. Can be cut into smaller servings.

Canine Cafe
125 Remount Road

"There are three faithful friends - an old wife, an old dog, and ready money."
Benjamin Franklin

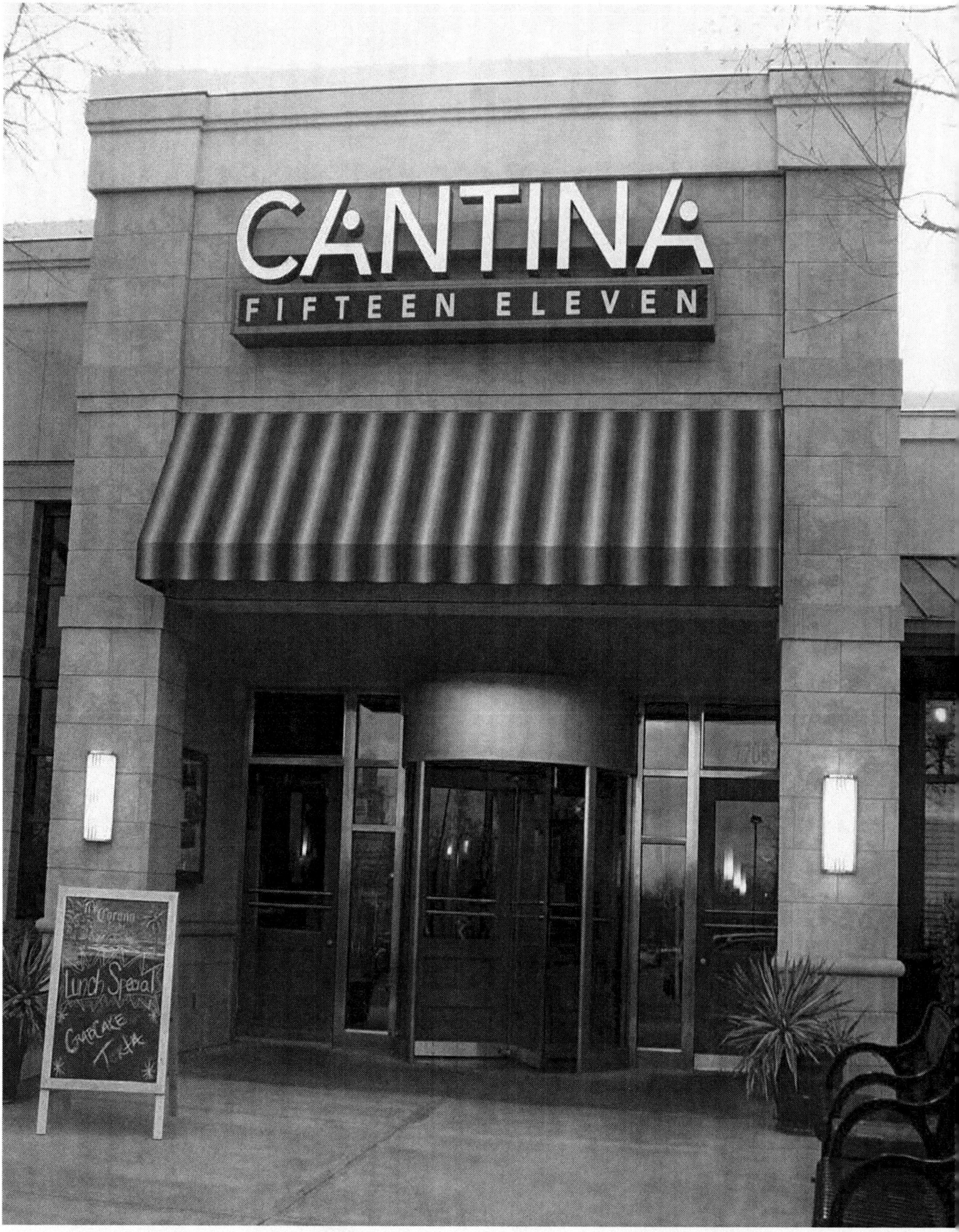
CANTINA
FIFTEEN ELEVEN
Lunch Special

Crab Salpicon (Tacos)

To understand the philosophy of Cantina is to know its owners. It all began with an appreciation for the way Mexican food is traditionally prepared. Unique by comparison, long before four walls were built, the inspiration for Cantina 1511 was born far from Charlotte in a place called Oaxaca, Mexico. Co-Owner Frank Scibelli, traveling on one of many trips to the region, became inspired to bring genuine Mexican cuisine to the Queen City. The evolution of Cantina 1511 was a highly involved labor of love that has resulted in one of Charlotte's most beloved dining establishments.

10 oz. jumbo lump crab meat
2 C. lettuce, shredded
3 C. cabbage, shredded
1 C. tomatoes, diced
1 C. white onion, thinly sliced
1 C. red onion, thinly sliced
4 Tbsp green onion, sliced
2 Tbsp extra virgin olive oil
12 cloves garlic, thinly sliced
2 avocados, pitted, peeled, small dice
4 pinches of salt
10 corn tortillas, warm
Juice of 2 limes

1. In a large mixing bowl, combine all ingredients except for the crab meat and the tortillas.

2. Combine and mix thoroughly. Taste and season accordingly.

3. Add crab and toss gently to incorporate crab meat.

4. Fill each warm tortilla with ⅓ C. of the mixture, and serve as a taco.

Signature Tastes of CHARLOTTE

Cantina Fifteen Eleven
1511 East Blvd & 7708 Rea Road

> "Have you ever watched a crab on the shore crawling backward in search of the Atlantic Ocean, and missing? That's the way the mind of man operates."
> H. L. Mencken

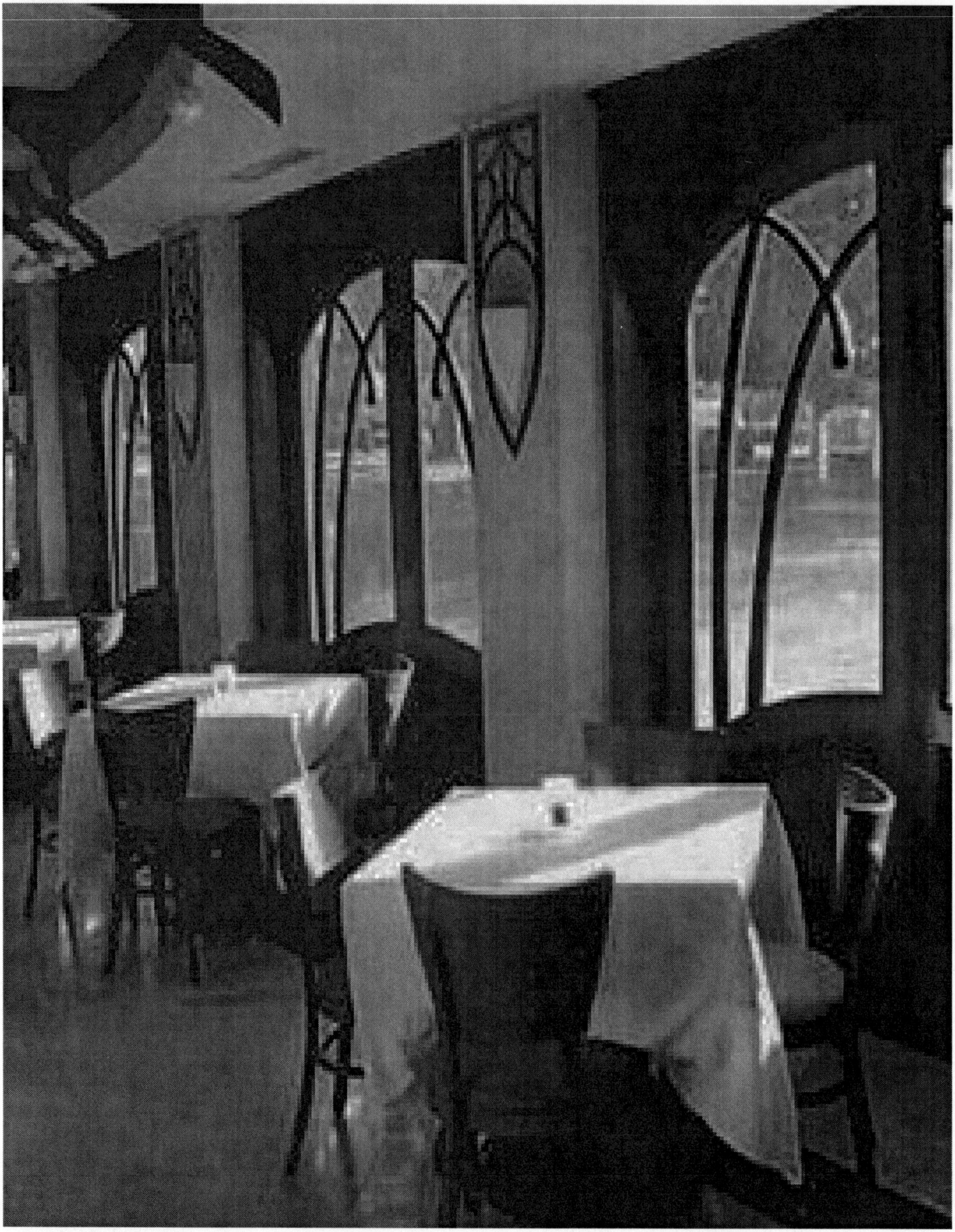

Mushroom Bolognese

At Carpe Diem, we take pride in providing you with gracious service. We want you to leave happy and satisfied, so all our staff are here to ensure an auspicious experience. We, the proprietors, sisters Tricia Maddrey and Bonnie Warford, are from Miami, Florida. Our interest in food grew from a love of the Latin and tropical flavors that influenced us growing up. These culinary influences have shaped our version of "new American" cuisine. When dining with us, we want you to truly "seize the moment" and let us take care of the details.

2 lb. mushroom stems, ground
2 C. shallots, minced
2 tsp garlic, minced
1 C. tomato paste
4 C. white wine
1 C. whole milk
1 C. marinara sauce

1. Grind the mushrooms through the small die on a meat grinder attachment of a mixer. Alternatively, pulse several times in a food processor fitted with a steel blade until the mushrooms reach a mealy consistency.

2. In a saucepan, sweat shallots and garlic in a small amount of blended oil.

3. Add ground mushrooms and cook until liquid has evaporated.

4. Add tomato paste, toasting briefly, before deglazing white wine.

5. Incorporate milk and marinara sauce.

6. Bring to a boil, then lower to a simmer.

7. Cook on low for 25 minutes.

8. Season to taste and serve on your favorite pasta.

"I am... a mushroom; On whom the dew of heaven drops now and then."
John Ford, American film director

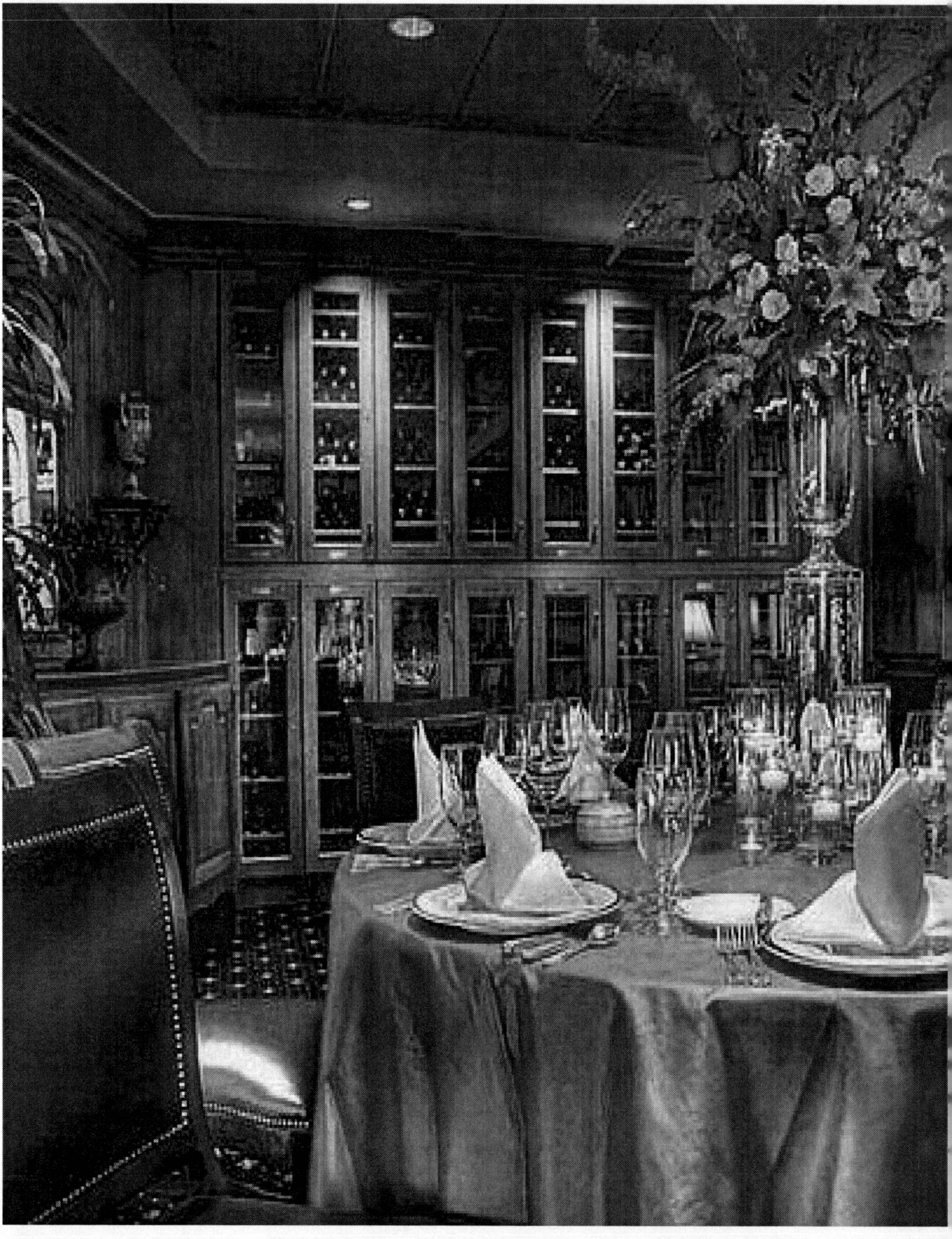

Ballotine of Duck with Roasted Apples & Pecans

Since its beginning in 1947, the Charlotte City Club has been a distinguished gathering place for the business, professional and social community to convene, entertain and dine. In this unique environment a special camaraderie develops among Members as they enjoy fine food and gracious personal service.

Signature Tastes of Charlotte

8 boneless duck breast, 6-7 oz. each
4 cloves garlic, smashed with side of knife
4 bay leaves
1 oz. fresh thyme
1 tsp fresh ground pepper
1½ lb. apples (Granny Smith or whatever is available)
⅓ C. roasted pecans
2 Tbsp roasted garlic

1. Clean the duck breast of any skin that covers more than the top of the breast. Using a boning knife, cut a lengthwise pocket in the breast meat, just under the skin. Make shallow, intersecting cuts just through the skin. Rub duck with garlic, black pepper, thyme and bay leaf. Roast the pecans at 350°F for 8 minutes, and set aside.

2. Cut apples in ⅓ inch dice, and sauté over medium-high heat, just to lightly brown. Combine the apples, pecans and roasted garlic, season lightly with salt and black pepper. Divide the apple stuffing into 8 parts. Stuff each part into a duck breast through the pocket incision.

3. Heat a skillet over medium heat for 1 minute. Place duck breasts skin side down, and continue to cook until skin is golden brown, and it begins to crisp. Remove excess fat from skillet. Transfer skillet to a 400°F oven for 5-7 minutes, or until duck is medium rare, and internal temperature registers 120°F.

4. Let rest for 5 minutes on a roasting rack. Slice slightly on the bias. Suggest serving with a mushroom risotto and a port wine demi glace.

Charlotte City Club
121 W. Trade Street, #3100

"The Church has never changed its teaching on the sanctity of human life - it didn't make up a rule for the convenience of a particular time like a rule at a country club as the Governor would have us believe."
Wellington Mara

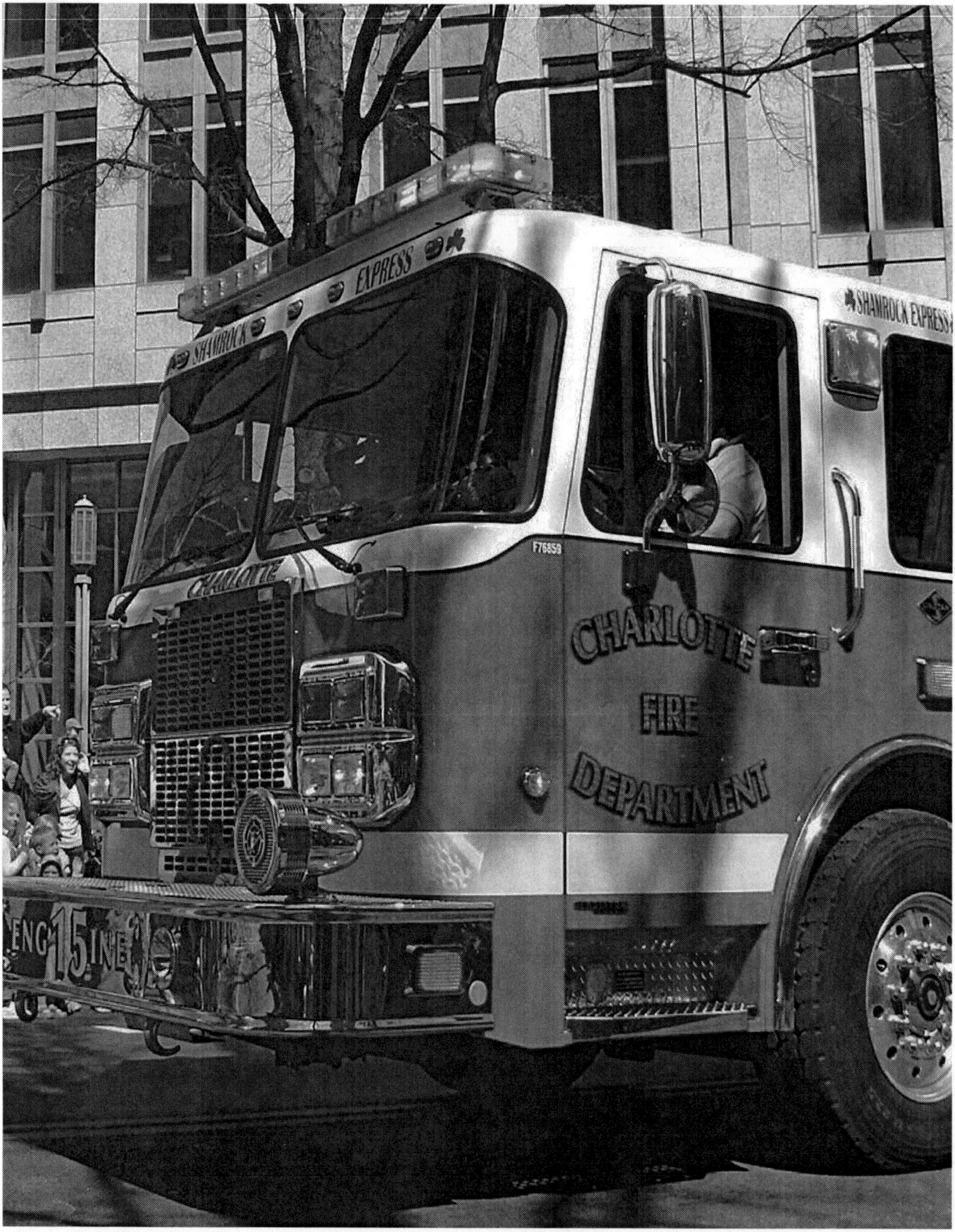

Station 39's Carolina BBQ

Signature Tastes of Charlotte

The Charlotte Fire Department operates out of 41 Fire Stations and provides fire protection for approximately 300 square miles. (Station 42 under construction). With 1,164 full-time positions, 1,044 are fire suppression personnel, 41 Engine Companies and 15 Ladder Companies, Charlotte Fire Department responded to over 93,000 calls for service in 2010.

Ingredients:

- 6-8 lb. Boston butt (trimmed)
- 1 Tbsp olive oil
- 2 Tbsp cracked black pepper - or to taste
- 2 Tbsp Red Monkey tres chili and cilantro powder
- 2 Tbsp Red Monkey smoked paprika and roasted garlic
- 1 Tbsp Captain Wetta's Magic Dust (2 Tbsp of regular chili powder is acceptable substitute)
- 2 Tbsp garlic powder
- 1 Tbsp Italian seasoning
- 1-1½ qts. chicken stock (enough to cover ¾ of butt in crock pot)
- 1 (18 oz.) bottle of Budweiser Smokey BBQ sauce
- ¾ bottle KC Masterpiece Hickory BBQ sauce
- 1 Tbsp Gravy Master

Directions:

1. Turn on grill to high.

2. Trim and rub olive oil on Boston butt. Cover all sides of pork with seasonings and rub in.

3. Put butt on grill for approximately 3-5 minutes (depending on size) and then repeat on all sides, until well seared and has achieved nice caramelization.

4. Put butt in crock pot set on high, and add BBQ sauces and chicken stock.

5. Add 1 Tbsp Gravy Master, cover and cook for 3½ - 4½ hours until internal temperature reaches 165°F, or meat falls off the bone.

6. Remove pork, and transfer to cutting board. Pull apart or chop, depending upon your preference. Add pork to the choice of sauces - Eastern Carolina (vinegar based) or Western Carolina (traditional sauce)

Eastern: Take a 6 oz. ladle of drippings from the crock pot and mix with pork. Add 8 oz. of Scotts BBQ sauce - (it's vinegar based, so it's thin.) Add 3 Tbsp Sweet Baby Ray's BBQ sauce, and serve on a bun with coleslaw.

Western: Take 6 oz. ladle of drippings from crock pot, and mix with pork. Add 10 oz. Sweet Baby Ray's BBQ sauce, and serve on a bun with coleslaw.

Chief Jon B. Hannan, by Firefighter Jeff Nixon, of Station 39

Charlotte Fire Department

> "You have to do something in your life that is honorable and not cowardly if you are to live in peace with yourself, and for the firefighter it is fire."
> — *Larry Brown*

Charlotte Fire Department
Chief Jon B. Hannan

Chicken and Arugula

Fire apparatus are vehicles designed to carry firefighters and their equipment to the scene of an emergency. Every Charlotte Fire Department engine company is a triple combination class A pumper. Our Engine Companies carry water, hose, ground ladders, and are equipped with a minimum of a 1500 gallon per minute fire pump. In addition to firefighting equipment, all Charlotte engines have life-saving EMS equipment, and an assorted cache of basic haz-mat, and rescue equipment.

Signature Tastes of Charlotte

1 lb. sliced boneless, skinless chicken breasts
4 thin slices pancetta - coarsely chopped
2 shallots (2 oz.), peeled and thinly sliced
2 cloves garlic, minced
¼ C. Kerry Gold pure Irish butter
⅓ C. drained and chopped oil packed sundried tomatoes
½-¾ lb. orecchietta pasta
(means "little ears" - any small pasta is fine)
Salt and pepper to taste
3 C. cleaned and roughly chopped arugula
1½ C. shaved or grated Dubliner Cheese
2 Tbsp toasted pine nuts

1. Sauté chicken, pancetta, shallots, and garlic over heat for about 10 minutes, or until they are cooked through.

2. Remove from skillet and keep warm.

3. Melt butter in same skillet for 1 minute, or until it starts to turn golden brown - DO NO BURN.

4. Add chicken mixture, tomatoes, and cooked pasta to skillet, and heat through.

5. Season with salt and pepper. Stir in arugula and pine nuts, and toss lightly.

6. The most important step ...ENJOY!

Chief Jon B. Hannan, by Firefighter Jeff Nixon, of Station 39

Charlotte Fire Department

"Writing became an obsessive compulsive habit but I had almost no money so I thought about being an urban firefighter and having lots of free time in which to write or becoming an English teacher and thinking about books and writers on a daily basis. That swayed me."
David Guterson

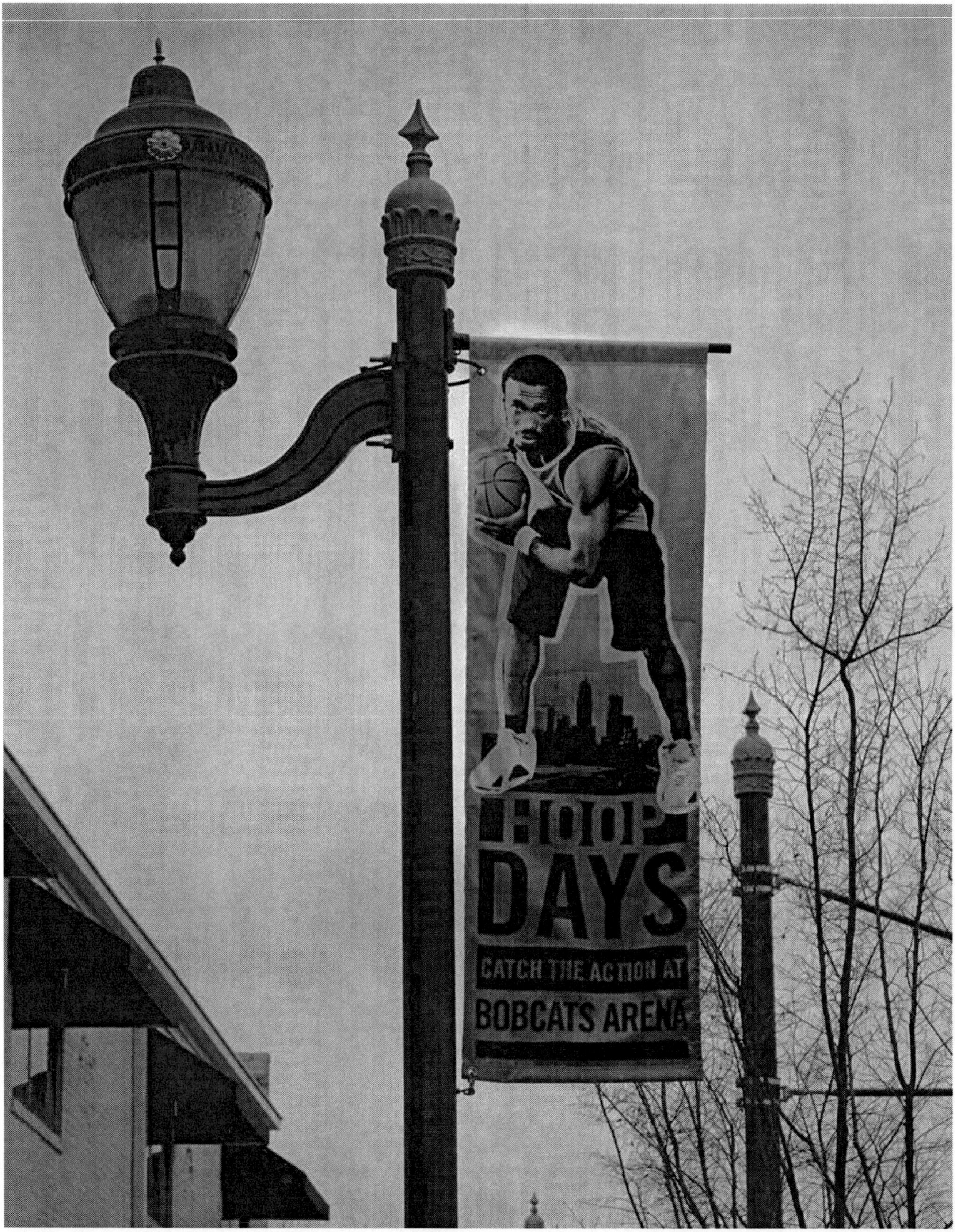
HOOP
DAYS
CATCH THE ACTION AT
BOBCATS ARENA

Pepper Crusted Tenderloin with Madeira Demi-Glaze

Signature Tastes of CHARLOTTE

With an organization-wide vision of Southern hospitality and world-class customer service, the Charlotte Regional Visitors Authority (CRVA) seeks to ensure that the visitors and events that come to the area have a positive experience. Guided by three main mission objectives, the CRVA markets by bringing visitors and events to the Charlotte region, manages by making the visitors' experience positive and the events successful, and maximizes by marketing and managing in a way that continues to bring visitors and events back to the region.

Pepper Crusted Tenderloin:
5 oz. cut Black Angus Tenderloin
Cracked back pepper
Roasted Garlic
Olive Oil

Madeira Demi-Glaze:
1 Tbsp butter
½ medium shallot, finely diced
⅓ C. chopped wild mushrooms
1 oz. Madeira wine
3 oz. demi-glaze (available at grocery stores)
½ oz. whole butter

Pepper Crusted Tenderloin:
1. Crust tenderloin steak with roasted garlic and olive oil.

2. Crust with cracked peppercorns. Sear in hot skillet on both sides to medium rare.

Madeira Demi-Glaze:
1. Sauté the shallot in butter until translucent.

2. Add the mushrooms, sauté, and add the Madeira.

3. Reduce by ⅔. Add the demi-glaze, and reduce heat.

4. Finish with ½ oz. piece of whole butter, adjust seasonings, and serve.

CHARLOTTE REGIONAL VISITORS AUTHORITY
501 SOUTH COLLEGE STREET

"Fish and guests stink after three days..."
Stanley W. Siler, on family coming to visit

61

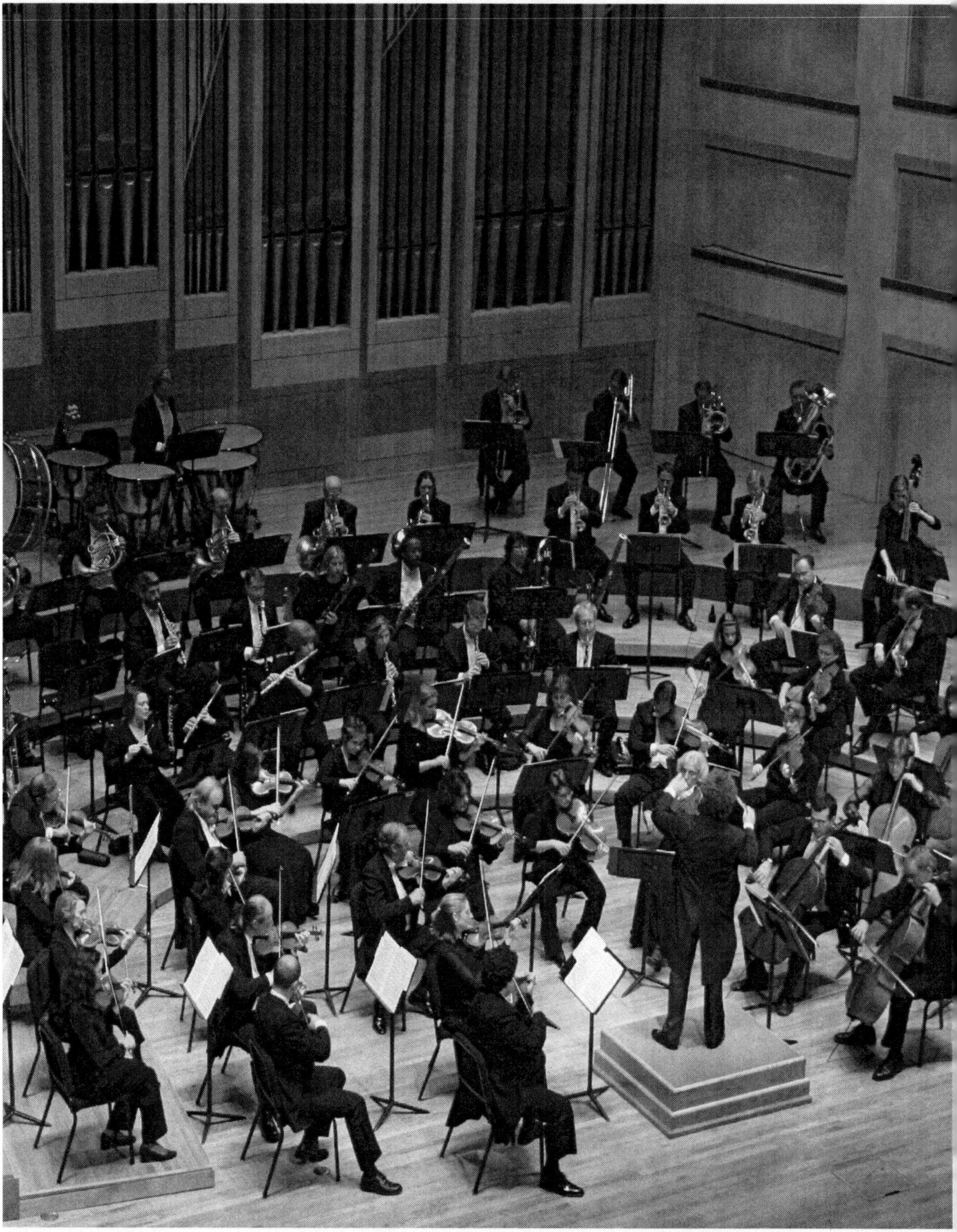

Explosion Pie

Founded in 1932, the Charlotte Symphony is the largest and most active professional performing arts organization in the central Carolinas, giving some 100 performances each season and reaching an annual attendance of more than 200,000 listeners. Now in its 79th season, the orchestra employs 62 musicians on full-time contracts and is led by the acclaimed conductor Christopher Warren-Green, who began his inaugural season this fall.

3 lb. skirt steak or stewing steak
½ lb. kidney, preferably ox
1 onion, chopped
olive oil
1 Tbsp Worcestershire sauce
1 pt. beef stock
5 medium-large potatoes, cubed
1 lb. carrots, cubed
1 leek, sliced in chunks
1 turnip, cubed
2 parsnips, cubed
salt and pepper to taste
1 sheet puff pastry to cover

1. Fry the onion in olive oil until soft and transfer to a large casserole.

2. Brown the meat in batches and add to the casserole. Cover with the stock.

3. Add the Worcestershire sauce and seasoning, bring everything to a boil, and then cook in a slow oven (300°F) for 2 hours.

4. Add the diced vegetables and potatoes and continue cooking for another 30 minutes.

5. Roll out the puff pastry.

6. Transfer the mixture to a 5 pint pie dish, and cover with the pastry.

7. Decorate the top with the left over scraps of pastry - a great job for the children.

8. Bake in the oven at 400°F for 20-25 minutes, until the pastry is well risen, crisp and golden.

This is a recipe by Director Christopher Warren-Green's wife, Rosie Warren-Green, and loved by everyone.

Signature Tastes of Charlotte

The Charlotte Symphony
Two Wells Fargo Center, 301 South Tryon Street, Suite 1700

"Musicians labor our entire lives to create compelling performances. If not for the support of dedicated subscribers and passionate listeners like you, it would all be for naught. The music is alive because you are there to hear it."
Christopher Warren-Green

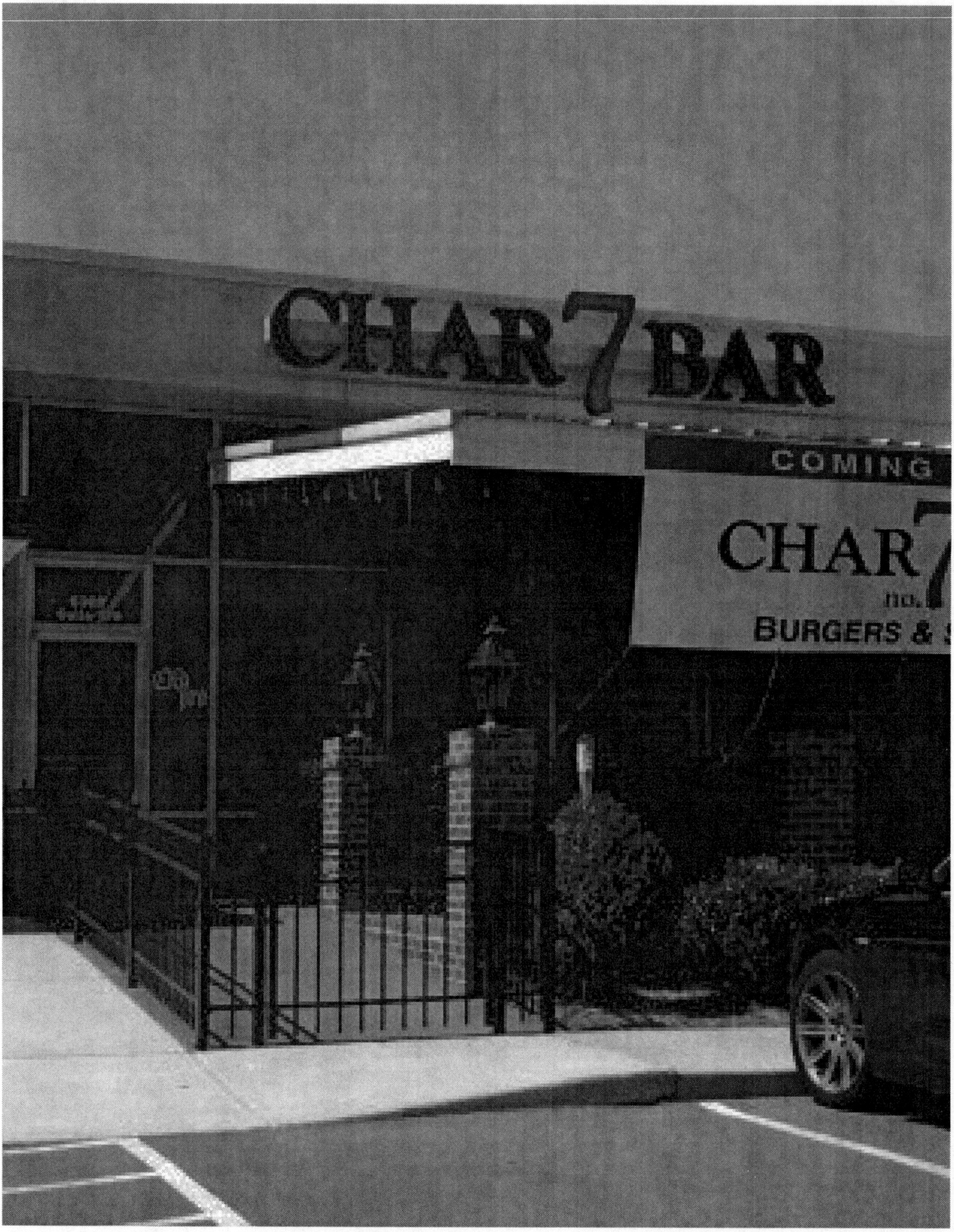
CHAR 7 BAR
COMING
CHAR 7
BURGERS &

Char Bar No. 7 Sauce and Signature Sandwiches

So, why is the name of the place CharBar No.7? Where are the other 6? This happens to be our FIRST CharBar and hopefully one of many. That question seems to arise more than often, and more than often we simply don't know.... From the beginning, we liked the number 7, but wanted to include CHAR in the name as well. We strive to be the best neighborhood bar around.

Char Bar No. 7 Sauce:
32 oz. of Honey Mustard
16 oz. of Sweet Baby Ray's BBQ Sauce
4 oz. Texas Pete hot sauce

Char Bar No. 7 Sauce:
Combine honey mustard, Sweet Baby Ray's BBQ Sauce and Texas Pete Hot Sauce. Mix well.

Leap Year:
A Leap Year is so-named because you should really only have one once every 4 years. Cook and top your favorite hamburger meat with American cheese, bacon and a fried egg. Then slather some garlic aioli on a hamburger bun that is stout enough to stand up to the delicious and decadent mess that this burger becomes after the first bite.

Bomber:
Have your butcher thinly shave some ribeye steak. Grill it off and pile it high on foccaccia bread that has been generously coated with chipotle mayo. On top of the steak goes provolone cheese, grilled salami, grilled onions and tomato slices. Close your eyes while you're experiencing this sandwich and you can almost see Philadelphia.

"I promise you this, you will not be let down by the food. If you are looking for a great place to relax, eat some food, or watch a game, let it be our pleasure to invite YOU to CharBar no. 7. We will give you a premium level experience for a mid-level price - every time. Come on in and let me prove it to you."
Tyler Hager, Founder

Chocolate Cream Cake with Vanilla Bean Sauce

Signature Tastes of Charlotte

WTVI is proud of its long history of service and involvement in the Charlotte communities. Our culture is supported by shared core values. We feel that everyone at WTVI can make a difference. On August 27, 1965, WTVI began broadcasting at 7 PM with a children's show called WHAT'S NEW and a 60-minute program of folk singing with Pete Seeger and Joan Baez.

Chocolate Cake:
4 oz. semisweet chocolate
¼ C. freshly brewed coffee
6 eggs, separated
¼ C. granulate sugar, plus 2 Tbsp, divided
1 Tbsp vanilla extract
¼ C. Godiva liqueur
Powdered sugar
1 C. heavy cream

Chocolate Glaze:
10 oz. dark chocolate, finely chopped
¾ C. heavy whipping cream
2 Tbsp corn syrup
1 Tbsp butter

Vanilla Sauce:
1 C. heavy cream
1 vanilla bean, split lengthwise
⅓ C. sugar

1. Preheat oven to 350°F. Line the bottom of a 17½" x 12½" sheet pan with aluminum foil. Butter and flour.
2. In a microwave at low power, melt the chocolate with the coffee, stirring in between until smooth.
3. In the bowl of an electric mixer fitted with a wire whip, beat the egg yolks with ¼ C. of sugar and the vanilla on medium high, until the batter forms a thick ribbon-like consistency. Gently fold the egg mixture into the chocolate.
4. In a separate, very clean bowl of an electric mixer, whip the egg whites on medium high until frothy. Add the remaining sugar, and whip to stiff peaks. Fold ⅓ of the whites into the chocolate mixture, then the remaining whites, creating a light chocolate cake batter.
5. Scrape the batter into the prepared pan, and bake for 25 minutes, or until a toothpick inserted comes out clean. Cool on a wire rack for 10 minutes. Run a knife around the pan to loosen the cake.
6. Dust a kitchen towel with powdered sugar. Place a sheet pan on top of the cake and invert the cake onto the cake rack. Gently remove the foil. Lay the prepared kitchen towel on the cake. Place a cake rack over the towel and cake, and invert it again to the right side up. Brush the cake with the liqueur.
7. On the long side of the cake roll, roll the towel and cake together into a jellyroll cylinder.
8. In an electric mixer fitted with a wire whip, ship the cream until it forms soft peaks. Using an offset spatula, spread the whipped cream evenly over the cake. Re-roll the cake using the towel as a guide. Wrap in aluminum foil and refrigerate for 3 hours.

Chocolate Cream Cake with Vanilla Bean Sauce

While Bonnie admittedly doesn't cook, her husband certainly can put on a show, especially with these desserts. They are gracious hosts, inviting me into their home (and set for the show) for photos, and to lavish me with these gloriously rich and wonderful desserts. Chef Phil served 600 guests this dessert on the back lot of Universal Studios, in Burbank, CA, during a Wolfgang Puck organized event for Meals on Wheels. While this is a time consuming recipe, it is well worth the effort.

Chocolate Cake:
4 oz. semisweet chocolate
¼ C. freshly brewed coffee
6 eggs, separated
¼ C. granulate sugar, plus 2 Tbsp, divided
1 Tbsp vanilla extract
¼ C. Godiva liqueur
Powdered sugar
1 C. heavy cream

Chocolate Glaze:
10 oz. dark chocolate, finely chopped
¾ C. heavy whipping cream
2 Tbsp corn syrup
1 Tbsp butter

Vanilla Sauce:
1 C. heavy cream
1 vanilla bean, split lengthwise
⅓ C. sugar

For the glaze:
1. In a large mixing bowl, place the chopped chocolate. In a saucepan, heat the cream, corn syrup and butter until hot. Pour in the bowl with the chocolate, and gently stir to melt the chocolate. DO NOT MAKE BUBBLES. Stir gently, until the chocolate reaches between 86-88°F, at which point it is getting a little thicker.
2. Unwrap the chocolate cake, and place it on a wire rack. Pour the melted chocolate evenly over the cake to cover the cake completely. Chill.

For the vanilla sauce:
1. Fill the bottom of a double boiler with 2 inches of water, and place over medium heat. Fill a mixing bowl with ice water, and set aside.
2. In a saucepan, bring the cream, corn syrup, and vanilla to a simmer. Remove from heat. Remove the vanilla beans halves. With a paring knife, scrape the vanilla beans to get the tiny specs inside the vanilla bean. Return them to the cream.
3. In a mixing bowl, whisk the egg yolks and sugar together, pour the vanilla cream into the egg mixture, and whisk to combine. Set this bowl over the double boiler. Using a wooden spoon, stir until you no longer see any of the tiny bubbles. Remove from the heat, and place the bowl into the ice water.

To serve:
Cut the cake into 2-3 inch slices. Place a slice standing up on dessert plate, ladle vanilla sauce around the cake.

"A good upbringing means not that you won't spill sauce on the tablecloth, but that you won't notice it when someone else does."
Anton Chekhov

Chef Phil Anderson....with his wife's permission.

The other chef of this couple, Bonnie Jones

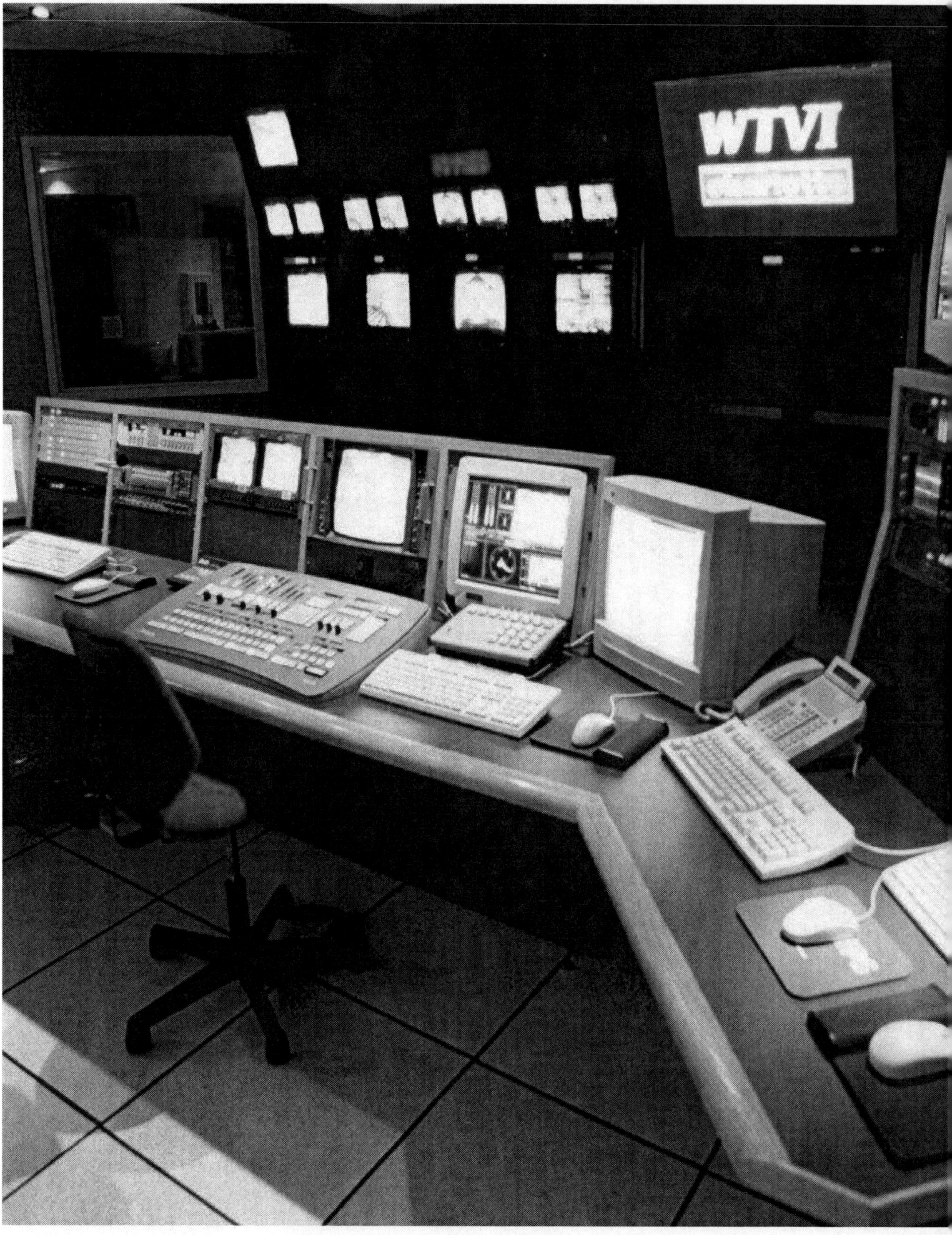
WTVI

Caramel Chocolate Glazed Praline Tart

Signature Tastes of CHARLOTTE

Tart shell:
1¾ C. flour
⅓ C. sugar
1½ sticks butter, cut in small pieces
2 egg yolks
2 Tbsp heavy cream
½ tsp vanilla

Caramel filling:
1 egg
4 egg yolks
3 C. heavy whipping cream
1 ¾ C. sugar
3 Tbsp butter, diced

Chocolate Glaze:
2 oz. bittersweet chocolate
2 Tbsp heavy cream
1 tsp vanilla extract

Praline Cream:
2 Tbsp butter
1 C. sugar
½ C. toasted almonds
1 C. heavy whipping cream

1. Mix the flour and sugar in a food processor. Add butter a little at a time, until incorporated into pea sized beads. Still using short pulses, add the yolks, cream and vanilla until the dough comes together. Remove from the bowl, shape into a disk, wrap in plastic, and refrigerate.
2. Place parchment paper on a cookie sheet. Place a 10½" x 2" spring form pan on the prepared sheet pan. Roll the dough to 14 inches. Using the rolling pin, carefully roll up the dough around the pin, and unroll it over the spring form pan. Using your hands, press the tart shell into place. Remove the excess dough.
3. Line the tart shell with aluminum foil, and use pie weights to hold the dough in place. Blind bake at 375°F for 30 minutes. Uncover, and bake for 3-4 minutes more. Remove, and cool. Lower the oven heat to 300°F.

Caramel filling:
1. In a mixing bowl, whisk the eggs together. Set aside.
2. In a sauce pan, bring the cream to a simmer, and remove from heat.
3. In a heavy bottomed deep pan, over medium heat, place the sugar evenly across the bottom. Stir to be sure all the sugar is melted. Remove from heat.
4. Pour the warm cream into the caramel and whisk until incorporated. Add butter. Pour caramel cream into the egg mixture, slowly at first, then totally whisking as you pour. Strain.
5. Pour into the tart shell and bake for 50 minutes. Cool on a cake rack for 30 minutes. Then, chill completely for 2 hours in the refrigerator.

Chocolate Glaze:
1. Melt the chocolate, cream and vanilla extract in a microwave on low power, for small increments of time, stirring in between, until chocolate is smooth.
2. Pour evenly over chilled caramel tart. Return to the refrigerator.

Praline Cream:
1. Butter the bottom and sides of a 17½" x 12½" inch sheet pan. Put the sugar into a saucepan, and cook over medium heat to a rich amber color, stirring to be sure all sugar has melted. Add chopped almonds, and cook 1 more minute. Pour onto the prepared sheet pan. Let cool, and break into pieces.
2. In an electric mixer, using a wire whip, whip the cream until it forms stiff peaks.
3. In a food processor, process the almond brittle into praline texture. Fold ⅔ of the praline mixture into the whipped cream. Add this whipped cream praline onto the top of the chocolate glaze, then sprinkle with the remaining praline. Refrigerate at least 2 hours before serving.

Chef Phil served this dessert a the Hacienda De Los Morales in Mexico City during a chefs' tour.

The Chef's Wife- Bonnie Jones and her husband Chef Phil Anderson on WTVI TV

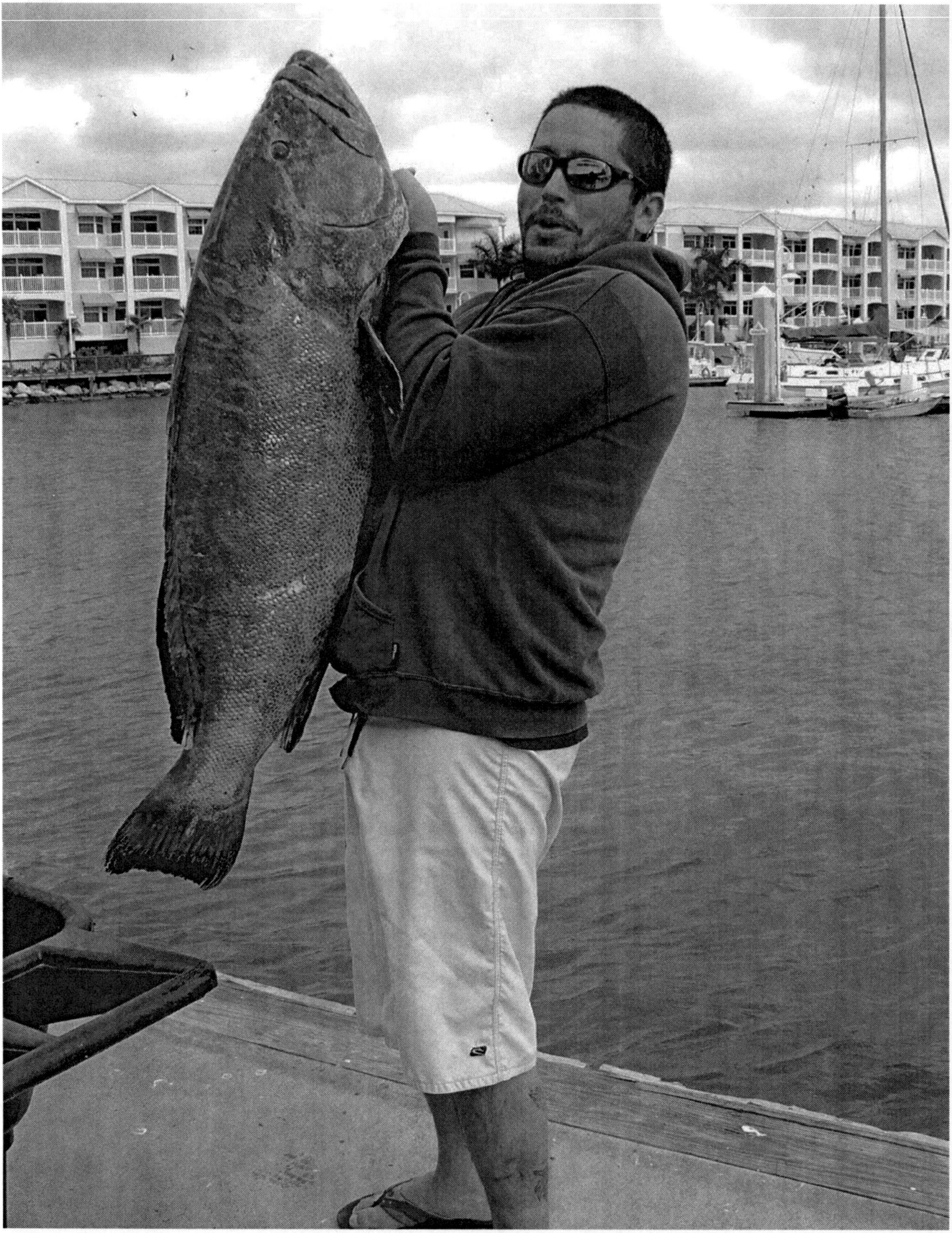

Pan Roasted Grouper with Parley Horseradish Mojo

Signature Tastes of CHARLOTTE

Bill Ryan's trademark phrase with this much needed fish market, "Turning seafood lovers into fishianados every day," is right on the mark. Considering that we're at least 3 hours away from the ocean, it's a real treat for Charlotteans to have an actual fish market offering such superior selection. As if that's not enough, Bill offers specially prepared dishes such as this, and is there to answer any of your questions about your seafood. Can't get that at the local grocery store fish counter.

Mojo:
⅛ C. freshly grated horseradish
½ C. chopped fresh parsley
¼ C. chopped chives
1½ shallots, minced
1 oz. red wine vinegar
¾ C. olive oil
¼ tsp cumin
Salt and pepper to taste

Grouper:
1 (6-8 oz.) portion of grouper, approximately 1 inch thick, per serving
kosher or sea salt and pepper to season
2 Tbsp olive oil
2 Tbsp cold butter
2 sprigs fresh thyme
1 clove garlic, crushed
squeeze of lemon

1. Mix all mojo ingredients and let stand at room temperature for minimum of one hour. Yields 1½ C.

2. Season flesh side of grouper with kosher or sea salt and black pepper. Heat 2 Tbsp olive oil to medium-high in a heavy gauge or cast iron pan.

3. Place fish, seasoned side down, in pan for approximately 2 minutes, or until a nice golden brown. Flip fish over, and reduce heat to medium.

4. Add the cold butter to the pan along with the thyme and the garlic. Tilt the pan slightly, so that the butter, garlic, and thyme pool in the corner of the pan.

5. With a large spoon, scoop the melted butter over the fish for approximately 2½ minutes. The butter will start to brown and become foamy. Squeeze lemon over the fish, and continue to ladle butter over it for another 1½ minutes.

6. Remove fish from the pan, and let rest for 2-3 minutes. Check for doneness. If the fish is not cooked to desired doneness, place into a 400°F oven for a few minutes until fish flakes easily.

7. Spoon 1-2 Tbsp of Parsley Horseradish Mojo over top of the fish, and serve immediately.

CLEAN CATCH FISH MARKET
6300 Carmel Road 2820 Selwyn Ave., #150

"It's no fish ye're buyin', it's men's lives..."
Sir Walter Scott

THE COMMON MARKET

Bridget's Chicken-less Chicken Salad

The Common Market is your stop for eclectic, neighborhood convenience. A modern twist on the general stores of our past, the Common Market offers fresh deli sandwiches, cold beer, an extensive wine selection, urban provisions, knicks & knacks, and most importantly, a community connection. We work hard to be a part of your neighborhood, your life. Conveniece is the easy part.

(2) 8 oz. packs baked tofu, diced (Soyboy - Tofulin is what we use at Common Market)
(1) 14 oz. pack extra-firm tofu (such as Nasoya), well drained and crumbled
1 small red pepper, diced
1 small red onion, diced
2 ribs celery, diced
1 tsp celery seed
½ tsp black pepper
1 Tbsp dill weed
1½ C. Vegan Mayo (Veganaise or Nayonaise

1. Drain and pat dry the extra-firm tofu, and crumble into a large mixing bowl.

2. Combine the remaining ingredients, except vegan mayo, work it all together together with hands.

3. Add vegan mayo and mix until blended.

4. This is great as a sandwich, a vegetable dip, or in lettuce wraps!

Open since 2002, Common Market has has been become a mainstay of the Plaza-Midwood neighborhood. As a neighborhood convenience store and deli, we cater to the urban provision needs of our 'hood.'

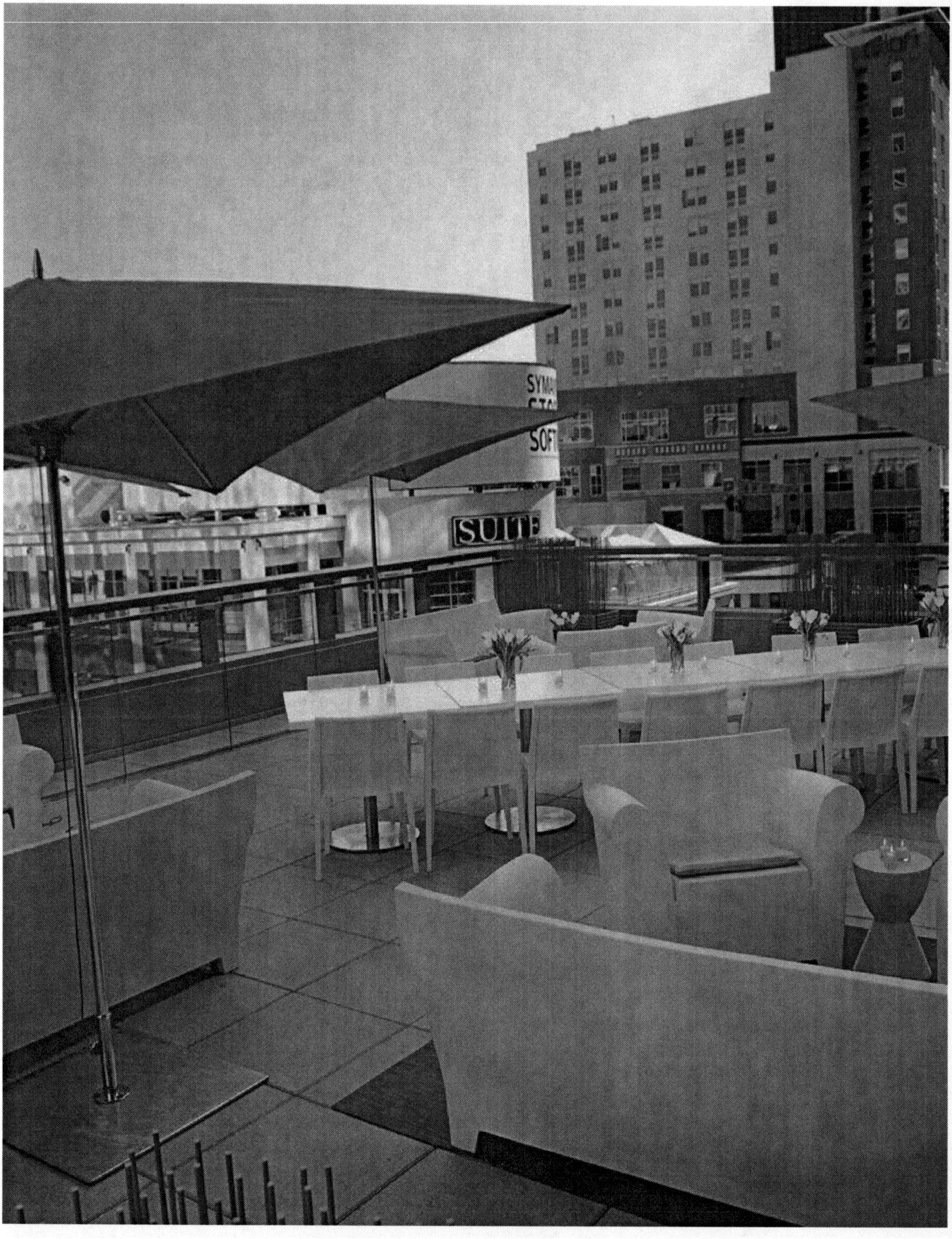
SUITE

Pecan Crusted Carolina Trout

Signature Tastes of CHARLOTTE

As British-based Compass Group PLC dates back to 1941 –with the foundation of 'Factory Canteens Ltd' in England– it's rather amusing to note that Compass Group's beginning in the US began with the acquisition of another canteen, Canteen Corporation, located in Spartanburg, SC with 1 billion in revenues during this time. The following year, Compass Group relocated its headquarters to Charlotte, NC. We are now one of the largest foodservice providers in the world. All in beautiful Charlotte, North Carolina.

4 (5-6 oz.) Carolina trout fillets (scaled, P-boned and trimmed)
1 C. pecans, lightly toasted and chopped
1 C. panko bread crumbs
1 Tbsp corn oil

½ C. yellow wax beans (Trimmed to 1 inch pieces on the bias, and blanched)
2 Baby yellow carrots (Peeled, blanched, and quartered)

200 grams (less than 1 C.) whipped sweet potatoes w/goat cheese
1 lb. sweet potato (Baked in skin and pureed)
4 oz. goat cheese

100 grams (less than ½ C.) picked Frisee (white and yellow parts only)
100 ml (just under ½ C.) Scallion Beurr Blanc
Amaranth Cress

1. Beat sweet potato and goat cheese together until smooth. Set aside.

2. Combine pecans and panko crumbs. Heat the oil in a non-stick skillet.

3. Season trout fillets with salt and pepper. Dredge flesh side of trout in pecan and panko mixture, pressing gently to help adhere. Sear trout, crust side down first.

4. Heat whipped sweet potato and goat cheese in pan. Reheat carrots and yellow wax beans in seasoned water.

5. On a hot plate, drag sweet potato puree through the top middle of the plate. Place the trout, crust side up, on end of the sweet potatoes.

6. Arrange carrots and wax beans to the right of the trout fillet. Dress the plate with the Scallion Buerre Blanc. Garnish with Amaranth Cress. Serve.

Yield: 4 servings.

Executive Chef, Tom Matterface-2400 Yorkmont Road

Compass Group

"There's no taking trout with dry breeches."
Miguel de Cervantes

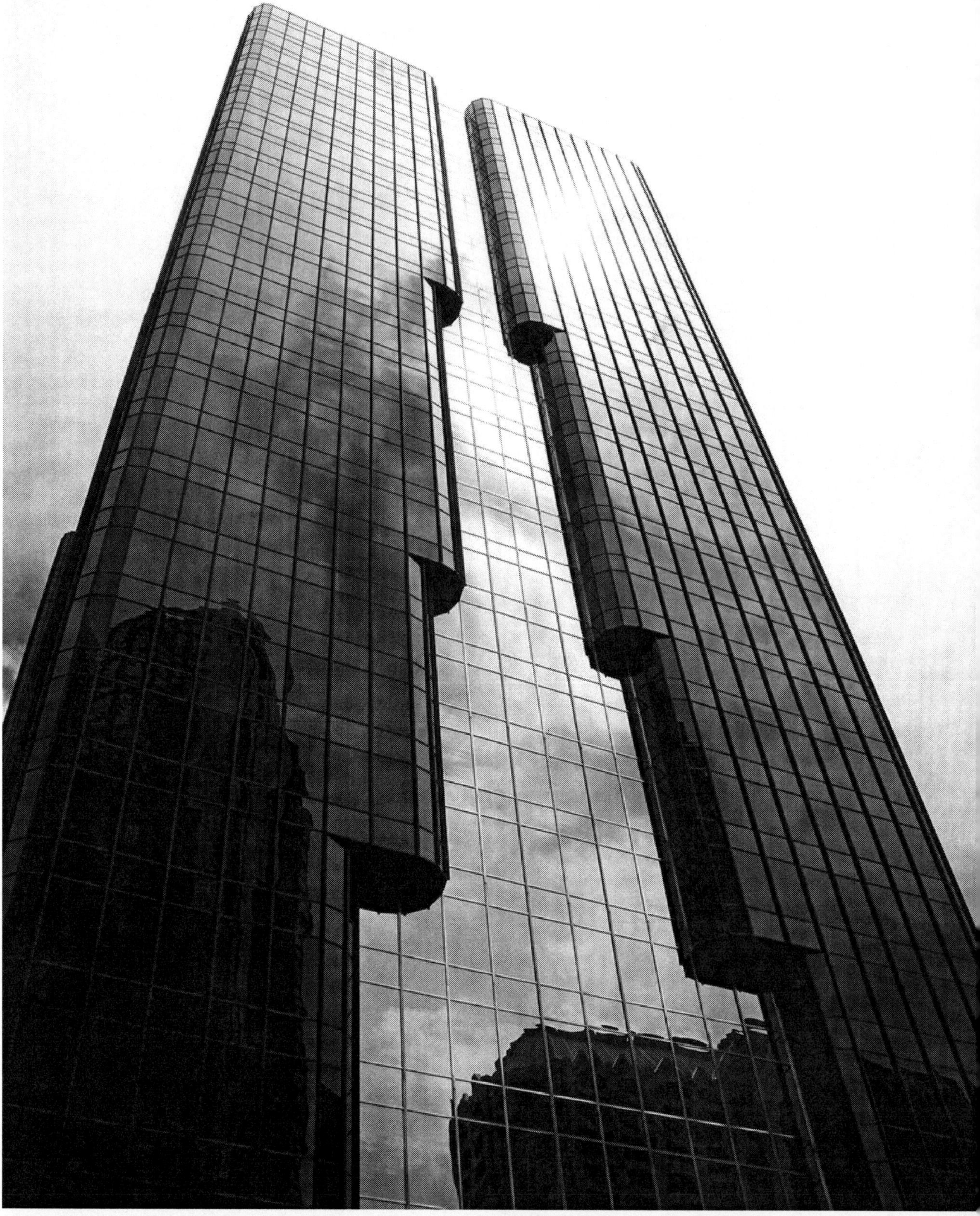

Fresh Strawberry Cake

Compass Group is committed to the communities in which we live and serve. These commitments have been formally recognized as 'Compass in the Community' since 1996. We encourage associates to get involved in our communities and we recognize their community-based efforts and successes each year. A panel of Compass Group judges reviews the community projects and rewards the associates with a monetary donation to the organization of their choice.

Vanilla Cake:
- ¾ C. large egg whites
- 4 oz. heavy cream
- 1 Tbsp vanilla extract
- 15.75 oz. cake flour
- 1 lb.+ 1 oz. sugar
- 1 Tbsp baking powder
- ¼ tsp baking soda
- ½ tsp salt
- 10 oz. unsalted butter at room temperature
- 9 oz. buttermilk

Strawberry Filling:
- 1 gal of strawberries, rinsed, hulled
- Approx. 1 lb. sugar

Butter cream:
- 1 lb. cream cheese, chilled
- 4 oz. unsalted butter, room temp
- 7 oz. powdered sugar
- Pinch salt
- 1 Tbsp vanilla
- ¾ C. egg whites
- 1 ⅔ C. sugar

Whipped cream:
- 1 qt. whipping cream or heavy cream
- ¾ C. sugar or powdered sugar, to taste
- 1 Tbsp vanilla extract

1. Preheat oven to 350°F. Prepare cake pans. Combine egg whites, heavy cream and vanilla in a bowl, whisk and set aside. In a mixer bowl place next 5 ingredients, mix to combine. Add buttermilk and butter and mix on low to blend then on medium speed until light and fluffy (approx. 2 minutes).

2. Add egg white mixture in 2 additions beating after each. Divide between cake pans and bake for 25-35 minutes depending on size of cake pan used and your oven. Cool completely. Slice each layer in half giving you 6 layers.

For Strawberries:
1. Put strawberries in large bowl and mash with a pastry blender until they are all broken up, and stir in sugar and refrigerate until needed.

For Butter Cream:
1. Beat cream cheese until fluffy. Add butter, salt and vanilla beat again until light and fluffy. Add powdered sugar mixing until fluffy. Set aside. Combine egg whites and sugar over a bain marie, stirring to dissolve sugar. Bring to 140°F.
2. Remove from heat and beat on high speed until mixture is just barely cool. Begin adding cream cheese mixture in small amounts until all is added and mixture is fluffy.

For Whipped Cream:
1. Whip cream until soft peaks form, and then begin adding sugar (either one) and vanilla. Whip until stiff but has fluffy peaks.

"One must ask children and birds how cherries and strawberries taste."
Johann Wolfgang von Goethe

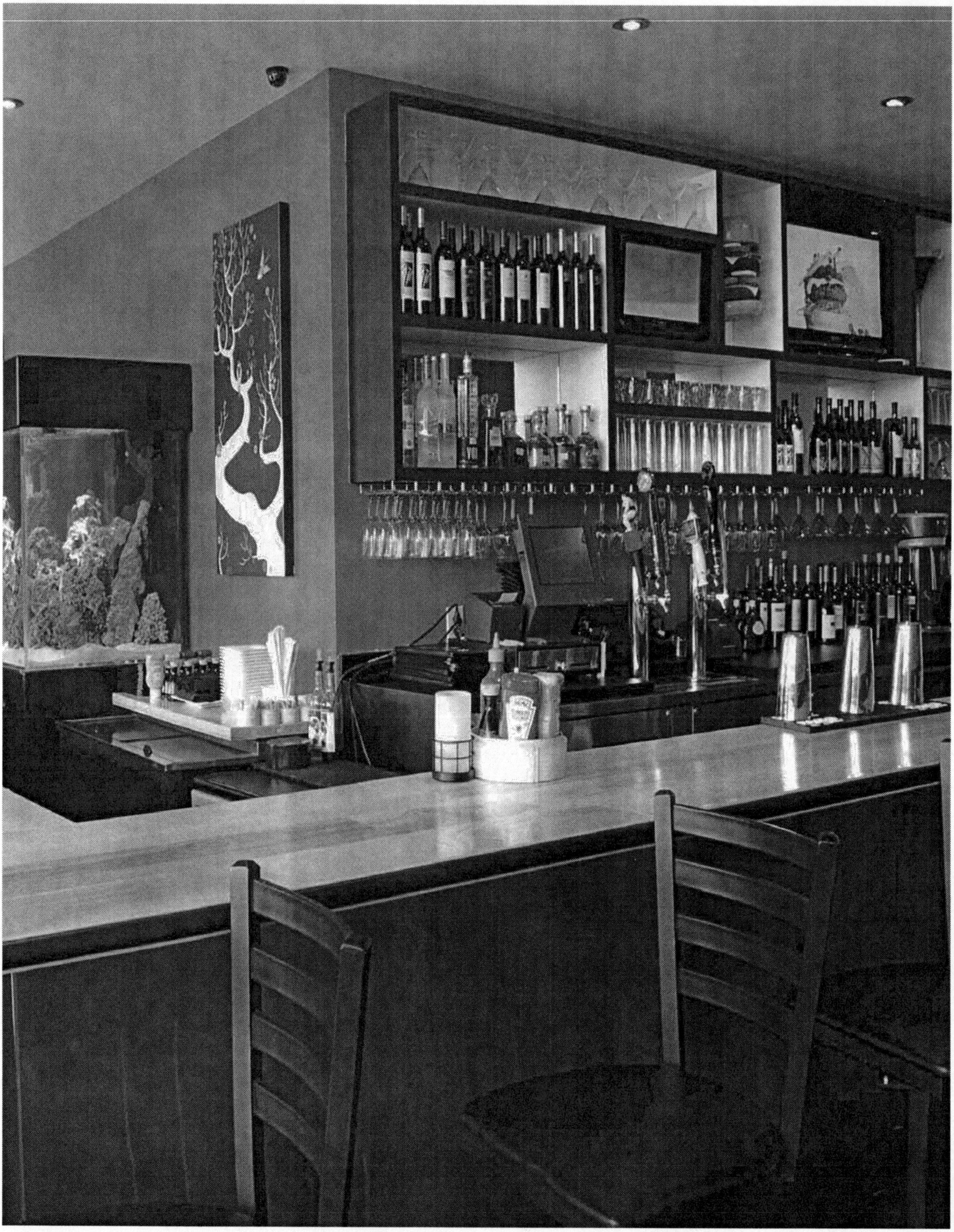

Thai Cucumbers

The Cowfish is a one-of-a-kind dining experience, thriving on its ability to fuse two niche products seamlessly on the same menu. Certainly unusual, absolutely great! The first and only "Sushi Burger Bar"! The Cowfish brings to the world the first restaurant focusing on offering both the best sushi AND the best burger in town. Fresh, innovative and delicious, the sushi segment of the menu is powered by the success of sister company, eeZ Fusion & Sushi. All natural, creative and hearty, the burgers entice with fresh, never frozen, ingredients and bold flavors.

10 cucumbers, peeled and seeded (Halved, lengthwise, scoop out seeds with spoon)
2 Thai Chilis, finely chopped
1 Tbsp Sambal Oeleck (Thai chili paste)
½ red onion
2 C. white vinegar
1 ½ C. water
1 ½ C. granulated sugar
1 Tbsp sea salt
½ C. honey
1 Tbsp chopped fresh cilantro

1. Thinly slice cucumbers on a ⅛" thick bias.

2. Peel onion, halve, and slice in ⅛" thick slices.

3. Remove the stems from the Thai Chilis and mince. Wear gloves, and thoroughly wash hands afterward.

4. Combine Thai chili, sambal, vinegar, water, sugar, salt and honey. Mix well.

5. Add sliced onion and cucumbers. Allow to rest in the refrigerator for 12-48 hours.

6. Serve over mixed lettuce and garnish with chopped cilantro.

Signature Tastes of CHARLOTTE

COWFISH SUSHI - BURGER - BAR
4310 SHARON ROAD, SOUTH PARK MALL

> "Sometimes sushi is just superb, and other times there's nothing like a great big steak. It depends where your taste buds are at the time."
> *Francesca Annis*

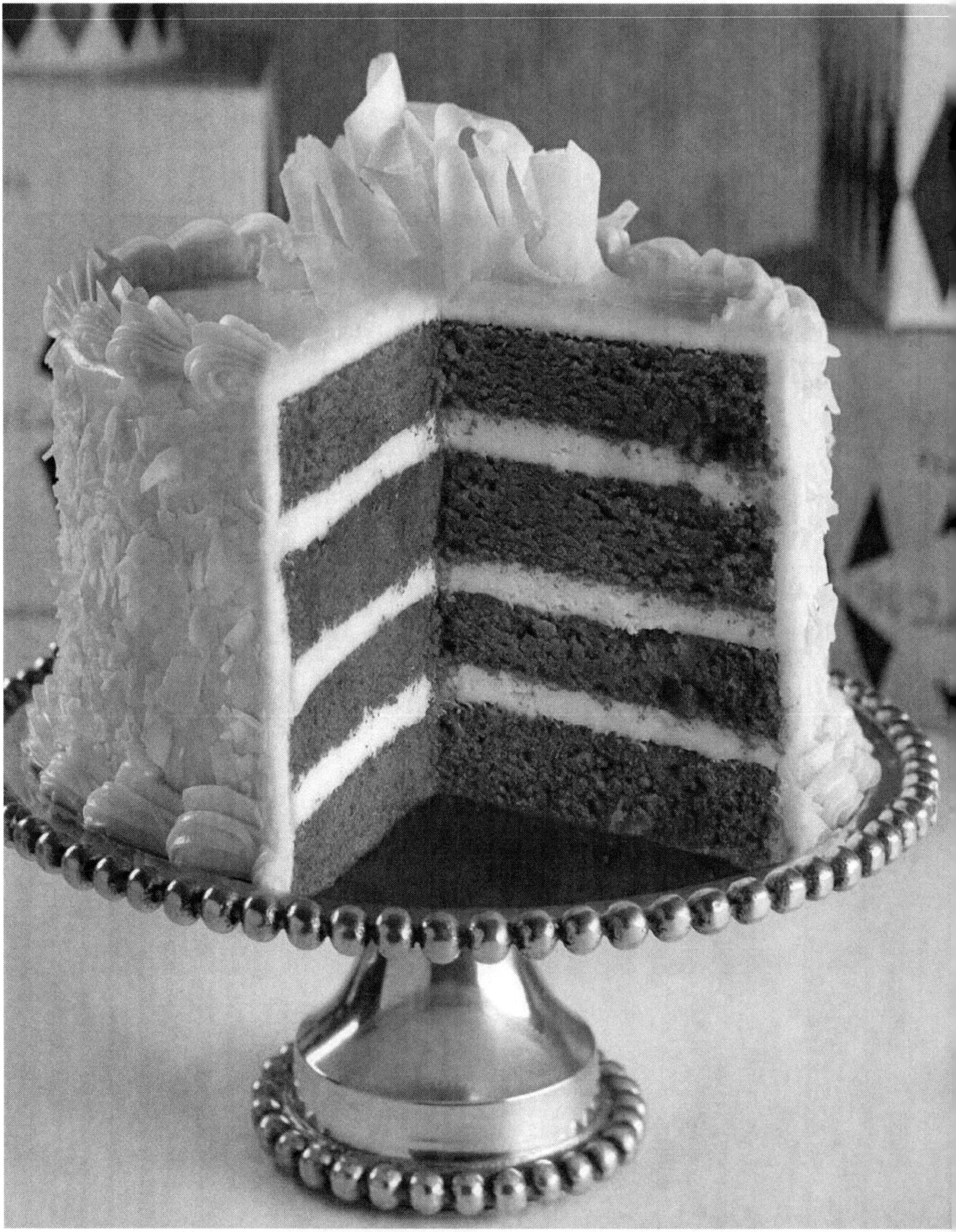

"The Scarlett Letter" Red Velvet Cakes

Signature Tastes of Charlotte

Crave represents a new breed of Charlotte evening entertainment: A world-class dessert boutique that naturally evolves into an upscale lounge, catering to the desires of Charlotte's late night enthusiasts. With a focus on providing decadent desserts, sensational cocktails, and savory small bites, Crave Dessert Bar aspires to be the Queen City's guilty pleasure of choice. Crave's dessert menu features an abundance of classic and seasonal selections, paired with wines by the glass from various parts of the world.

2 ½ C. flour
½ C. unsweetened cocoa powder
1 tsp baking soda
½ tsp salt
1 C. unsalted butter, softened
2 C. sugar
4 large eggs
1 C. sour cream
½ C. milk
1 oz. bottle of red food coloring
2 tsp Madagascar vanilla extract

Mascarpone Cheese Frosting:
8 oz. Mascarpone cheese, softened
¼ unsalted butter, softened
2 tsp Madagascar vanilla extract
16 oz. confectioner's sugar

1. Preheat oven to 350°F.

2. Mix flour, cocoa powder, baking soda and salt in a medium bowl. Set aside.

3. Beat butter and sugar in large bowl with electric mixer on medium speed for about 5 minutes, or until light and fluffy. Beat in eggs, one at a time.

4. Mix in sour cream, milk, food coloring, and vanilla. Gradually beat in flour mixture on low speed until just blended. Do not overbeat.

5. Spoon batter into muffin tin, lined with paper cup cake liners, or sprayed with non-stick spray. Bake 20-25 minutes. Allow to cool completely before frosting.

For Frosting:
1. Beat Mascarpone cheese, butter and Madagascar vanilla extract in a large bowl until light and fluffy. Gradually beat in confectioners' sugar until smooth.

2. Frost cupcakes with Mascarpone cheese frosting.

Crave Dessert Bar
500 W. 5th Street Suite 120

"A bad review is like baking a cake with all the best ingredients and having someone sit on it."
Danielle Steel

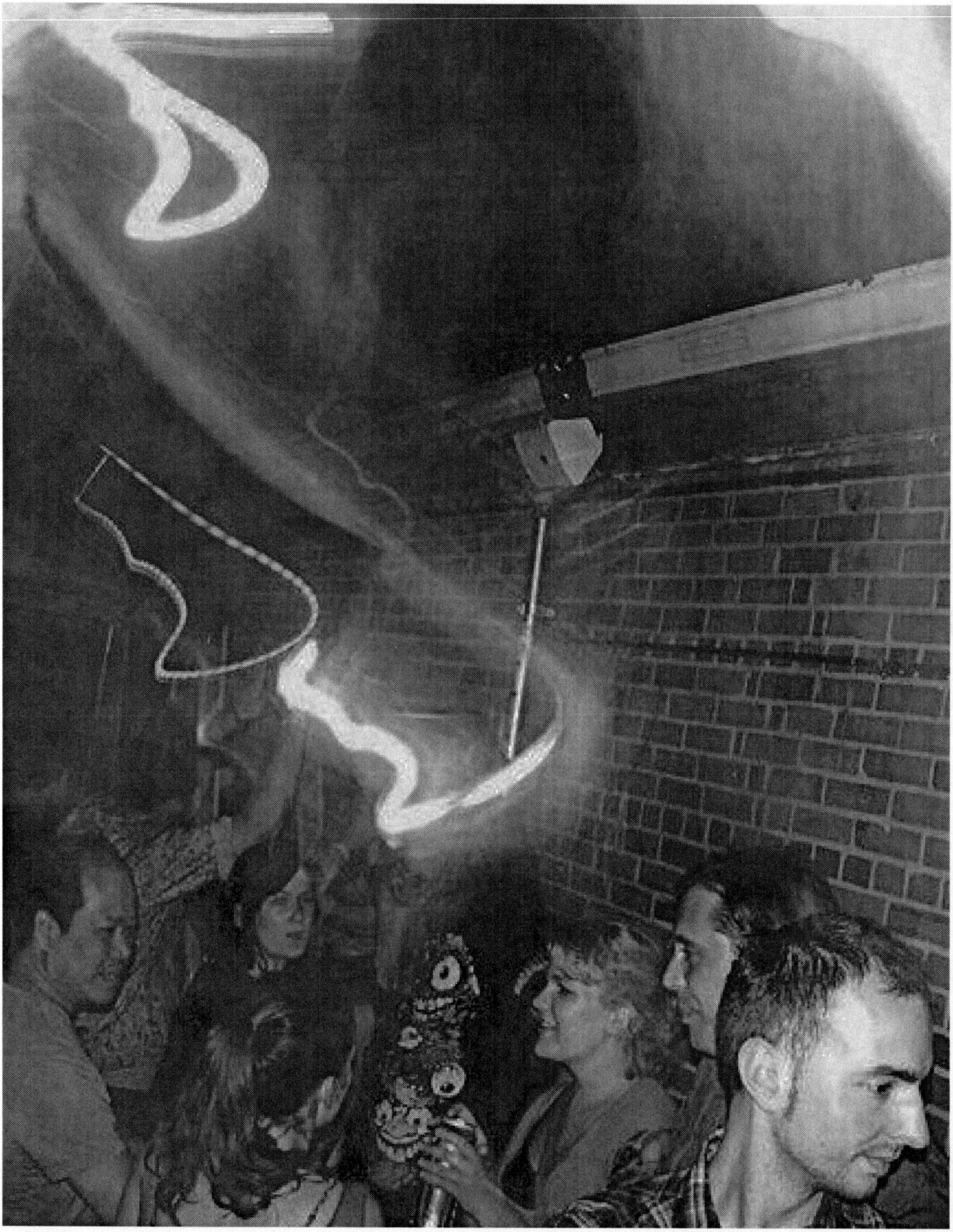

Thai Lemon Grass Sauce

Cuisine Malaya is "Charlotte's Home to Authentic Malasian Cuisine." Our cuisine is one of the infusion of primarily six major Asian and Continental cultures (Malays, Chinese, Indian, British, Dutch and Portuguese.) We proudly call ourselves the original fusion cuisine, as we have been doing fusion cuisine since the 1500s. Come and join us in celebrating and experiencing our proud heritage.

For Tofu, Chicken, Shrimp, Beef or fish/shellfish stir-fry

½ stem of lemon grass
2 oz. fresh ginger, sliced
½ clove garlic, sliced
1 whole dry or fresh red chili pepper

For Tofu, Chicken, Shrimp, Beef or fish/shellfish stir-fry

1. Blend all of above ingredients in grinder.

2. Stir fry blended ingredients with ½ C. vegetable broth.

3. Add 1 tsp madras curry powder, you choice of protein and/or vegetables (such as sliced tomatoes, onions, and asparagus).

4. Add ½ tsp of fish sauce if using seafood.

"What is sauce for the goose may be sauce for the gander but is not necessarily sauce for the chicken, the duck, the turkey or the guinea hen."
Alice B. Toklas

CUSTOMSHOP
Handcrafted Food

Customshop Mussels, Chorizo, Shishitos & Beer

Starting with the highest quality raw ingredients, Customshop's handcrafted dishes are meticulously prepared. Owner and Executive Chef Trey Wilson utilizes the sous vide method to slow cook proteins and vegetables, enhancing their natural flavors and textures. Customshop is committed to supporting local, organic farm ventures by bringing our guests the freshest, sustainable foods in the area. Weekly menu changes are tailored around the seasonal availability of produce, with sea options created around the weekly catch of our local fisherman, Rock Stone.

Ingredients:

- 1 lb. in-shell mussels, thoroughly cleaned
- 3 oz. Spanish chorizo sausage, minced
- 6 whole fresh shishito peppers
- 2 scallions, chopped
- 1 C. Catawba Valley Brewing Co. Farmer Ted's Cream Ale
- 2 oz. basic tomato sauce
- 1 oz. butter

1. Sauté peppers and scallions in olive oil on medium heat, until they start to brown.

2. Add tomato sauce, and cook, uncovered, 30 seconds.

3. Add chicken stock and beer, reduce sauce by half. Add mussels, cover and cook 1 minute (or until mussels open.)

4. Add butter, toss and serve immediately.

Notes: PEI mussels are rope-cultured, but are high quality, and available year-round.
Shishitos are relative mild peppers of Japanese origin; hotter or milder peppers may be substituted if desired, or if Shishitos are unavailable. Farmer Ted's Cream Ale has crisp floral qualities, and a creamy texture which is perfect for this. We use it because it's local, but you may substitute any quality Belgian-style beer of your choice. Salt to taste! Both mussels and chorizo have naturally high salt contents that are released in the cooking process. This dish is great with grilled focaccia or garlic bread to sop up the delicious sauce remaining after you've devoured the mussels.

Signature Taste of Charlotte

Customshop
1601 Elizabeth Avenue

"Beer, it's the best damn drink in the world."
Jack Nicholson

87

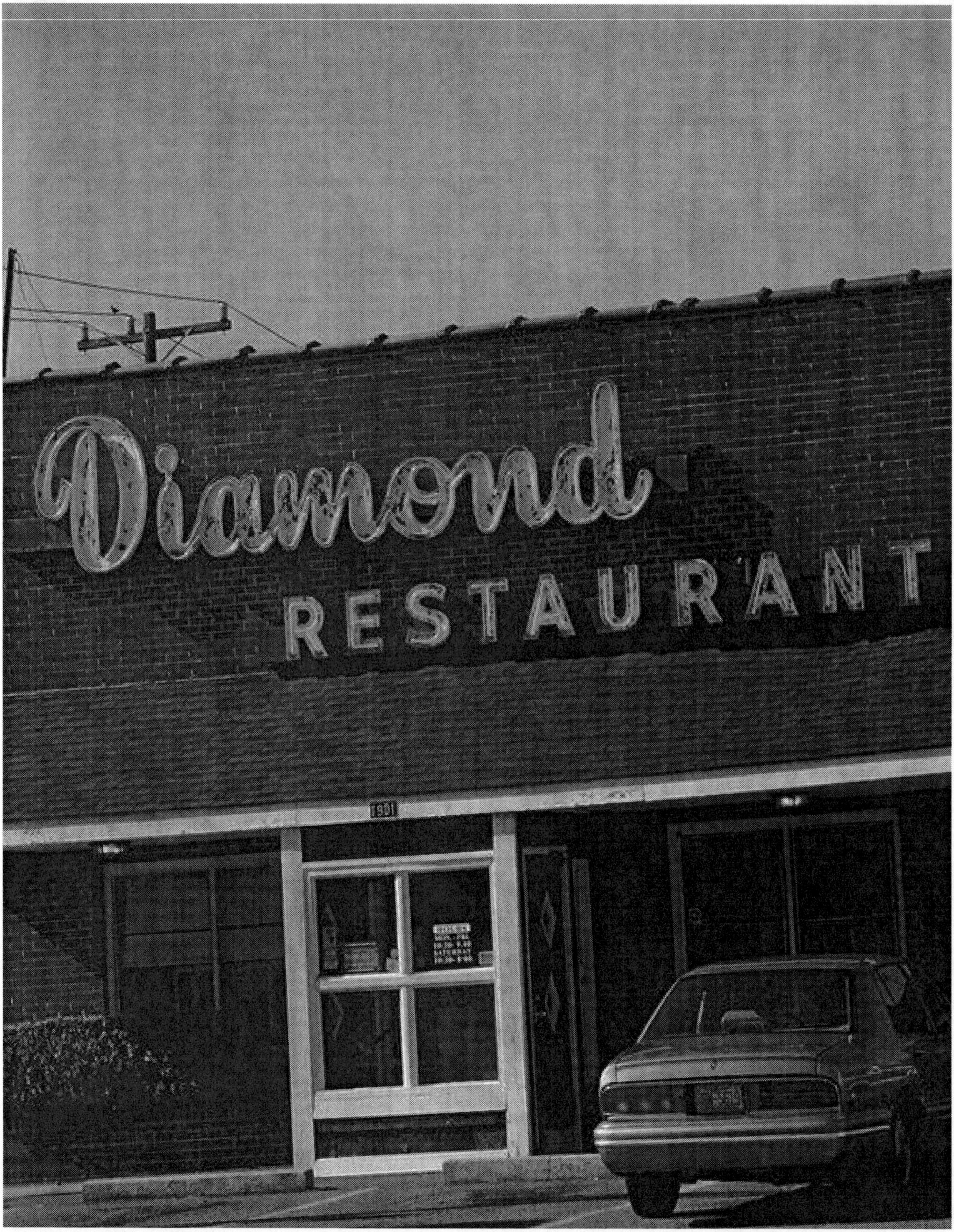
Diamond
RESTAURANT
1901

Collard Greens

Originally the Diamond Soda Grill, the snug brick diner was conceived in 1945 by founders Flonnie and W.A. James. Mrs. James was the beating heart of the Diamond, a Marshville, NC native who loved to cook and serve and had a personality for hospitality.. With respect to her past and previous caretakers, the Diamond has been polished and buffed to meet a new generation and welcome back an older generation and carry on the legacy of Just One Big Happy Family.,

Signature Tastes of Charlotte

The Diamond Restaurant
1901 Commonwealth Avenue

2 yellow onions, diced
6 cloves garlic, minced
1 tablespoon olive oil
4 C. chicken stock
2 bunches or about 5 lb. of collard greens, washed and stems removed
6 slices of bacon
1 large slice of fatback (salt pork)
1 spring fresh thyme or ½ tsp dried thyme
Salt and pepper to taste
1 teaspoon crushed red pepper
¼ C. cider vinegar

1. Render bacon in a large stockpot. When crispy, remove from pot and reserve.

2. Add olive oil to bacon grease and sauté onions and garlic until soft.

3. Add chicken stock, fatback, vinegar, thyme, salt and pepper and bring to a boil. Add chopped or torn greens.

4. As greens cook down, add hot water if needed. Simmer until tender, about 45 minutes.

5. Remove fatback and thyme. Chop or crumble reserved bacon and stir it to pot at end, and serve with some of the pot liquor and Texas Pete hot green pepper sauce on the side.

"I wanna sit behind the scenes and see nothin' but the greens."
Method Man

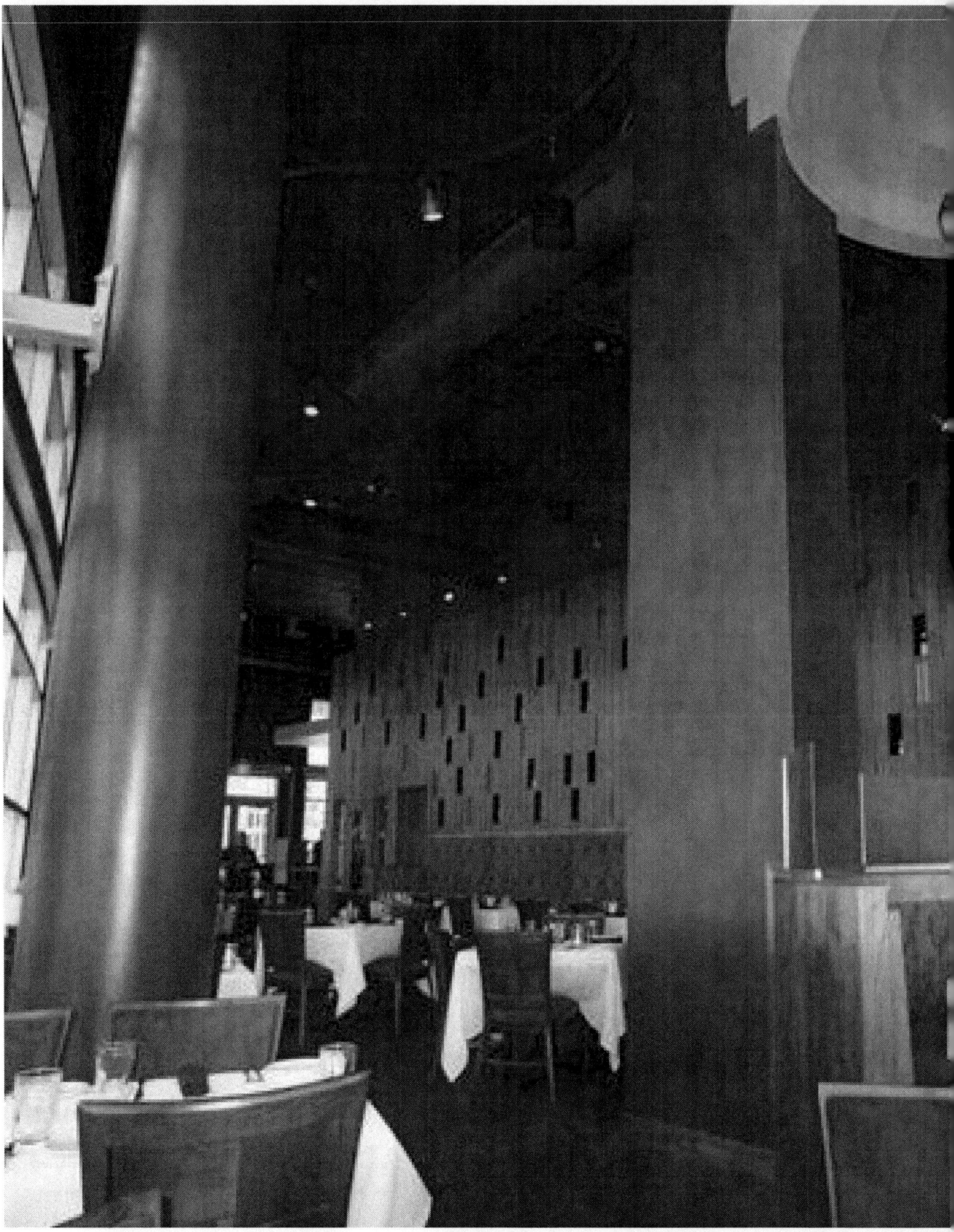

Pan Seared Scallops with Shallot Jam & Roasted Tomato Vinaigrette

The philosophy at Dressler's Restaurants is simple: Everyone who walks through our doors is either already a friend, or will be. By embracing that theory, the Dressler's know that every guest will have exceptional service, outstanding food and hopefully will know that whenever they walk into a Dressler's, that they are coming home. In addition, by having a local Chef, Jon and Kim know that they have a handle on the culinary pulse of the city, offering regional favorites all the while making sure that every diner can find that "one dish" that makes the dining out experience worthwhile.

1 lb. Scallops
3 Tbsp canola oil

Shallot Jam:
2 Tbsp vegetable oil
4 large shallots, thinly sliced
¾ C. balsamic vinegar
⅓ C. light brown sugar
Pinch of salt

Roasted Tomato Vinaigrette:
2 tsp minced shallots
2 Tbsp smooth Dijon mustard
Pinch of salt and ground black pepper
¼ C. champagne vinegar
1 tsp honey
1 tsp chopped fresh thyme
3 medium vine ripe tomatoes
¾ C. vegetable oil

For Shallot Jam:
1. Saute sliced shallots in the oil. After shallots are tender, add the vinegar, sugar and pinch of salt.
2. Turn the heat down to medium low, and reduce until all ingredients a jam-like consistency.

For the Roasted Tomato Vinaigrette:
1. Roast whole tomatoes on a grill or in a 400°F oven until soft and skin is browning. Remove from oven, set aside to let cool.
2. While cooling, whisk all ingredients but the oil in a bowl. Set side.
3. Chop the tomatoes, and add to the vinaigrette. Slowly add the oil while whisking to emulsify the ingredients.

For the Scallops:
1. Heat large enough saute pan on medium high heat, and add canola oil. When the oil starts to shimmer, add a few scallops at a time to the pan.
2. Cook scallops on one side for about 2 minutes, or until there is a nice brown crust. Flip the scallops over, and cook 1 more minute.
3. Remove to a warm plate for serving with the Shallot Jam and the Roasted Tomato Vinaigrette.

"With scallops, it's where you get them. We get them live in the shell. I'm willing to share our connection with the White House. This could be the start of a beautiful love affair with the scallop."
Eric Ripert

the Fig Tree
restaurant
at the Lucas House

Chilled Spicy Cantaloupe and Minted Honeydew Melon Soup

Welcome to The Fig Tree Restaurant. We opened in March, 2005 after nearly a year of renovations and upgrades to the historic Lucas House, a 1913 Craftsman Bungalow in Charlotte's Elizabeth neighborhood. As a Chef owned and operated restaurant, our goal is to provide a unique dining experience building on our seasonal French and Italian cuisine, an international wine list and unsurpassed service. We look forward to serving you.
Owners Greg Zanitsch & Sara Scheidler

Spicy Cantaloupe Soup:
1 cantaloupe, peeled, seeded, and rough chopped
2 oz. simple syrup
1 lime, zest and juice
1 orange, zest and juice
1-2 Tbsp chili paste
¼ tsp crushed red pepper flakes
¼ tsp white pepper
2 Kaffir lime leaves
Salt to taste

Minted Honeydew Melon Soup:
1 honeydew melon, peeled, seeded and rough chopped
1 Tbsp honey
6 oz. simple syrup
1 lemon, zest and juice
1 orange, zest and juice
1/4 tsp white pepper
10 mint leaves, chiffonade
Salt to taste

Spicy Cantaloupe Soup:
1. In a food processor, puree all ingredients except for the Kaffir lime leaves.

2. Push through a sieve, add lime leaves and refrigerate for 4 hours.

3. Remove lime leaves before serving.

Minted Honeydew Melon Soup:
1. In a food processor, puree all the ingredients except for the mint leaves.

2. Push through a sieve, add mint leaves and refrigerate for 4 hours.

3. To serve. pour Minted Honeydew Melon Soup in a bowl. In the center, pour the Spicy Cantaloupe Soup until equal amounts.

4. Pour in center 1 oz. of heavy cream and garnish with fresh mint sprig.

Signature Tastes of CHARLOTTE

The Fig Tree Restaurant
The Lucas House, 1601 East 7th Street

"Success to me is having ten honeydew melons and eating only the top half of each slice."
Barbra Streisand

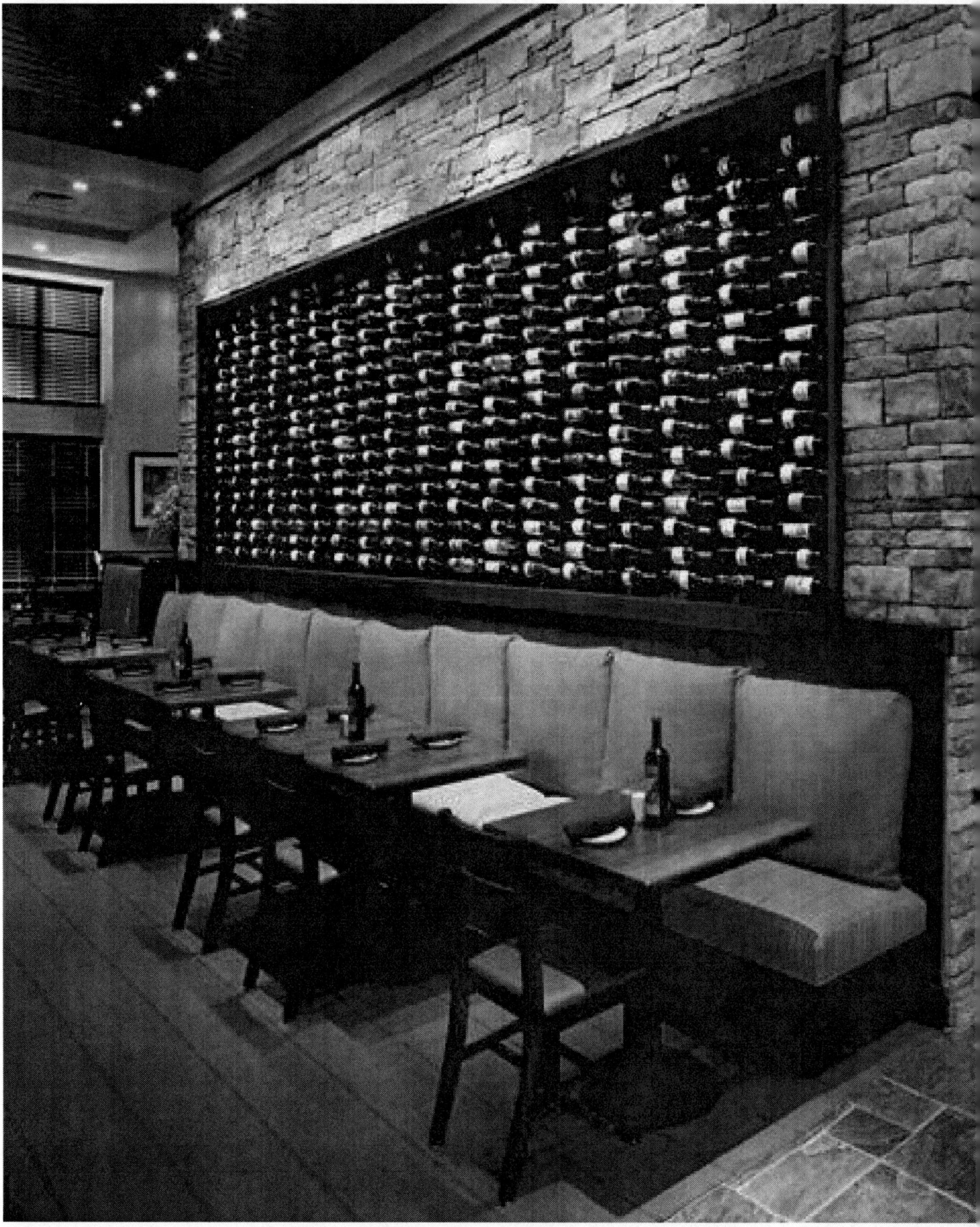

Firebirds Pecan Crusted Trout

Firebirds Wood Fired Grill introduced a taste of Colorado to the Carolinas when it first opened its doors in Charlotte, North Carolina in December of 2000. The restaurant is the creative concept of owner and restaurateur, Dennis Thompson, who regularly travels out west. He fell in love with the feel of the area as well as the food. Drawing from those experiences, he developed Firebirds.

4 trout filets
4 Tbsp canola oil
1 C. buttermilk
1 C. finely chopped pecans
1 C. panko bread crumbs
¼ tsp salt

1. Preheat oven to 400°F.

2. Place buttermilk into a shallow bowl. Combine finely chopped pecans, panko bread crumbs and salt in a separate shallow bowl.

3. Heat a saute pan on medium high heat and add the oil.

4. Dredge the trout filets in the buttermilk and shake off excess buttermilk; then place them into the pecan crust mixture. Press firmly with your hand to completely coat each filet. Add the trout to the saute pan skin side up and saute until brown, approximately 3 minutes.

5. Remove the trout from the saute pan by flipping it over and placing it onto a baking sheet. Bake for approximately 3 minutes until the fish is firm and flaky.

6. Place on a serving platter along with the Tortilla Slaw and Peach Salsa. Garnish with a sprig of cilantro and extra pecans!

Signature Tastes of Charlotte

Firebirds Wood Fired Grill
13850 Ballantyne Corporate Place, Suite 450

"We do a little bit of everything you can do with a pecan."
Keith Ellis

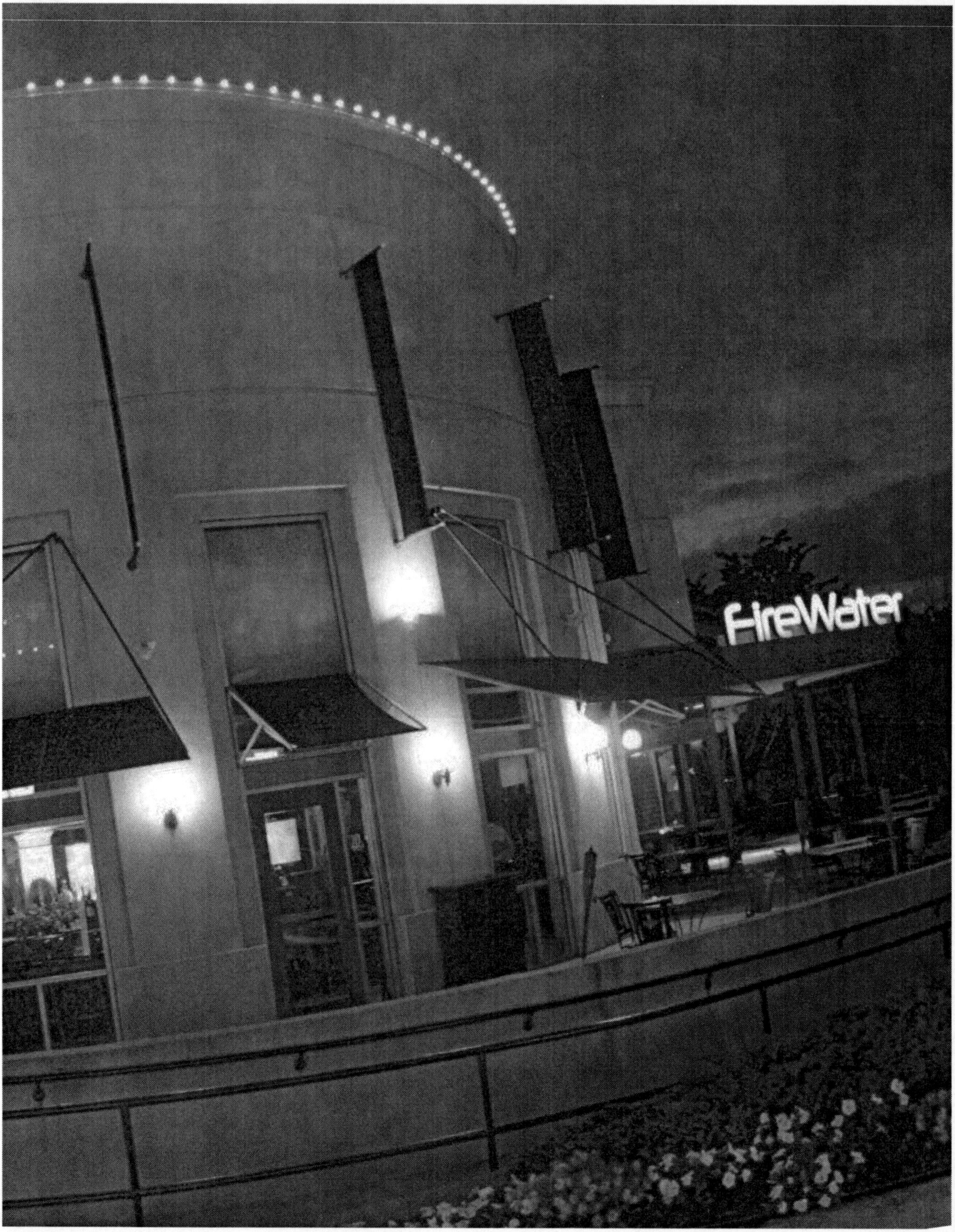
FireWater

Tuna Tartare Trio

Firewater sets the standard for casual, upscale dining in the Charlotte University City area. Our eclectic American cuisine, extensive wine list and contemporary atmosphere are perfect for intimate or group dining. We boast sushi grade Tuna, as well as the best steak in a modern, yet, romantic setting. Our outdoor patio offers an expansive view of the lake and an unforgettable experience. We are north Charlotte's premier location for corporate dinners, group luncheons, rehearsal dinners and intimate wedding receptions.

Mayonnaise:
2 oz. egg yolks
2 C. oil
2 Tbsp lemon juice
2 tsp minced garlic
Orange Sauce
(2) #10 cans mandarin oranges
3 qts. orange juice
6 lbs white sugar
2 Tbsp red food coloring
zest of 4 oranges
Wasabi Aioli:
8 oz. wasabi powder
water as needed
2 C. mayonnaise
Soy Mandarin:
1 C. soy sauce
2 Tbsp zanthum gum
2 C. orange sauce
2/3 C. mayonnaise
zest of 2 oranges
½ C. black sesame seeds
Lemon Caper Garlic:
½ C. capers
1 C. green onions
4 oz. roasted garlic
zest of 2 lemons
3 Tbsp lemon juice
1/3 C. house mayonnaise
8 oz. chopped tuna
3 fried won tons
2 oz. sprouts

Homemade Mayonnaise:
1. Mix the yolks with the lemon juice and the garlic in a blender. Slowly add the oil while mixing to emulsify the mixture until smooth.
2. Season with salt and white pepper. Let cool.

Orange Sauce for Mandarin Soy Sauce:
1. Cook the mandarins, juice and sugar down to a thick syrup consistency. Remove from the heat.
2. Test a small portion in the freezer for consistency. If correct, add the food coloring and pulse 2 times in the blender, so small chunks of the orange remain.

Wasabi Aioli:
1. Mix the wasabi powder with just enough water to smooth the mixture into a paste, then add the mayonnaise.

Soy Mandarin:
1. In a mixer, combine the soy sauce, zanthum gum, and orange sauce. Blend until smooth.
2. Mix in the mayonnaise. Fold in the sesame seeds and orange zest. Let cool overnight before using.

Lemon Caper Garlic:
1. Chop ingredients and mix together until smooth.

Assembly:
1. Mix a little of each sauce with 2 oz. of tuna. Use ring molds for each flavor, and place the won ton on top of the tuna.
2. Top with sprouts. Garnish plate as desired.

Signature Tastes of CHARLOTTE

FIREWATER
8708 JW CLAY BLVD.

"I really look at my childhood as being one giant rusty tuna can that I continue to recycle in many different shapes."
Augusten Burroughs

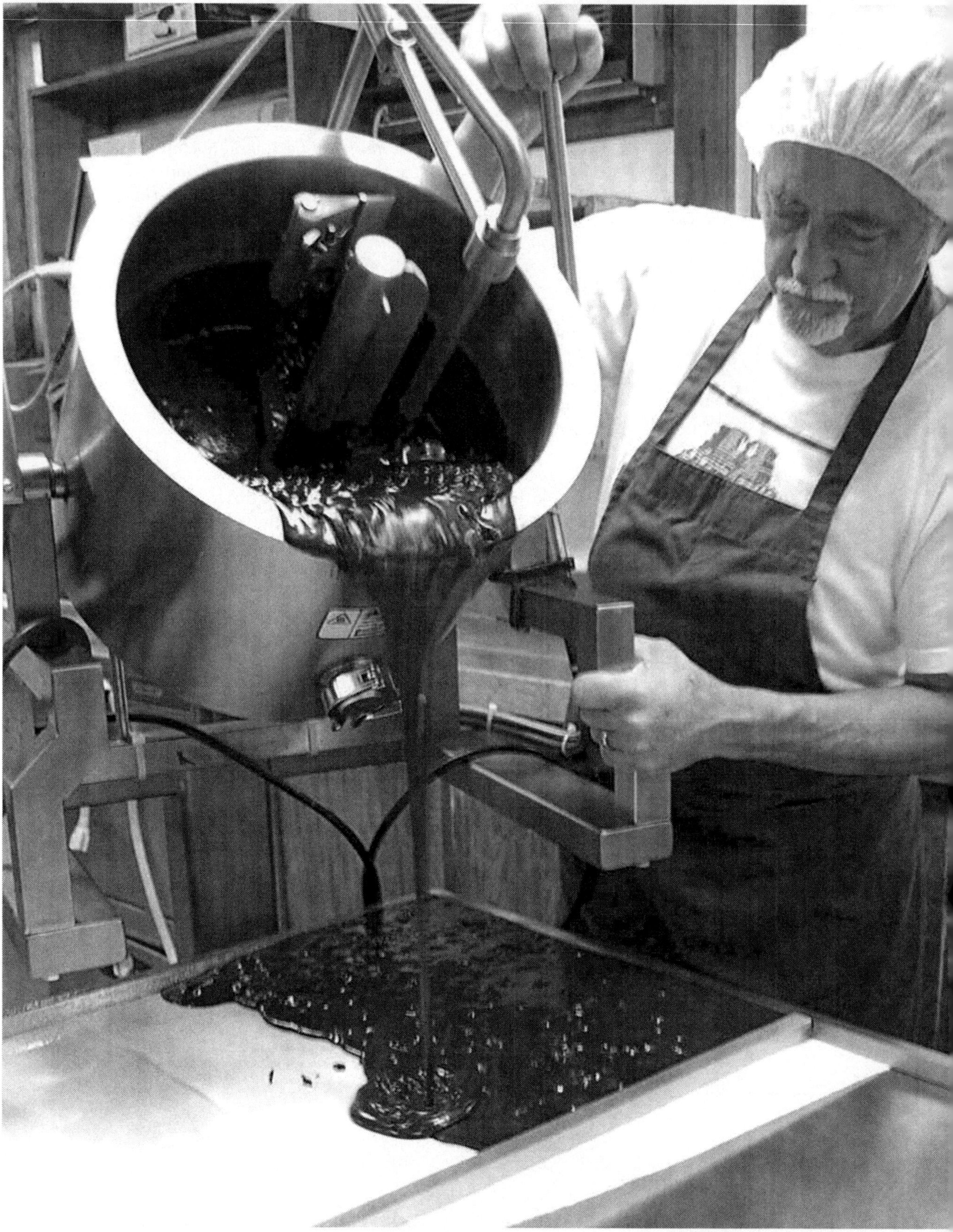

Sour Cream Fudge

Signature Tastes of CHARLOTTE

Those familiar with Shiela will no doubt agree that she is a member of this community who, as she proudly admits, "bleeds Charlotte." Famous throughout the city for board service at the Children's Speedway, Charities, Hospitality Tourism and the Chamber of Commerce, the city of Charlotte is certainly better because of her service and contributions. This recipe is courtesy of Shiela's beloved mother, Juanita Hicks

1½ C. sugar
⅔ C. sour cream (or 8 oz. container)
½ C. margarine
8 oz. white chocolate (or 6 oz. bag white chocolate chips)
1 tsp vanilla
¾ C. toasted pecans or walnuts

1. Butter sides of heavy 2 qt. saucepan.

2. Mix sugar, sour cream, and margarine, and cook over medium heat to a full boil.

3. Boil 5 minutes, or until candy thermometer reads 238°F. Remove from heat.

4. Stir in white chocolate and vanilla. Stir until smooth and creamy, about 3 minutes.

5. Add nuts and stir in, incorporating evenly.

6. Pour into buttered 8" x 8" x 2" pan. Refrigerate, and cut into pieces when cooled.

Shiela H. Fletcher
Partner of Pavilion at Epicenter, Charlotte Resident since 1999

"EXISTENCE, n. A transient, horrible, fantastic dream, Wherein is nothing yet all things do seem: From which we're wakened by a friendly nudge Of our bedfellow Death, and cry: "O fudge!"
Ambrose Bierce

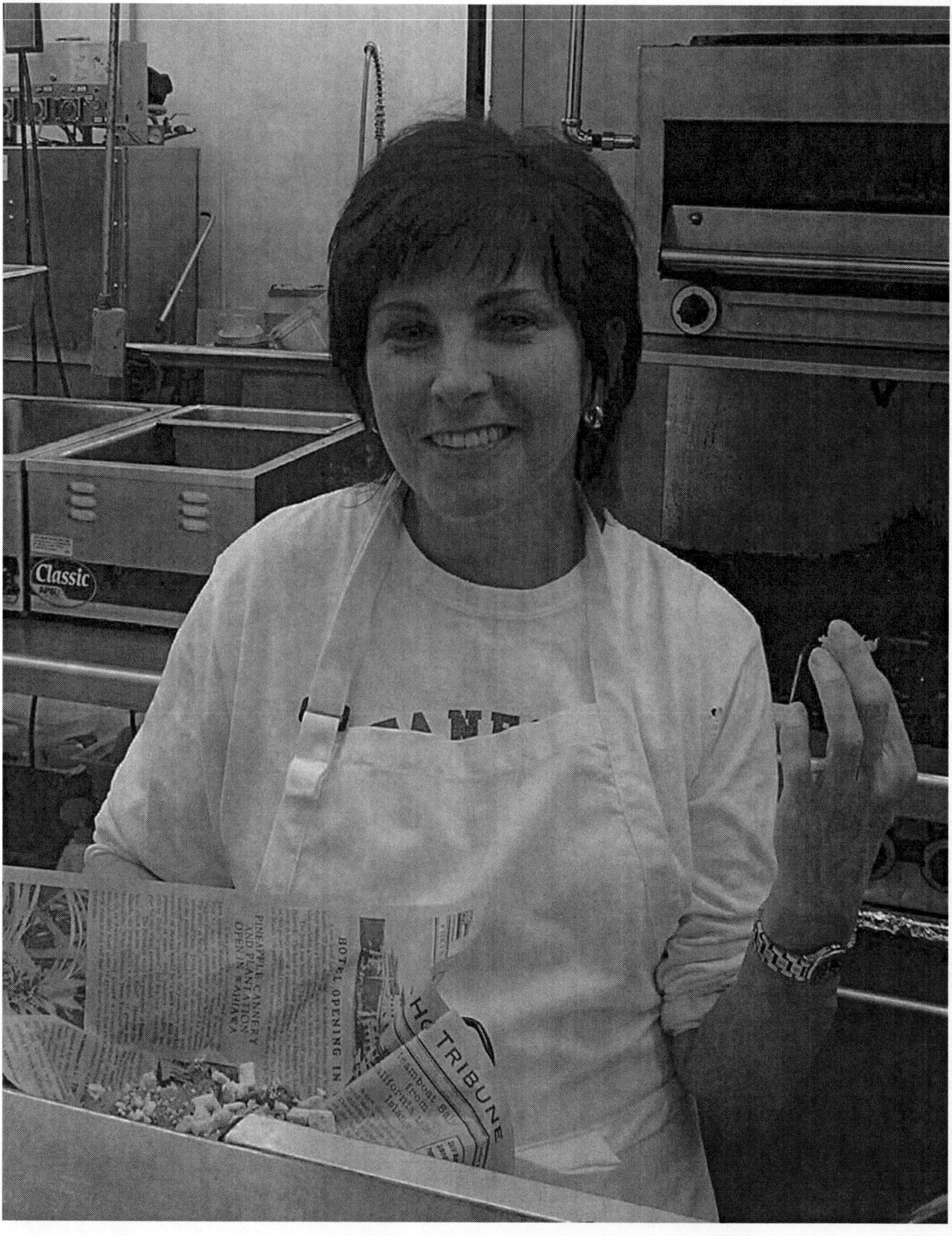
Classic
HOTEL OPENING IN
TRIBUNE

Fran's House Roast Chicken

I opened this restaurant to fill a void: inexpensive, eclectic dishes designed to satisfy both grazers and hearty eaters in a fun, welcoming and casual environment. My mission is to prepare fresh and carefully crafted food and to serve it in a manner that nurtures the spirit as well as the body, capturing the essential meaning of hospitality. Happy Eating!

(1) 4-5 lb. chicken, cut into 8 parts

Herb Rub:
- 3 Tbsp garlic, minced
- 4 Tbsp paprika
- 4 Tbsp lemon pepper
- 1/8 C. chopped fresh rosemary
- 1/8 C. chopped fresh thyme
- 1 1/2 C. canola/olive oil blend
- 2 Tbsp lemon zest
- 2 Tbsp lime zest

Roasted Root Vegetables:
- 4 extra-large carrots, or 6 regular sized carrots, peeled
- 5-6 red bliss potatoes, washed, but not peeled
- 3 turnips, peeled
- 3-4 cloves garlic, finely minced
- 1/2 C. parsley, finely chopped
- Salt and pepper

1. Combine all the ingredients for the herb rub, and rub well over all the chicken parts. Place on parchment-lined baking sheet. Sprinkle with extra paprika, herbs, and zest.
2. Place in preheated 425°F oven for the first 10-12 minutes, then reduce heat to 350°F, and continue roasting for 15-20 minutes, or until meat thermometer reads 160°F when inserted into chicken. Serve with Roasted Root Vegetables

Roasted Root Vegetables:
1. Preheat oven to 400°F. Cut veggies into irregular pieces that are a little bit bigger than what you would consider "bite-sized." The point is to have these look rustic, not perfectly similar, but close enough in size that they will look well together in a rustic way.
2. In a large bowl, toss together the carrots, potatoes and turnips with 3/4 of the garlic and parsley. Season generously with salt and pepper. Spray a baking sheet with cooking spray and arrange the veggies on the tray so that they are not overlapping and too crowded. Otherwise, they will steam instead of roast, and won't caramelize.
3. Cut the onions into sixths, being careful to keep each piece together as much as possible. Don't over think this, because they will fall apart some. Toss them with the remaining garlic, parsley and more salt and pepper.
4. Place on a separate, well sprayed baking pan. Pop both pans into the oven. Allow to bake without looking for about 10 minutes, then check them, giving stir from time to time, so that all sides brown. The onions will be finished first, only taking about 20 minutes. The other veggies will require about 30 minutes. They are done when they can be easily pierced with a fork or knife, and when they are a lovely golden brown. Some edges of the onions may scorch a bit, but remove them as they are ready, just a bit at a time, to avoid a problem.

Signature Tastes of CHARLOTTE

Fran's Filling Station
2410 Park Road

"A Jewish woman had two chickens. One got sick, so the woman made chicken soup out of the other one to help the sick one get well."
Henny Youngman

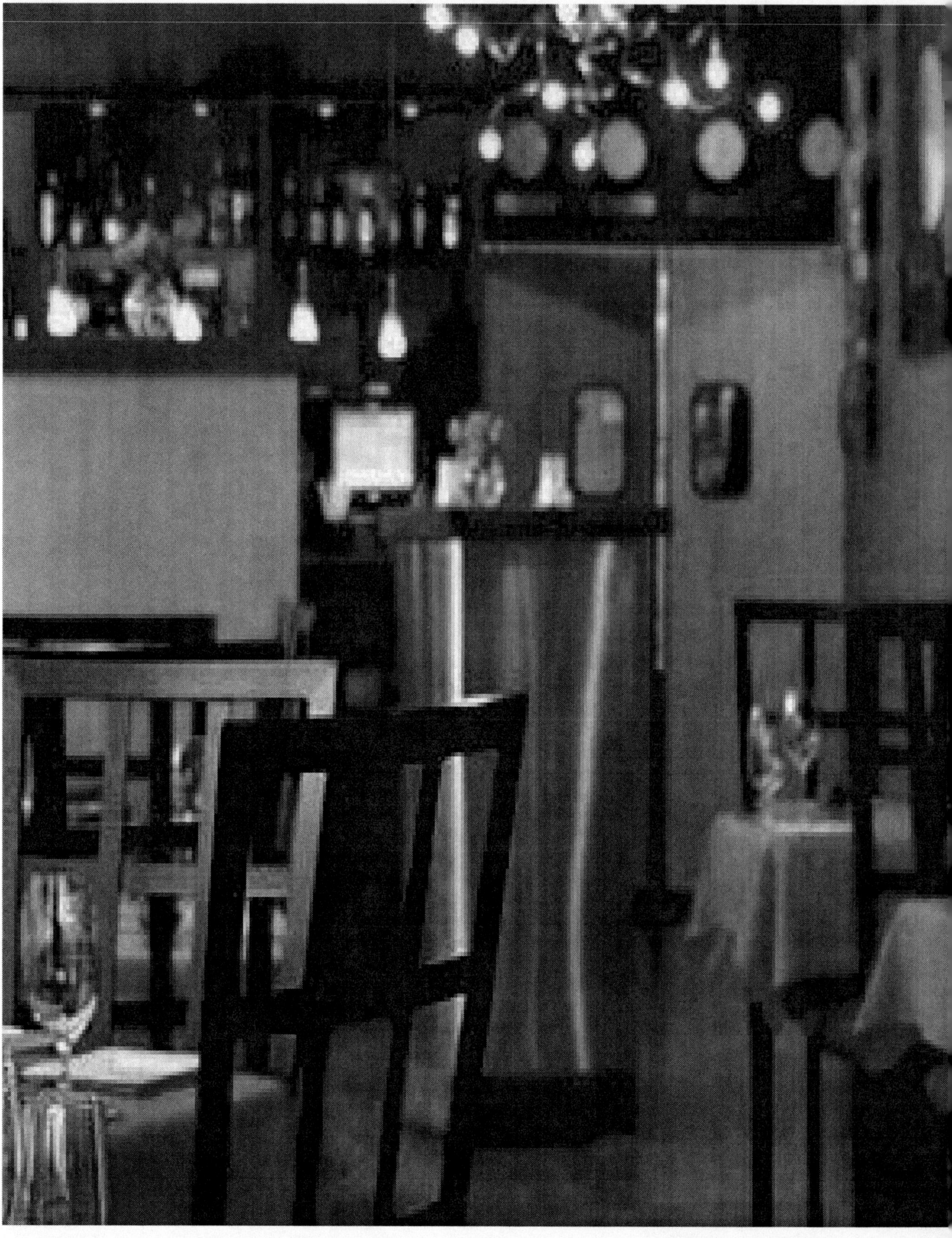

Diver Scallops Crudo with Mango Salsa & Arugula

While growing up in Nice, France, Bernard knew his calling would be in the culinary industry. From the age of 15, his influences included both his grandfather Pastry Chef and father who owned a fish shop. Dreaming of working in America, Bernard accepted a position in the cruise industry and met his wife, Shannon, an essential partner in bringing their restaurant to life. There is no one favorite style of cooking that defines Bernard's efforts in the kitchen and the essential ingredient is literally the love and passion he brings to each dish.

8 Scallops (size U/10 Dry)
½ oz. Micro Arugula (From Tega Hill Farm)
1 fresh ripe mango
1 shallot
1 lime
½ C. extra virgin olive oil
Salt and pepper to taste

1. Reserve your scallops in the cooler. Meanwhile, peel the mango and shallot. With a chef's knife, dice the mango and shallot very thinly. Add them into a small pastry bowl.

2. With a zester on top of the bowl, zest the lime, then cut in half and squeeze in its juice. Add seasoning and olive oil and mix together. Reserve in the cooler.

3. Slice each scallop with a paring knife, ¼ inch thick maximum. You should be able to slice approximately 5 per scallop.

4. Take 4 dinner plates, pour a touch of olive oil on each plate. With a brush or your hand, spread the oil on the surface. Then, arrange scallops (2 scallops per person/10 slices) on each plate.

5. Once the plates are filled with the scallops, season with salt and pepper. Use a tablespoon to delicately spread the sauce/salsa on the scallops uniformly.

6. Arrange arugula on top. "Et voila! Bon appetit!"

Signature Tastes of CHARLOTTE

GLOBAL RESTAURANT
3520 TORRINGDON WAY

"Personal transformation can and does have global effects. As we go, so goes the world, for the world is us. The revolution that will save the world is ultimately a personal one."
Marianne Williamson

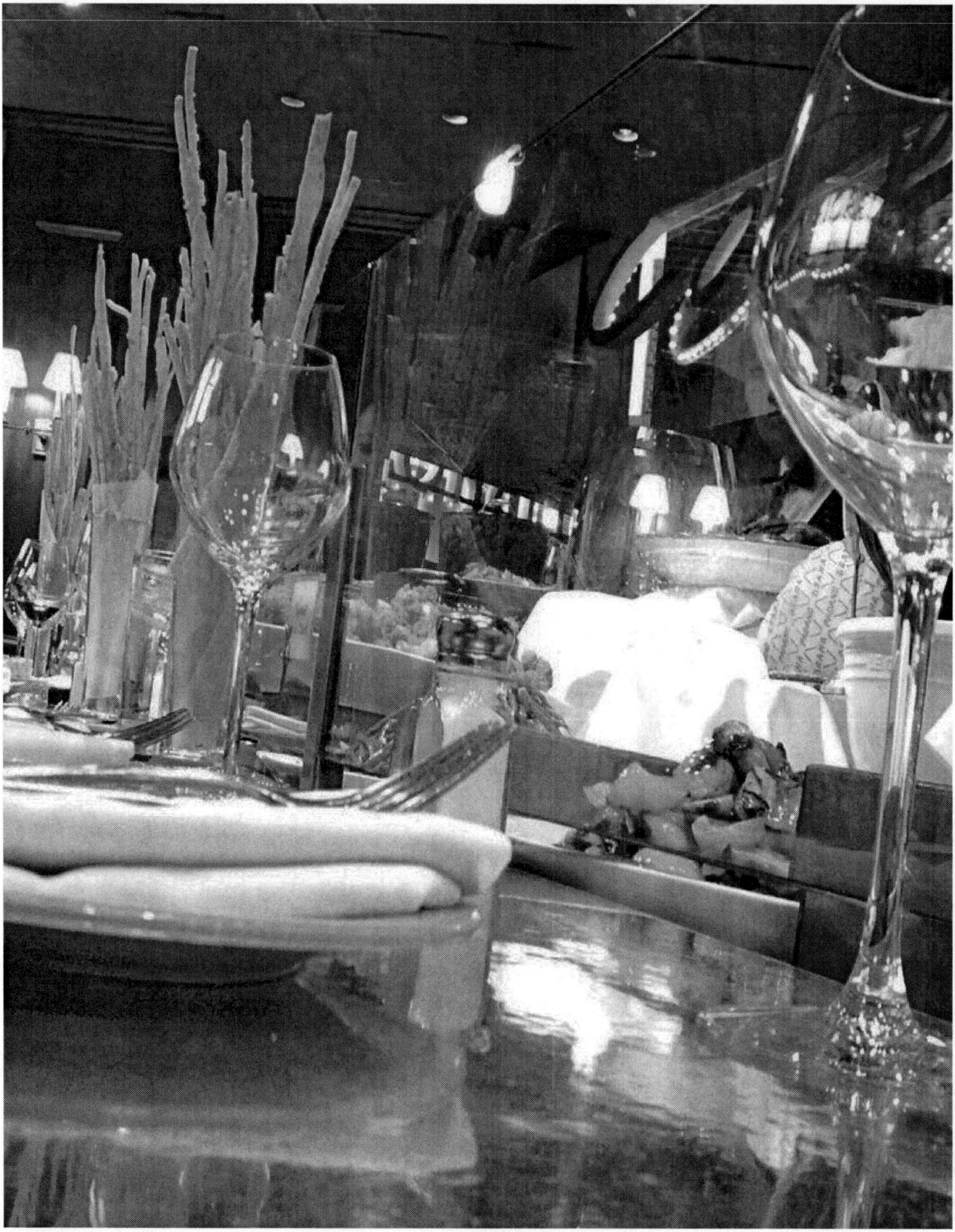

Chocolate Chip Cheesecake

Signature Tastes of CHARLOTTE

The Greater Charlotte Hospitality & Tourism Alliance (HTA) is a full time association representing more than 800 businesses in the greater Charlotte area. The organization was established in October 1994 by the leaders of different segments of the hospitality industry. This combined organization was created to respond to the need for a full time and privately funded organization which was required to represent this growing industry with a commitment to proactively influence decisions, eliminating industry related challenges and maximizing opportunities for our remarkable industry.

Crust:
¼ C. butter, melted
1½ C. Oreo cookie crumbs (approximately 18 cookies)

Filling:
(3) 8 oz. packages cream cheese, softened
1 can sweetened condensed milk
3 eggs
2 tsp vanilla
1 C. mini milk chocolate chips
1 tsp flour

For the crust:
1. Remove filling from the Oreos and crush. Combine butter and cookie crumbs.

2. Press into bottom of a 9" springform pan.

For the filling:
1. In a large mixing bowl, beat cream cheese until fluffy.

2. Add condensed milk, eggs and vanilla, and mix well.

3. In a separate bowl, combine ½ C. of the chocolate chips with 1 tsp flour. Toss to coat, and stir into cream cheese mixture.

4. Pour over crust, and sprinkle remaining ½ of chocolate chips on top.

5. Bake for 1 hour at 300°F, or until cake springs back when lightly touched. Cool to room temperature and then chill until serving.

Hospitality & Tourism Alliance 301 South McDowell Street, Suite 1106

Greater Charlotte HTA

"Because you don't live near a bakery doesn't mean you have to go without cheesecake."
Hedy Lamarr

QUEEN
CHARL
95657

License plate from the 1960's
to celebrate the city.

HICKORY TAVERN

Chicken Salad

Signature Tastes of CHARLOTTE

Founded in 1997, the Hickory Tavern network has grown to include businesses in 13 communities throughout North Carolina and Spartanburg, SC. Our unique brand of casual dining, lively bar atmosphere, and sports enthusiasm provides the perfect destination no matter what the time of day. We are constantly growing so if you don't have a Hickory Tavern near you right now stay tuned - there may be one coming to your neighborhood soon!

3 lbs. seasoned, cooked chicken, diced into ¾ inch cubes
½ Tbsp tarragon leaves
⅙ C. celery, finely diced
¾ C. halved grapes
¾ C. chopped dried cranberries
1¼ C. mayonnaise
1½ Tbsp olive oil

1. Chop Craisins until they are small and fine.

2. In a large mixing bowl whip mayonnaise, olive oil and tarragon leaves until smooth.

3. Add in chicken, celery, Craisins and grapes into bowl.

4. Mix all ingredients in a mixing bowl until they are evenly incorporated.

5. Refrigerate overnight to allow the flavors to meld.

Yield: 36 oz

The Hickory Tavern
Chef Monte Olson - 12220 Copper Way, Ste. 210

"Love, like a chicken salad a restaurant has, must be taken with blind faith or it loses its flavor"
Helen Rowland, English-American writer

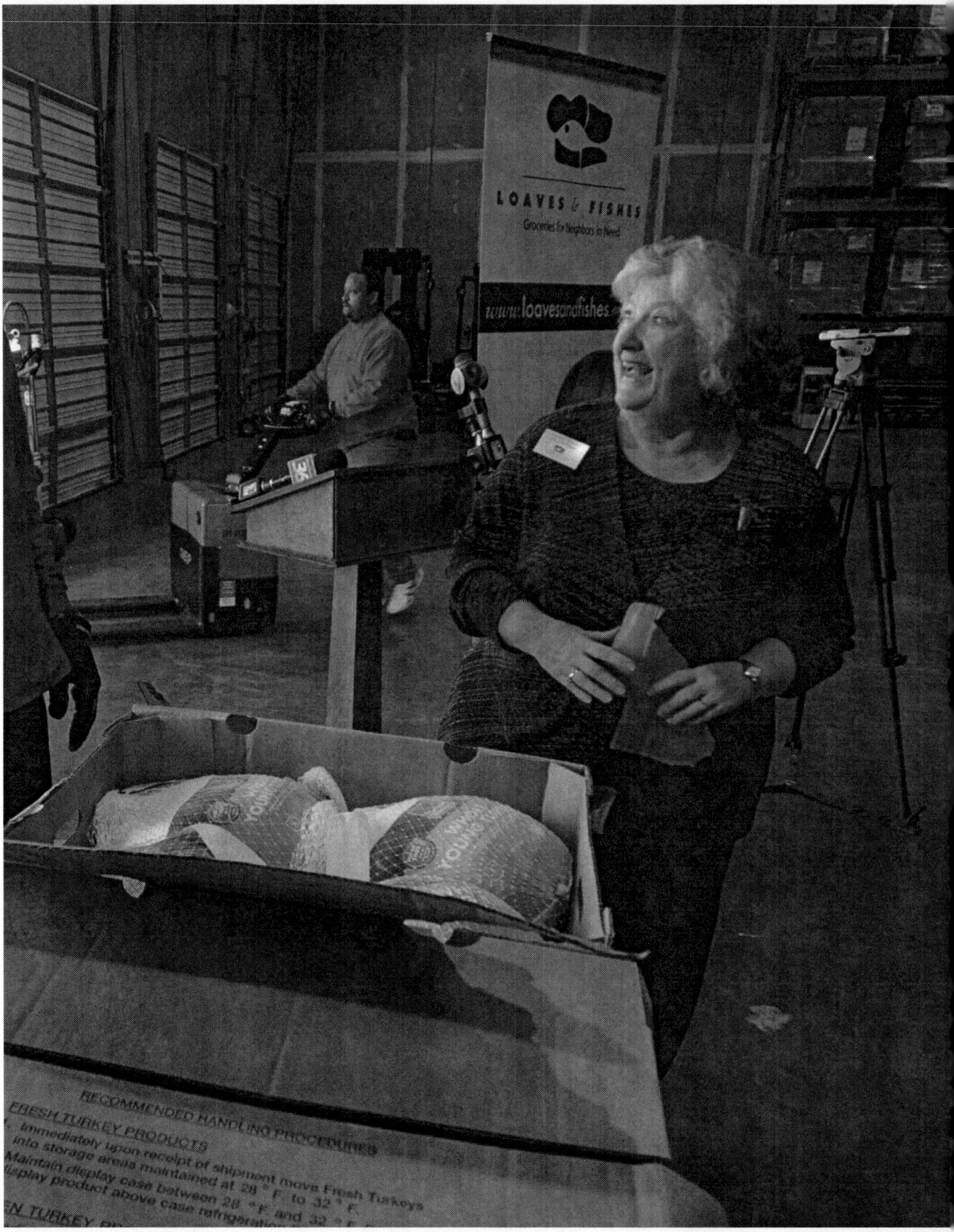
LOAVES & FISHES
Groceries for Neighbors in Need
RECOMMENDED HANDLING PROCEDURES
FRESH TURKEY PRODUCTS

Walnut Wonder Cake

Loaves & Fishes provides a week's worth of nutritious groceries to individuals and families in a short-term crisis. In 2010, Loaves & Fishes provided groceries to 110,336 people. Loaves & Fishes is a 501(c)(3) nonprofit, nondenominational organization, founded and operated by local religious congregations and community organizations. It grew out of an effort in 1975 at Holy Comforter Episcopal Church to respond to the growing hunger problem in Mecklenburg County North Carolina and continues to expand to meet that need.

2 C. sifted flour
1 tsp baking powder
1 tsp baking soda
½ tsp salt
1 C. butter, softened
1 C. sugar
2 eggs
1 tsp vanilla
1 C. sour cream

⅓ C. brown sugar
¼ C. granulated sugar
1 tsp cinnamon
1 C. chopped walnuts

1. Sift together the first 4 ingredients. Set aside.

2. Cream together the butter, sugar, eggs and vanilla. Add 1 C. sour cream to the creamed mixture, alternating with the flour mixture. Begin and end with the dry ingredients.

3. Combine the brown sugar, sugar, cinnamon and walnuts.

4. Spread half the batter in a greased and floured 9" x 13" pan. Sprinkle half the nut mixture over the batter.

5. Pour remaining batter over, and sprinkle remaining nut mixture as a topping. Bake at 350°F for 35 minutes.

Signature Tastes of CHARLOTTE

BEVERLY HOWARD, EXECUTIVE DIRECTOR, LOAVES & FISHES

"Having cakes as a business certainly changes things for me - I don't now sit at home doing a cake for the fun of it anymore. But it's an extremely happy and pleasureable business to run because people are generally buying cakes for celebrations."
Jane Asher

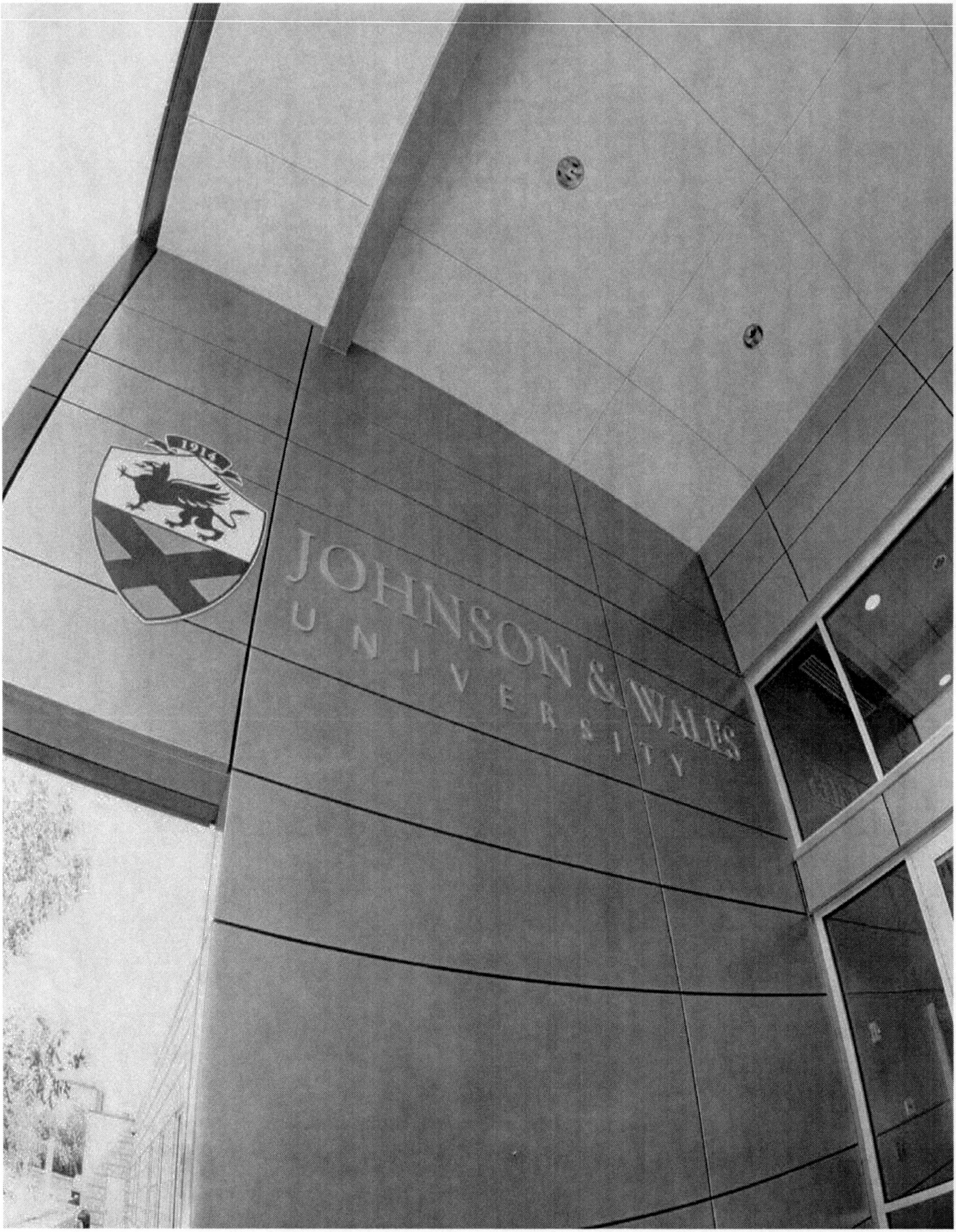
1914
JOHNSON & WALES
UNIVERSITY

Tangy Melon with Shrimp

When we have barbeques at home, the boys love making this dish, peeling the shrimp, pulling off their heads, and deveining them. Chopping up the melon, squeezing the honey from the bottle and mixing it all together with their hands (washed, of course.) It's also a sure fire winner with the family and friends alike. Cantaloupes are a good source of vitamin C. and beta carotene ... add shrimp, and you have a finished dish high in calcium and lean protein. It's also, ever-so-easy to knock up!

1 clove garlic, crushed
1 Tbsp organic honey
2 tsp nam pla (Thai fish sauce)
1 Tbsp grated lime zest
Juice of 2 limes
1 medium sized Thai red chili, finely diced
6 oz. cooked and shelled shrimp
2 oz. unsalted roasted almonds, lightly chopped
1 small canteloupe melon, peeled and chopped into 1 inch dice, or scooped out in balls
2 Tbsp chopped cilantro
1 Tbsp chopped mint leaves

1. In a large bowl, combine the garlic, honey, nam pla, lemon zest, lime juice and chili.

2. Fold in the shrimp and almonds, add the melon and stir to combine.

3. Sprinkle with chopped cilantro and mint, stir in, and serve.

Signature Tastes of CHARLOTTE

Chef Mark J. Allison, Dean of Culinary Education-801 West Trade Street

Johnson & Wales University

"I want to go to culinary school because I love cooking. One day I'd love to open up a restaurant or cafe."
Mary-Kate Olsen

Diesel enjoying the 70 degree weather on the
dog friendly deck of Kennedy's
Photo by Kyle Dettloff

Kennedy's Shepherd's Pie

Kennedy's Premium Bar & Grill is the newest addition to the historic Elizabeth area of Charlotte. Located on the corner of 7th Street & North Caswell, open seven days a week, Kennedy's Irish Bar will provide the perfect atmosphere to enjoy spirits, great food and live entertainment. We are a New York owned and operated Bar! We invite all New York Transplants to enjoy drinks and food with us!!

Signature Tastes of Charlotte

Kennedy's Premuim Bar and Grill — 366 North Caswell

Ingredients:

- (2) 16.5 oz. cans beef broth
- 8 oz. Guinness
- 1 C. celery, diced
- 1 C. carrots, diced
- 1 C. onion, diced
- 2 C. sliced mushrooms
- 1-2 lb. flank steak, (adjust to desired amount)
- salt, pepper and garlic to taste
- 2 Tbsp corn starch
- ½ Tbsp water
- 3 whole potatoes, cooked, mashed and seasoned to taste
- 10 oz. shredded cheese

Instructions:

1. Sear both surfaces of the steak, then cut into bite size pieces. The meat shouldn't be cooked more than medium rare. Set aside.

2. Mix corn starch with water. Set aside.

3. Combine 1 can of the beef broth and Guinness in a pot, and heat to a boil. Once boiling, turn down so that the liquid is at a constant slow rolling boil. You want to let the broth reduce in the pot by 25%, or approximately 10-15 minutes.

4. Add the beef pieces to the broth, and let broth continue at a slow boil for another 10-15 minutes, until the meat is tender.

5. Add the celery, carrots and onions to the broth. Turn down to simmer. Add salt, pepper and garlic to taste.

6. Cover the pot and let simmer until all vegetables are tender. If at any point in this process your broth begins to dry up, add the 2nd can of broth. Once the vegetables are tender, add the mushrooms and simmer under a lid again until they are tender.

7. Once all the vegetables are tender, add the corn starch slurry slowly to the broth, whisking it in until it has reached your desired thickness. You're done!

8. Top it with mashed potatoes and cheese to complete. Serve in a casserole or individual ramekins.

"The shepherd's pies and pub pies are real close to what we got served when we were kids."
Don O'Brien

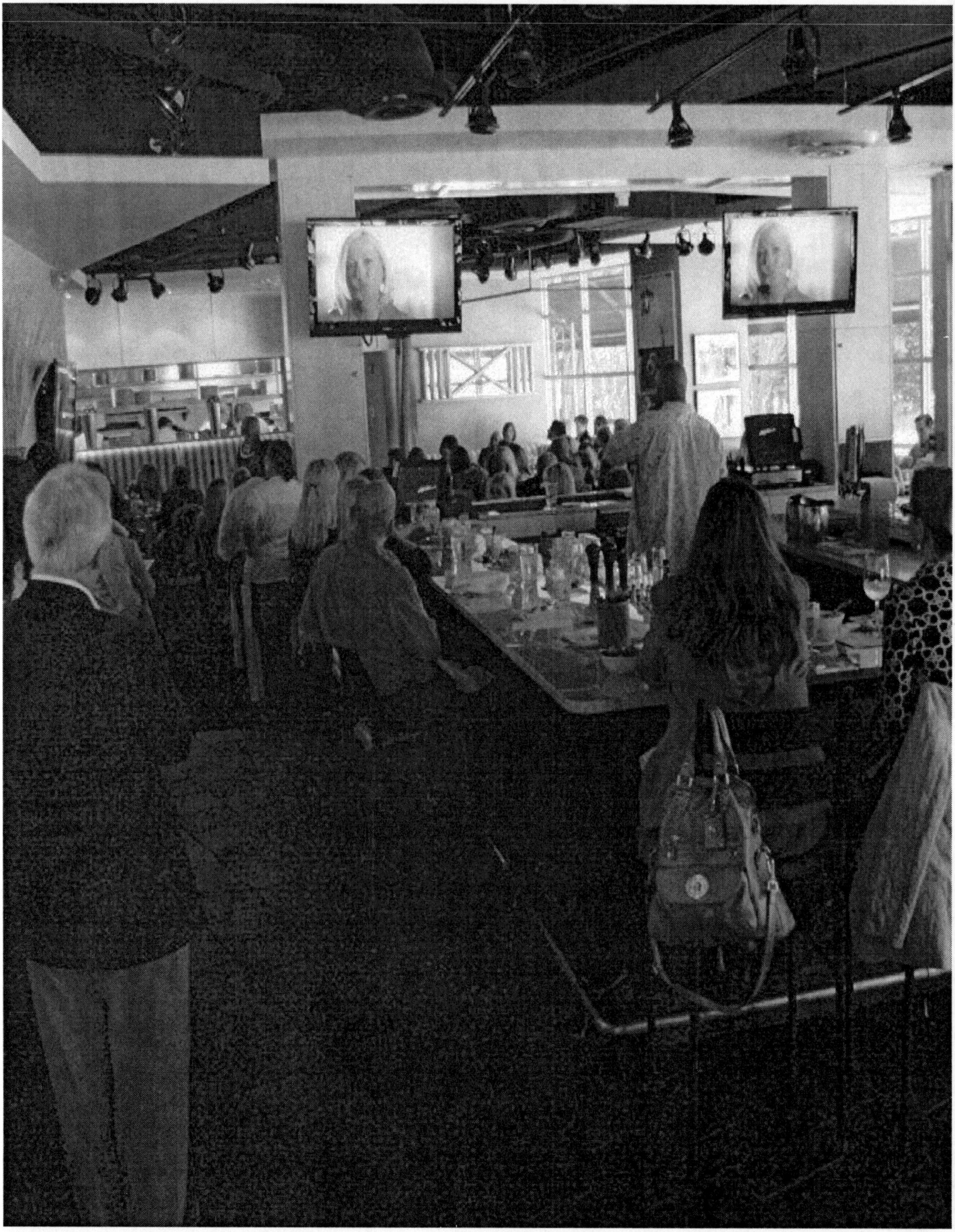

Pimento Cheese

The King's Kitchen is an outreach of Restoration Word Ministries managed by Jim Noble Restaurants that donates 100% of profits from sales to feed the poor in Charlotte, the region, and the world. Additionally, The King's Kitchen partners with area ministries to provide employment opportunities to Charlotteans in search of a new beginning. And while every penny of profit at The King's Kitchen has a higher calling, each bite of the food served to patrons, features Jim's signature "New Local Southern Cuisine."

4 lb. cheddar cheese, shredded
1 lb. Gouda cheese, shredded
3 C. roasted red peppers (24 oz.)
4 C. mayonnaise
3 Tbsp lemon juice

1. Clean the roasted red peppers, and dice them small.

2. Mix everything together in bowl and refrigerate.

Yield: 4 qts.

Signature Tastes of CHARLOTTE

Chef Sam Stachon, Owner Jim Noble-129 W. Trade Street, #100

King's Kitchen

"We're a not for profit restaurant serving up southern cuisine made with fresh, local ingredients from right here in our community. And the proceeds go back to the community, helping to feed those in need. So, come on in. Because when you dine, the whole community thrives."
Jim Noble, owner

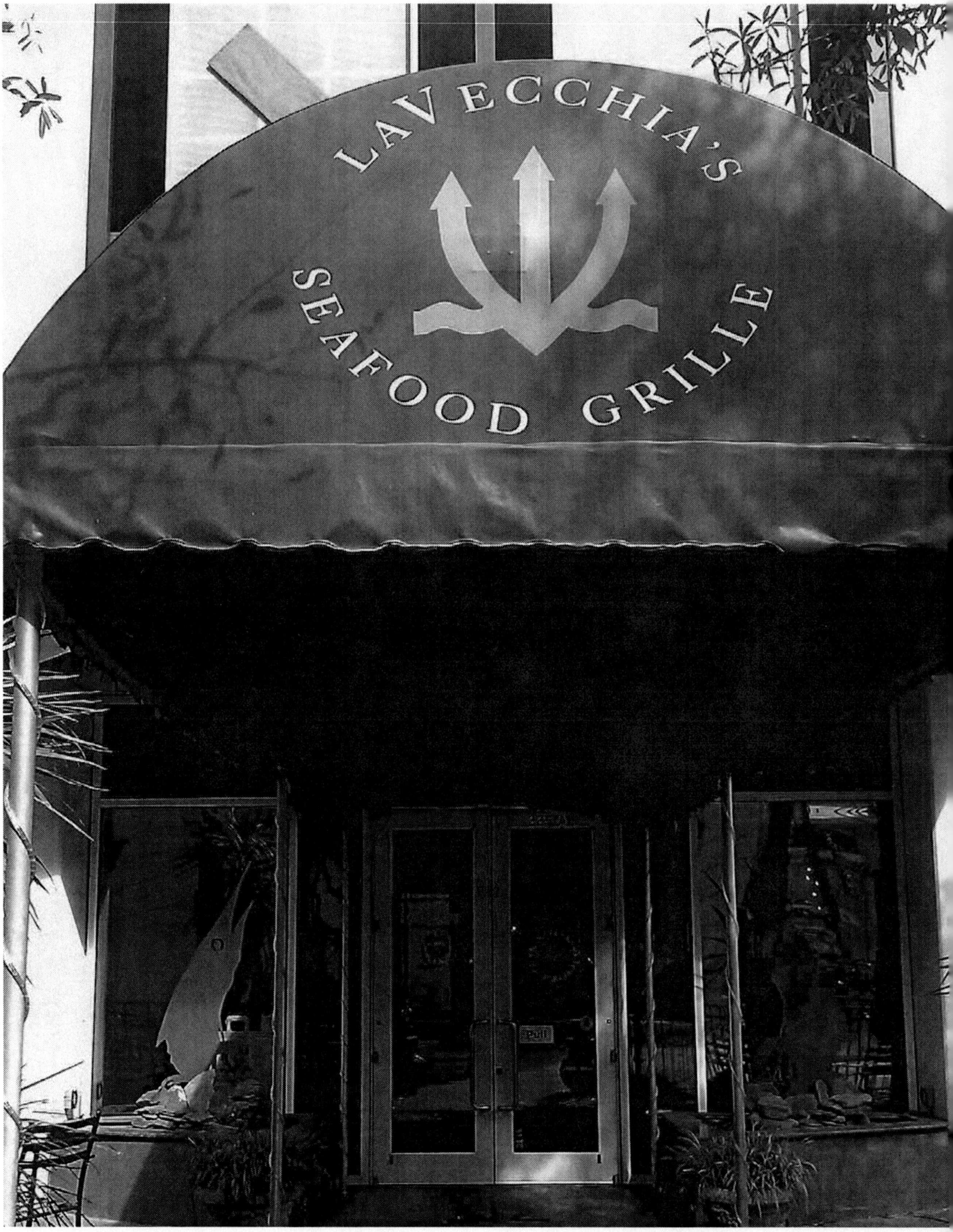
LAVECCHIA'S
SEAFOOD GRILLE

Crab Cakes

Since 1998 this award winning seafood restaurant is perfect for all sorts of gatherings. From birthday celebrations to large business functions, LaVecchia's Steak and Seafood offers the freshest seafood in uptown Charlotte, aged USDA Prime Steaks, great pasta dishes and a hip wine list. Affordable and stylish, LaVecchia's is ALWAYS good.

Base:
- 1 gal. mayonnaise
- 1 lb. liquid egg yolks
- ¾ C. Worchestershire Sauce
- ¼ C. Tabasco Sauce
- 4 lemons, zested and juiced
- 2 bunches, parslely, stemmed and minced
- 1 Tbsp white pepper
- 2 kosher salt
- ¼ C. Old Bay Seasoning
- 2 Tbsp Cajun Seasoning
- ¾ C. Dijon mustard

Crab Cakes:
- 5 lb. claw crab meat, drained, picked through
- 4 lb. lump crab meat, drained, picked through
- Crab cake base
- 4 qts. Panko crumbs
- 1 French baguette, processed in food processor into crumbs
- 3 lemons, juiced
- 3 limes, juiced

Base:
1. In a large mixing bowl, combine all ingredients until fully incorporated.

Crab Cakes:
1. In a large mixing bowl, combine all ingredients, and mix softly by hand until well incorporated, folding the mixture.

2. Place the mixture into the cooler to chill for at least an hour before handling.

3. Using a 3 oz. scoop to form the crab cake, place them onto a sheet tray. Using your hands, form into desired shape and perform standard breading procedure ... coat in flour, dip in egg whites, then coat in panko crumbs. These may be refrigerated until ready to cook.

4. Cook in a saute pan over medium high heat with very little oil, and brown both sides of the crab cake. Run into a hot oven on a sizzle platter for 3 minutes, and serve immediately.

"Because I wasn't going to do it. I'm just going for the crab cakes."
Linda Pierce

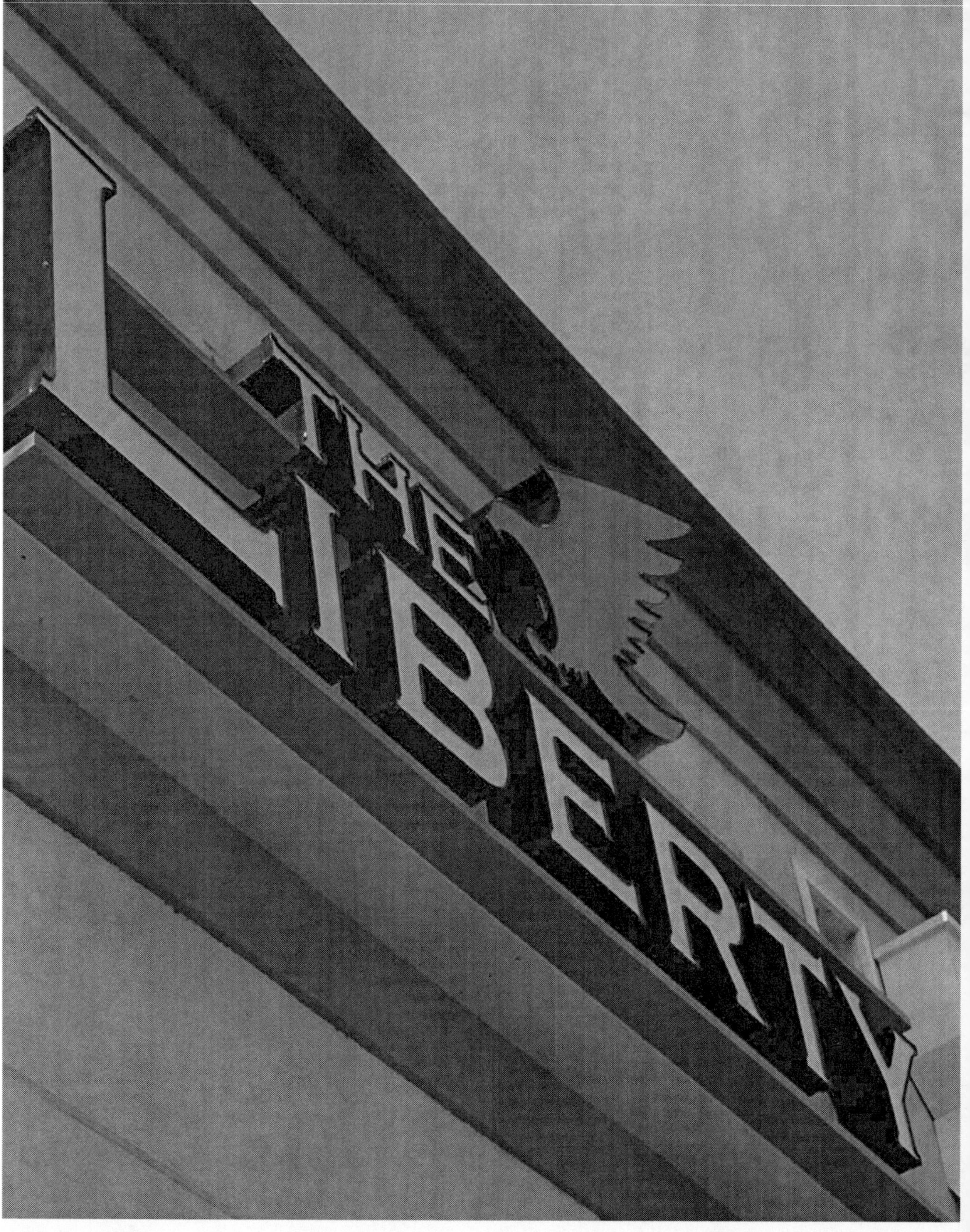
THE LIBERTY

Pork Belly with Sage, Garlic, Apple Sauce & Port Wine Reduction

The Liberty is Charlotte's first Gastropub. Our goal is to provide great food and drink at a reasonable cost. The first Gastropubs started in London as many top chefs turned away from the high costs of fine dining, wanting to do their food in a more casual setting. We also share this vision. We don't have a dress code, or for that matter, an ounce of pretension. We are casual enough for jeans and a tee shirt, but nice enough for a first date. We are a neighborhood establishment, with a light rail stop in our parking lot. We are unlike anything else in Charlotte. Welcome to The Liberty.

1 boneless pork belly
8 fresh sage leaves
1 clove garlic
Juice of 1 lemon
3 Tbsp salt
1 lb. Bramley apples, peeled and cored, and roughly chopped
½ cinnamon sticks
2 oz. butter
3 oz. red wine vinegar
5 oz. red wine
2 oz. port
4 Tbsp sugar
Extra virgin olive oil (to garnish)
Mustard cress (to garnish)

1. Look at the pork belly. If the skin is elastic and fresh, without being slimy or dry, then score it, drizzle with lemon juice, and cover with a very generous amount of salt. Leave for 10 minutes, then pat dry with absorbent paper towels.

2. Lay the belly, skin side down, and sprinkle with the sage leaves and garlic. Tie the whole belly with kitchen string.

3. Place in 460°F oven, until golden brown and crackled, approximately 25 minutes. Turn down to 320°F, and cook for 1-1½ hours. The belly should be tender. The belly is tender when a skewer slides easily into the meat when inserted.

4. Combine the red wine, red wine vinegar, Port and sugar in a saucepan, and heat and reduce until it almost coats the back of a soup spoon.

5. Remove from heat, and keep warm, or transfer to a squeeze bottle. Place apples in a large pot with the butter and cinnamon stick, and gently stew until soft. Put through a mouli or mash with a potato masher.

6. Have 6 warm plates ready. Remove string from pork, slice and put a slice on each plate, a dollop of apple sauce, a drizzle of extra virgin olive oil, and a few very delicate splashes of Port reduction. Sprinkle with a little mustard cress.

"A peasant becomes fond of his pig and is glad to salt away its pork. What is significant, and is so difficult for the urban stranger to understand, is that the two statements are connected by an and not by a but."
John Berger

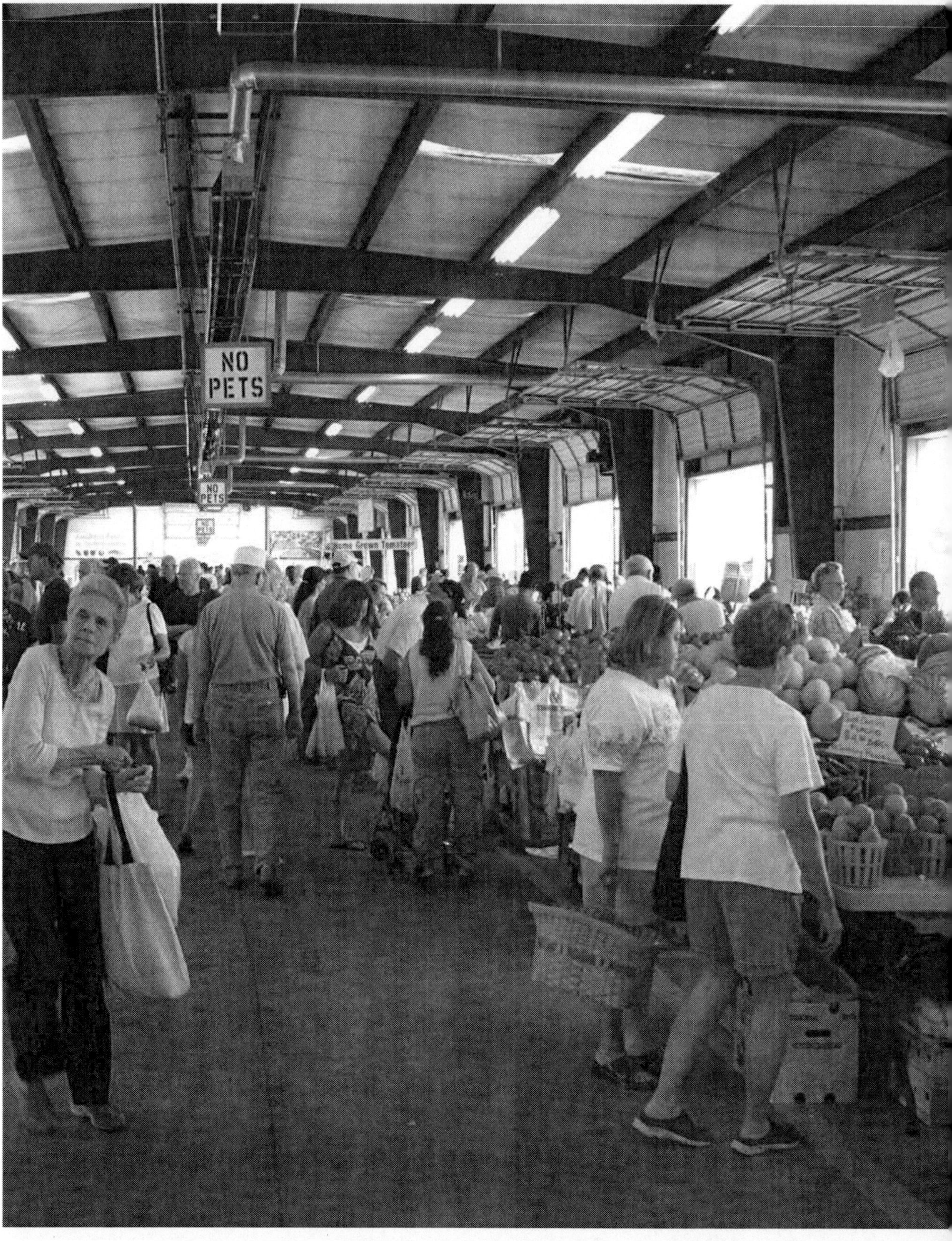
NO
PETS
NO
PETS

Old Fashioned Pound Cake

Pam Hyatt's Lit'l Taste of Heaven is a favorite stop for visitors to the Charlotte Regional Farmers' Market. Her signature fried pies are common treats there. Her prized pound cake is even offered at Price's Chicken Coop by the slice, having developed quite a following, inciting regular phone calls from people who purchased a slice at "The Coop" wanting to know where they can buy a whole cake. Yes, it's that good.

2 sticks, plus 6 Tbsp butter, softened
2¾ C. sugar
6 large eggs
3 C. all purpose flour
½ tsp salt
½ tsp baking powder
1 C. milk
1 Tbsp pure vanilla extract

1. Preheat oven to 325°F. Grease and flour a 10" tube pan.

2. Place softened butter in a bowl of mixer. Mix on medium speed until smooth. Add sugar and mix on low speed until incorporated. Mix on high speed until butter and sugar mixture is light and fluffy.

3. Stop the mixer and scrape down the bowl several times during the creaming process. Add the eggs, one at a time, beating on medium speed after each addition, making sure each one is incorporated.

4. Sift together the flour, baking powder and salt. Sift the mixture again. Add ⅓ of the flour mixture to the creamed mixture. Beat until incorporated.

5. Add ½ of the milk, beating until well incorporated. Add ⅓ of the flour mixture, then the remaining milk, ending with the last ⅓ of the flour. Beat well after each addition.

6. Add vanilla extract, and beat on high speed until incorporated and cake batter is smooth. Pour into prepared pan.

7. Place in preheated oven and bake for 1 hour and 15 minutes, or until cake is golden brown, and a toothpick inserted in the center comes out clean. Let cake sit in the pan for 5 minutes, then remove from pan and allow to cool on rack.

"These two statements are contradictory. If you can support the principles behind a program, how can you not support a program? It's like a pound cake without the butter."
Virginia Cutshall

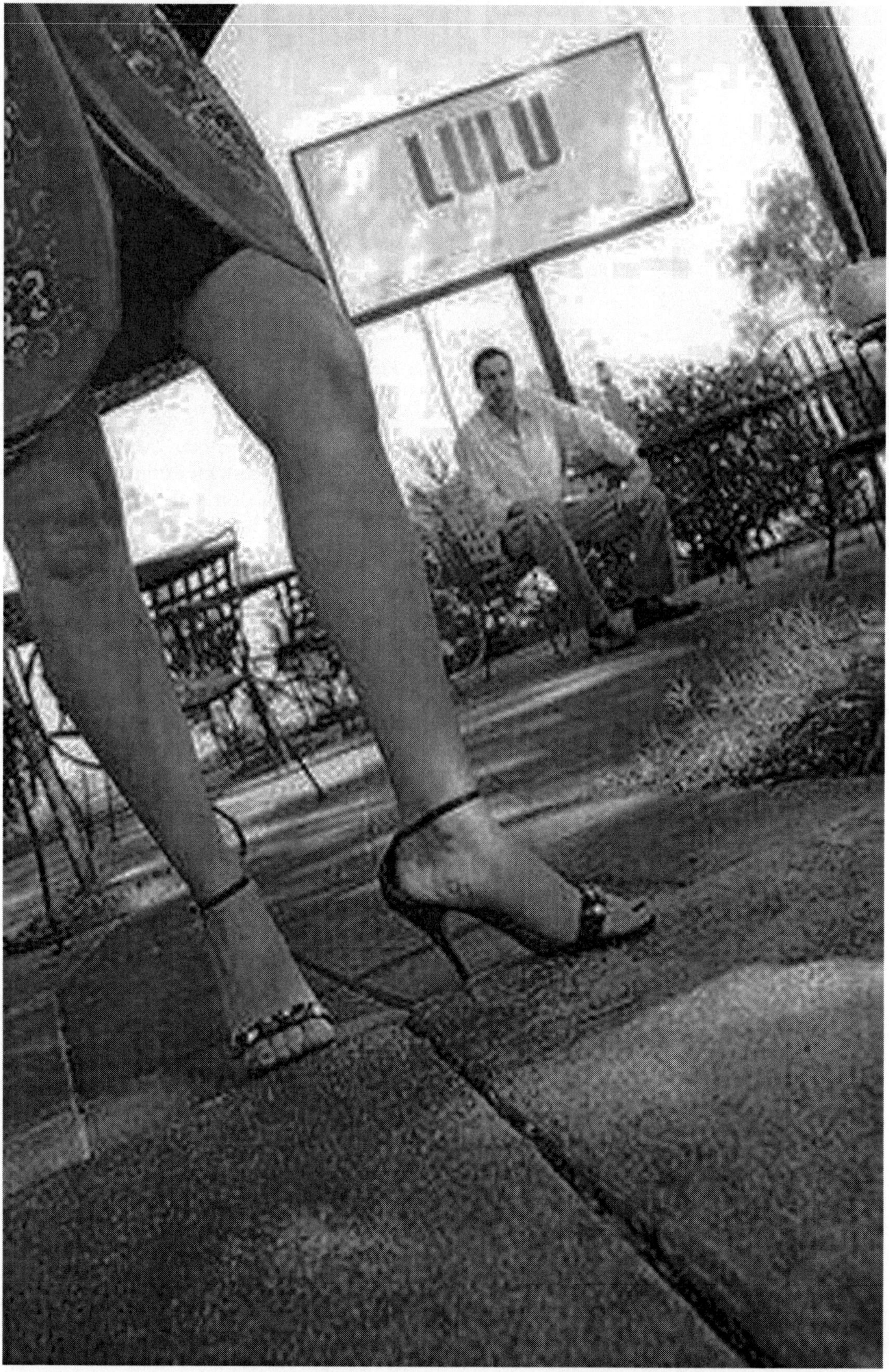
LULU

Fab's Pate

Signature Tastes of CHARLOTTE

Lulu is quaint and lovely, and even has a 'secret' lounge in the back that is totally unexpected. The service is personal, friendly, and attentive. Then, there's Fabs. Charming, talented, and interesting. It was through his personal invitation that I was able to indulge in the pate recipe he submitted. This is a mild, distinctive, heavenly mousse-like pate that rivals all others.

2 C. chicken liver
1 C. rabbit liver
1 C. forest mushrooms
3 shallots
5 cloves garlic
2 large spoonfuls of duck fat
salt and pepper
10 crushed juniper berries
2 carrots, chopped
brandy or dry sherry
about 2 C. heavy cream
milk
thyme

1. Combine the chicken and rabbit livers, rinse them well, and transfer to a container with 2 C. of milk, and let sit for 24 hours.

2. In a large pan, combine duck fat, shallots, garlic, thyme, crushed juniper berries, salt and pepper, chopped carrots, and forest mushrooms and bring to a high heat.

3. Saute until the shallots are golden. Season livers with salt and pepper. Tilt pan so that the fat falls to one side; add livers to the 'fat' side, and cook the livers until they are brown.

4. Deglaze with brandy or dry sherry. Reduce for about a minute, add cream, and reduce for about 5 minutes.

5. Remove the thyme stems, and let rest to cool.

6. Put all ingredients in a food processor, and blend. Transfer the mixture to a terrine, cover with plastic wrap, and refrigerate for 24 hours.

7. Serve with toasted slices of French bread, cornichons and Dijon mustard.

CHEF/OWNER FABRICE DINONNO-921 CENTRAL AVENUE

LULU

"I sometimes feel that more lousy dishes are presented under the banner of pâté than any other."
Kingsley Amis

Mac's
SPEED SHOP

Mac's Speed Shop Brisket

Signature Tastes of CHARLOTTE

Known as some of the best, if not the best beef brisket, anywhere, Mac's is the place to feed a craving for the the stuff. With 3 locations throughout the area at Lake Norman, Steele Creek, and South End, you're bound to know your way to one of them. Since some may consider a stop at Mac's Speed Shop a must, a look on their website gives a list of celebrities who must have agreed. Chef Kevin Kuruc does his duty, and keeps Mac's patrons coming back.

(1) 10-12 lb. whole beef brisket
1 container Mac's Spice Rub (Available at macspeedshop.com)
⅓ C. table salt
(1) 16 oz. jar Mac's Red BBQ sauce
Hickory wood chunks (or wood chunks of choice)

1. Trim the fat cap on top of the brisket to an ⅛ inch thickness. Turn the brisket over and identify the direction the strands of meat fiber are pointed. Flip the brisket over so the fat cap is up, and mark it so that after cooking, it can be sliced across the grain (strands.)

2. Rub liberally with Mac's rub and table salt. Wrap and chill for a minimum of 8 hours. (If you're not lucky enough to have Mac's rub, substitute 3 Tbsp coarse ground black pepper, ⅓ C. granulated garlic, and ¾ C. table salt.)

3. Pull brisket from refrigerator and bring to room temperature. Meanwhile, light your smoker and pre-heat to 225°F, per manufacturer's instructions. A water pan method is highly recommended.

4. Place brisket, fat cap up, on smoker surface, and close lid. Smoke, and maintain heat at 225°F for 10 hours, or until internal temperature reaches 198°F.

5. Pull brisket from smoker and double wrap in aluminum foil. Place wrapped brisket in a pan, so as to catch the meat's juices. Let rest, covered, for 1 hour. After 1 hour, remove the brisket, and place on a cutting board.

6. Slice across the grain in ⅛ inch thickness. Arrange on a serving platter. Mix the saved juices in equal proportions with Mac's Red BBQ sauce and drizzle over the sliced brisket. Enjoy!

CHEF KEVIN KURUC-223 ATHERTON STREET (CORPORATE OFFICE)
MAC'S SPEED SHOP

"This was a silly experiment. ... It has been well documented that great white sharks prefer brisket over bacon. These men had no business attempting such a dangerous experiment. I myself pioneered the study of great white shark food preferences and published the definitive work on the subject titled: Great White Shark Food Preferences: A definitive study."
George Burgess

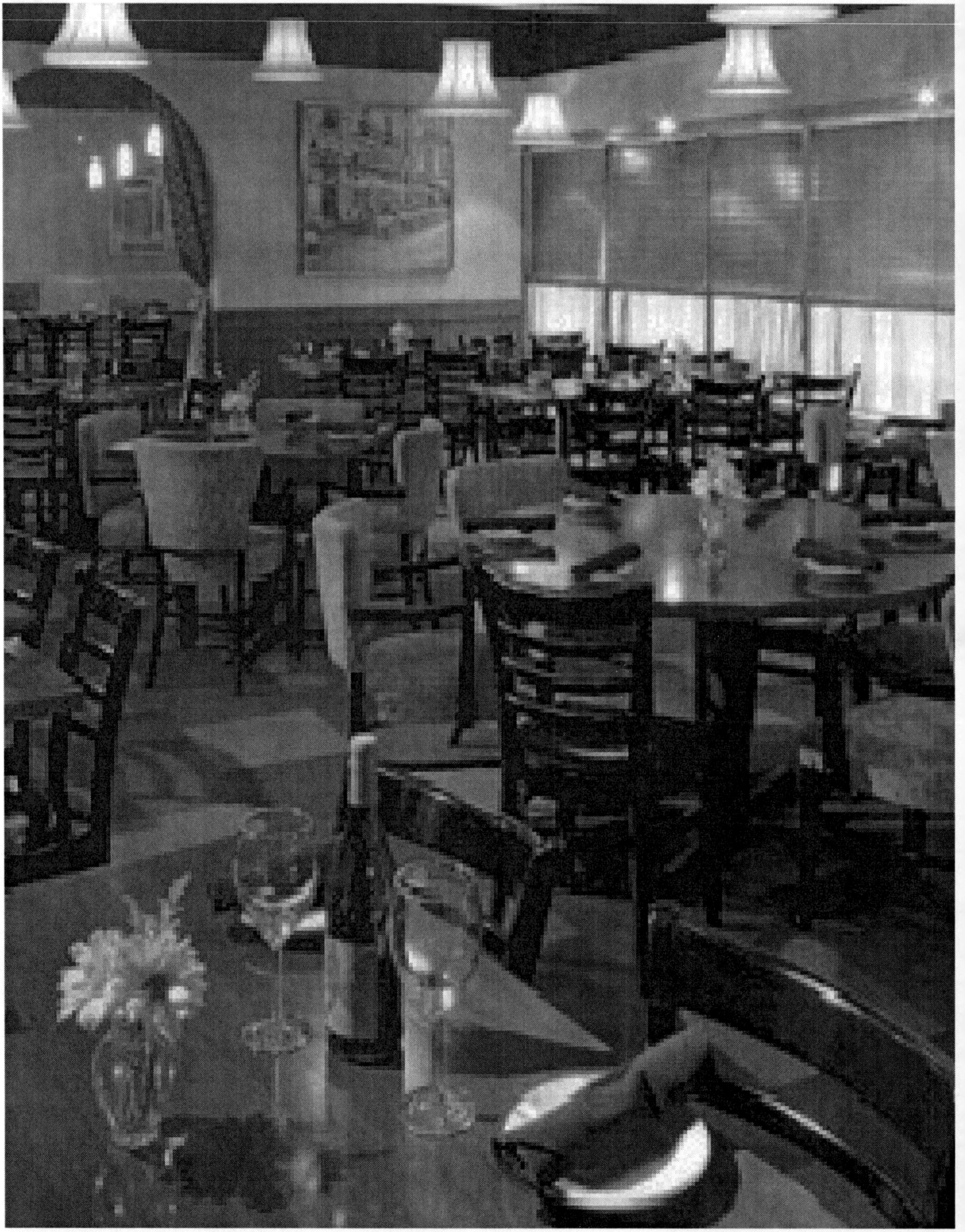

Pollo Carciofi

Owner Frank Scibelli, raised in the grand tradition of hearty family dinners, dreamed of owning a restaurant featuring Italian dishes he grew to love in his family's kitchen. Nearly 15 years has passed since he made that dream a reality and in that time, Mama Ricotta's has become the restaurant of choice for thousands of Italian food lovers. But despite the growth that comes with rising to the top of the list of Charlotte's most beloved restaurants, Mama Ricotta's has upheld unfaltering standards for food and service.

1 C. flour
2 lb. boneless, skinless chicken breasts
6 oz. extra virgin olive oil
8 oz. white wine
16 oz. chicken stock
1 16 oz. can artichoke hearts
4 oz. capers
4 oz. unsalted butter
2 lemons, (juice lemons, and reserve two halves)
Polenta
2 C. vegetables of choice
Italian Parsley, finely chopped

Polenta:
3 oz. mascarpone cheese
11 oz. chicken stock
5 oz. heavy cream
5 oz. water
4 unsalted butter
3 Tbsp Romano cheese, grated
3 Tbsp goat cheese
2 oz. yellow corn meal
pinch ground black pepper
1 tsp kosher salt

1. Dredge each chicken breast lightly in flour. Heat oil in large saute pan and sear chicken breast until golden brown on both sides. Do not remove chicken.

2. Deglaze the pan with the white wine. Let wine reduce by half. Add chicken stock and lemon juice. Place lemon halves in saute pan and simmer.

3. Add capers and reduce sauce by half. Add artichokes and continue to reduce for 3 minutes. Stir butter in until thoroughly mixed with sauce (sauce should be glossy). Salt and pepper to taste. Make sure chicken is thoroughly cooked (should have internal temperature of 165°F).

4. Spoon 8 oz. of polenta onto each plate with your vegetable of choice. Lay chicken over vegetables and polenta. Cover with Carciofi sauce. Finish the plate with light sprinkle of finely chopped Italian parsley.

Polenta:
1. Combine chicken stock, water, and heavy cream in medium sauce pan on high heat. Bring to boil.

2. Slowly add corn meal while whisking the mixture. Note: This step helps keep the polenta from forming lumps.

3. Reduce heat to medium-low and cook for 15 minutes. Stir mixture frequently. Add remaining ingredients. Stir well, and remove from heat. Serve immediately.

"The food here is created with the same passion and adventurous spirit I saw every day in my family's kitchen. Maybe it goes without saying, but family and friends deserve only the best."
Frank Schibelli, owner

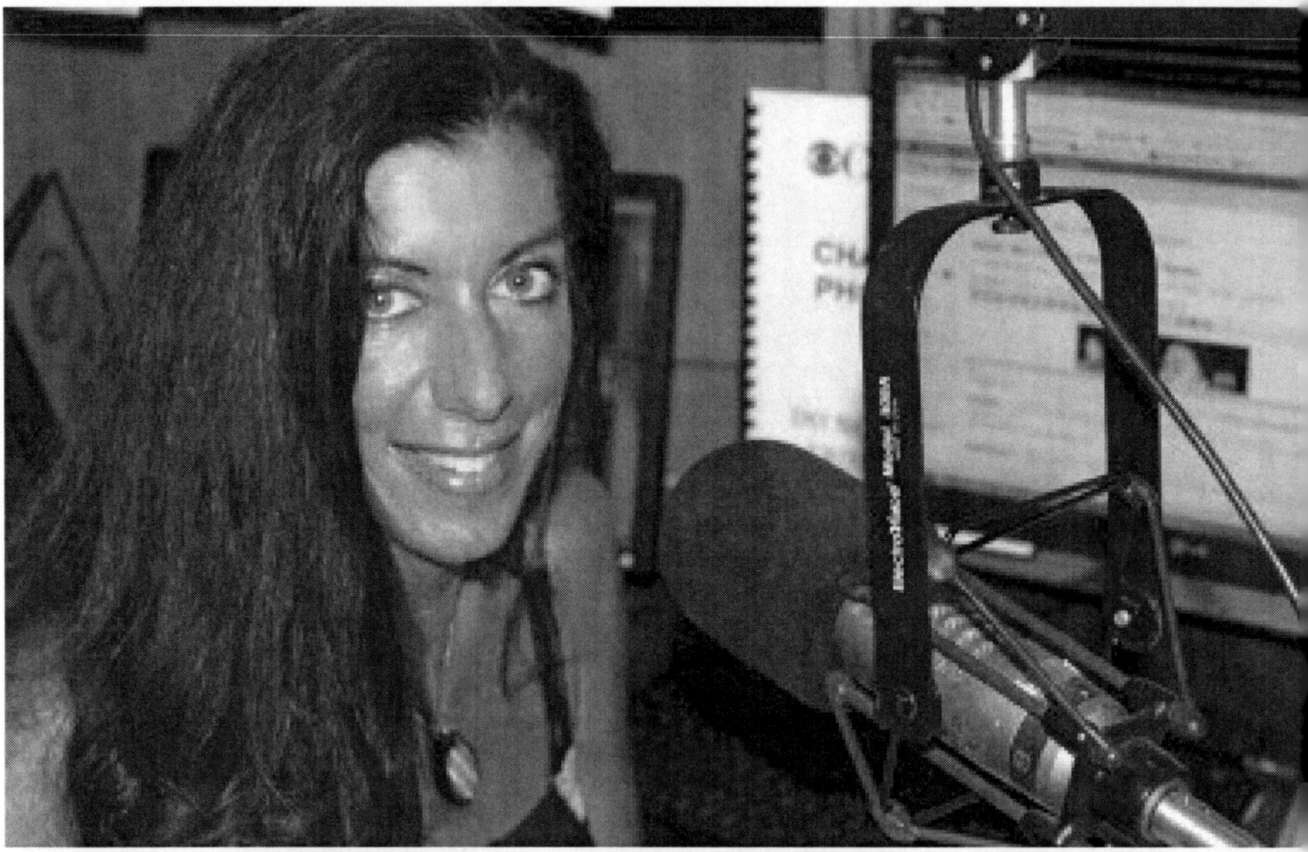

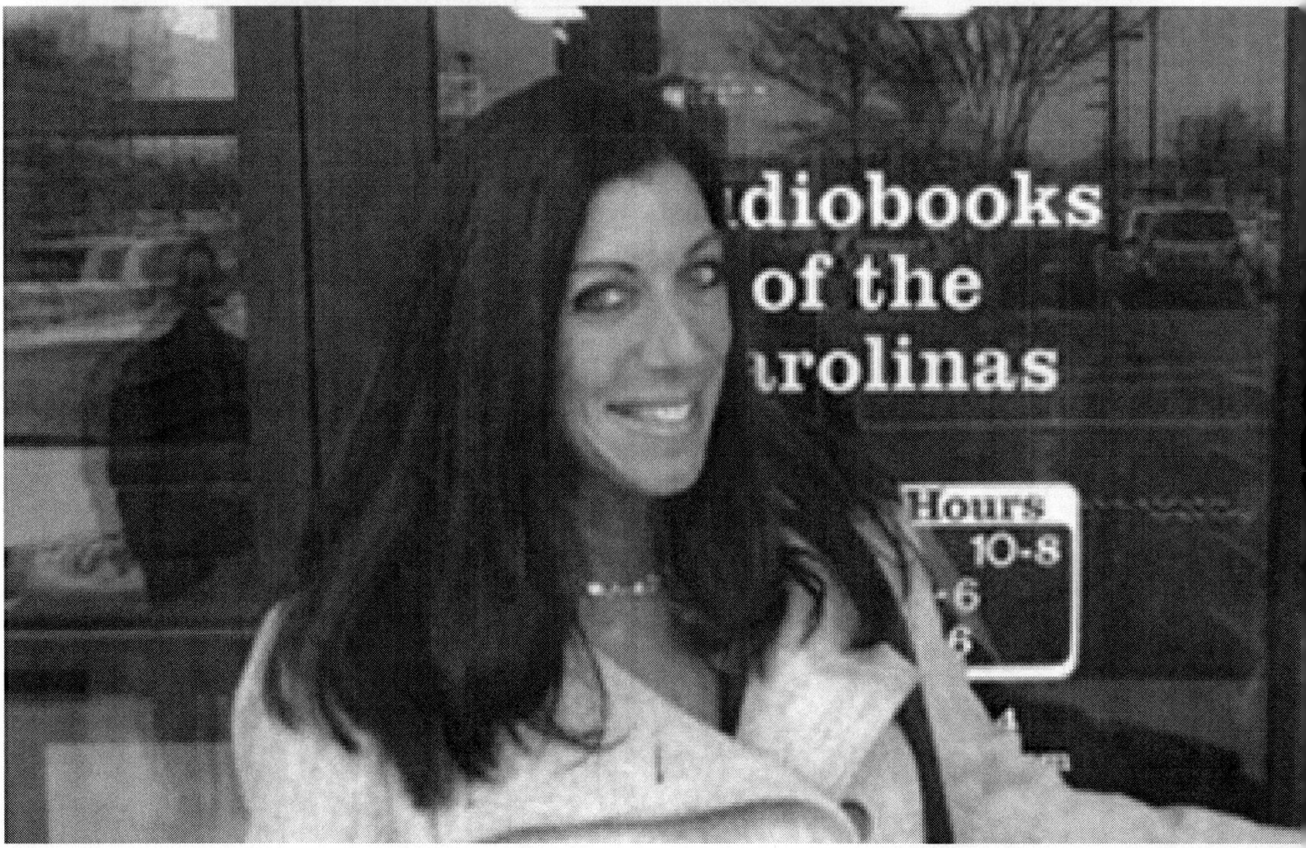
of the
Hours
10-8

Robin Marshall's Thanksgiving Feast

Signature Tastes of Charlotte

Robin is real. She's genuine. And, she knows a lot about the radio industry, as a voice over artist, and second generation DJ. She's been a national voice-over artist for the last 15 years, and on the air in New York City for 25 years. Somewhat recently coming to Charlotte, and sharing her warmth over our airways has been a gift to us. Considering all of this, all of the following is straight from Robin herself.

(1) 20 lb. turkey (or larger)
1 tin with handles to hold turkey

Green Bean Casserole:
4 cans French style green beans
2 cans (just in case) of those crispy onion thingy things that go on top of the green beans.
Milk

Sweet Potatoes:
2 large cans of yams
1 bag of small marshmallows
1 C. syrup

Mashed Potatoes:
2 boxed of powdered garlic potatoes
Butter
Milk
Boiling water

Veggies and lettuce for salad
2 cans cranberry sauce

Turkey:
1. Take stuff out of the turkey after it's defrosted. If you're anything like me, that turkey will be put in luke warm water in the tub, 3 hours before cooking time. I'm never on time with getting that stupid bird defrosted!
2. Rub butter all over the bird; add garlic, onion powder, seasoned salt, Adobo, and pepper. Roast at 350°F, covered for the first few hours, then cover with foil for the last hour or so.

Green Bean Casserole:
1. Mix milk with the green bean casserole
2. Read the directions on the can of onions to bake.

Sweet Potatoes:
1. Pour yams in a casserole, cover with marshmallows, and pour on syrup.
2. Add to oven 30 minutes before the turkey is done.

Mashed Potatoes:
1. Put them in the pot, and prepare 10 minutes before the bird is done.

Salad:
1. This is a MUST. It's the only way you won't feel guilty about feeding your kids that sweet potato concoction.
2. Just throw every vegetable you can think of into a bowl, add lettuce, and MAKE them eat it.

Cranberry Sauce:
1. Should be opened and chilled prior to meal.
2. Take a butter knife and slide it in the side of the can to help slice the cranberry roll out.
3. Slice up and serve.

Robin Marshall
On Air Mid-Days on CBS's K104.7

"Don't let me scare you off by saying, NOTHING is made from scratch! Are you kidding me? It if doesn't come in a box or a can with directions that I can see, I don't buy it. Any of you stodgy people out there, best come to terms with MY way that tastes as good as YOUR HOME MADE way, and maybe even better. Ask my 5 kids and the dogs."

Robin Marshall

Shane McDevitt CEO of McDevitt Real Estate Agency

California Shrimp Tacos (Made in Charlotte)

Signature Tastes of Charlotte

Shane McDevitt's real estate agency is a boutique firm, specializing in properties in Center City Charlotte and the popular surrounding neighborhoods. The McDevitt Agency is undeniably part of the vibrant energy and momentum proudly carrying this city forward. It seemed Shane was just waiting for an excuse to whip up these tacos to fulfill his craving, and admitted, he had to write it all down as he went along. Following the instructions for this recipe, you can't avoid having fun. We're glad Shane shared it with us.

1 can of corn (gold and white mix is my pref...)
1 can of black beans
1 can of petite cut diced tomatoes (*petite is a must and you can go plain, but I prefer to rock the Zesty Jalapeno style)
(1) 16 oz. package of shredded cabbage or dry coleslaw mix to add a little crunch
3 C. of Mexican blend shredded cheese
1½ lbs of medium sized shrimp
Ranch dressing
Hot sauce (Franks Red Hot tends to work the best)
Blackened Old Bay seasoning
Garlic Pepper
Fresh garlic
Fajita size flour soft tortilla shells
6 pack of Corona
A lime
A shot or several of tequila, depending how many people are helping you prepare...

1. Step one... put Jack Johnson on your stereo, turn it up, pop open a Corona, insert a lime, take a swig.
2. Drain all canned items until there's virtually no moisture left. I mean none!
3. Mix black beans, corn, and tomatoes in a bowl together. Add fresh crushed garlic cloves from a garlic press (as much as you can handle). The average Joe might use 2-3; I use 5. Stir up, throw a serving spoon in it, and set aside.
4. Next, empty a lot of ranch into a bowl... half a bottle or so. Unscrew the lid of the Franks Red Hot and pour in at least a good few tablespoons. I prefer more. Sprinkle in some garlic pepper and some blackened Old Bay seasoning. Stir all together, put a spoon in it, and set aside.
5. Grab a couple bowls and fill one with the shredded cabbage and the other with the shredded cheese.
6. (Shot of tequila can be inserted here. In your mouth, not in the cabbage!)
7. OK, now take the shrimp and throw them in a pan or wok over medium high heat. Sprinkle graciously with garlic pepper and blackened Old Bay seasoning. Cook em up! Then take em out, cut them in half, and put them in a bowl. TIME TO GRUB!
8. To keep your guests in the proper flow, you must line everything up in order. Tortillas, special sauce, shrimp, cheese, salsa mix, cabbage, hot sauce. Start at the front of the line, grab a tortilla, spread secret sauce all over it, put some shrimp on it, cover the whole thing in cheese. Now pop it in the microwave for 25 seconds. Return to the line, add a couple table spoons of salsa mix, sprinkle on enough cabbage to give it some crunch, and splat on a little hot sauce.

Owner, The McDevitt Agency-237 South Tryon Street

Shane McDevitt

"Actually lowering the cost of insurance would be accomplished by such things as making it harder for lawyers to win frivolous lawsuits against insurance companies."
Thomas Sowell

McNINCH HOUSE
Restaurant
★ ★ ★ ★ ★
Reservations Required
704-332-6159

Sea Scallops with Sweet Corn Risotto, Proscuitto and Basil

Experience true Southern hospitality in a turn of the century Victorian home in Charlotte's historic Fourth Ward. Since 1988, Chef and Owner Ellen Davis has created a culinary experience of a highly choreographed seven-course dinner by reservations only in elegant Victorian surrounding reminiscent of the leisurely, evening-long meals of that era. The McNinch House recently won its ninth consecutive Four Diamond designation from AAA, and is listed as one of the top "extraordinary" restaurants by Zagat's Dining guide.

6 ears fresh sweet corn, preferably Silver Queen
1 Tbsp olive oil
2 Tbsp butter, divided
1 large shallot, finely minced
¾ C. Arborio rice
½ C. dry white wine
½ C. corn puree
2 thin slices prosciutto
6 large 'dry pack' diver scallops
Extra virgin olive oil, or white truffle oil, for garnish
1 bunch fresh basil

1. Cut kernels off cobs by standing each ear on end and slicing down from top to bottom, cutting as close to cob as possible. Place corn kernels AND cobs in large pot and cover with water. Bring to a boil, then cover and turn down to simmer for 10 minutes. Remove kernels from water and reserve. Leave cobs in and allow to simmer for 30 minutes to 1 hour to make corn stock.
2. Warm 3 C. corn stock to a gentle simmer and keep warm.
3. In a large, steep sided skillet, warm 1 Tbsp olive oil and 1 Tbsp butter over medium heat. Once butter has foamed and subsided, add shallot to pan and saute until translucen, about 1 minute. Add Arborio rice to pan, stirring to coat, and cook until the rice has taken on a golden, pale color, about 2-3 minutes. Add wine to pan and do not stir, but allow rice to absorb the wine without agitation. Cook rice, stirring, until alcohol has been 'cooked out' and rice smells toasty. Add 1 C. of corn stock to skillet and stir, cooking until all liquid is absorbed. Continue adding stock to rice ½ C. at a time, stirring constantly, until rice is al dente about 15 minutes longer.
4. For corn puree, place half of the reserved corn kernels in a food processor with ½ C. of reserved corn stock. Blend on high speed until smooth, adding more stock as needed. Ideally, puree should be very smooth, but thick and creamy. Stir remaining reserved kernels and corn puree into cooked rice and salt and pepper to taste.
5. While rice is cooking, lay prosciutto slices on a cookie sheet lined with parchment or food spray, and place in 350°F oven for 8-10 minutes until crispy. Break into 1-2" shards and reserve.
6. Heat remaining 1 Tbsp butter in medium skillet over medium high heat. Salt and pepper scallops to taste, and sear in hot skillet for 3 minutes on each side, turning only once. Remove from pan to paper towel-lined plate.

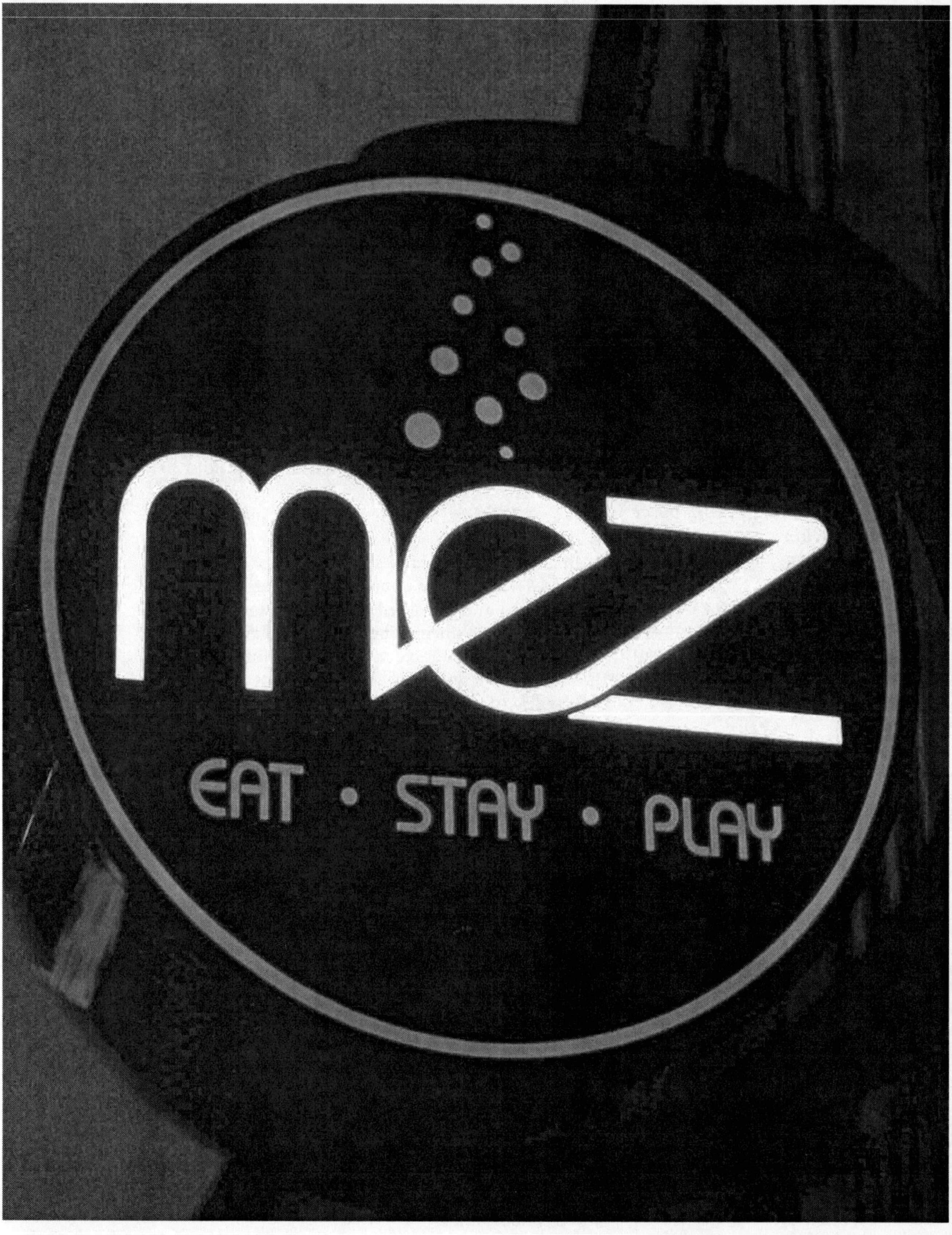
mez
EAT · STAY · PLAY

Seared Ahi Tuna on Ginger Lemongrass French Toast

Mez is a stylish, modern establishment in the heart of Uptown Charlotte serving a seasonal menu of globally-influenced cuisine. Shortly after opening in 2009, it received "Best Of" awards from both the Charlotte Observer and Charlotte Magazine, and in 2010 it was a Diner's Choice award winner on Opentable.com for its vibrant bar scene. The locals agree that Mez is the place to see and be seen, and the lively bar is a great place to enjoy premium beer and wine selections as well as specialty cocktails.

1 lb. tuna, cut into 4 4-oz. pieces
4 pieces of bread (Brioche, Challah, Egg bread or Texas toast) cut into 2x4 inch rectangles or 4" rounds
Micro cilantro or chives for garnish
Olive oil or clarified butter - enough to coat pans

Batter:
1 C. heavy cream or Half & Half
2 eggs
1 Tbsp lemongrass chopped, or 1 stalk chopped
2 Tbsp chopped fresh ginger
¼ salt

Rub for tuna:
1 Tbsp chopped ginger
½ tsp salt
¼ tsp pepper, or a couple turns of fresh milled pepper

Syrup:
¼ C. honey
1 Tbsp lemon juice

The batter for the French Toast for this recipe is best prepared a day or two before to allow the oils from the ginger and lemongrass to infuse into the egg mixture.

1. Add cream, lemongrass, ginger and salt to a pot. Allow to steep for 30 minutes on very low heat. Do not allow to reach a boil. Cool at room temperature for 20 minutes.
2. Whisk eggs in mixing bowl. Slowly add cream mixture to eggs while whisking constantly, so as to not allow the cream mixture to cook the eggs.
3. Allow enough time for the lemongrass and ginger oils to flavor the cream and egg mixture.
4. Before making the French toast, pour egg mixture through a fine strainer to remove lemongrass and ginger pieces.

Syrup:
1. Add honey and lemon juice to pan.
2. Cook on medium heat, and bring just to a boil. Remove from heat.

Tuna:
1. Mix the rub ingredients well, and rub into each piece of tuna.
2. In a pan, heated on high heat, add olive oil or clarified butter. Quickly sear tuna. Remove from heat.

French toast:
1. Soak bread in the egg mixture, flipping to coat both sides of bread.
2. Heat pan to medium heat, add olive oil or clarified butter.
3. Cook until each side of bread is golden brown, flipping only once.

"If you ever want to eat a tuna sandwich again, don't go to a tuna factory. I visited one where they had two lines: one was the human food line and one was the cat food line - and they didn't look any different."
Mark Mobius

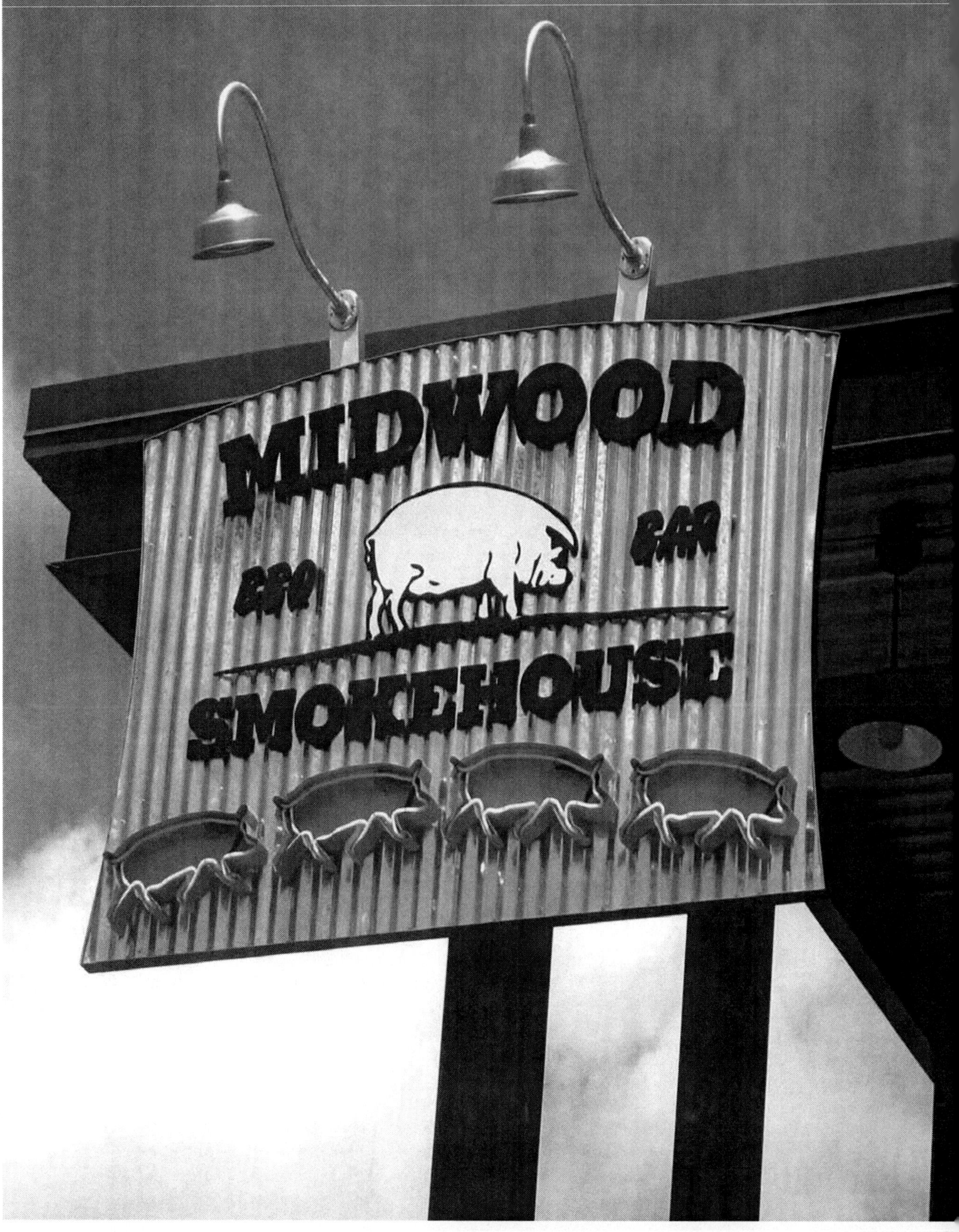
MIDWOOD
BBQ
BAR
SMOKEHOUSE

Smoked Stuffed Jalapenos

Originating in Mexico, the jalapeño is named after the town it came from, Xalapa, Veracruz. Christopher Columbus is responsible for bringing the pepper to Europe. The "aji" as it was called at the time, meaning "child", was renamed the "Calcutta Pepper" a German botanist named Leonard Fuchs. The pepper began to be cultivated in Spain and became an instant success. It is unclear in history how the pepper reached North America. But we are certainly glad it did!

12 - 2 inch jalapenos
12 oz. Monterey Jack Cheese
24 slices of bacon
24 toothpicks

1. Split pepper lengthwise and remove seeds (You may want to wear gloves to protect your skin, and anything else you may touch afterwards).

2. Cut the jack cheese into ½ oz. rectangles. Fill jalapeno with ½ oz. of Monterey Jack cheese.

3. Wrap each stuffed pepper with one strip of bacon. Secure with a toothpick (soak the toothpicks in water to prevent burning).

4. Preheat grill - set up indirect heat with low to medium heat. Place peppers on grill and add a few wood chips to achieve smokey flavor.

5. BBQ peppers until they are lightly roasted, or until bacon is fully cooked.

Signature Tastes of Charlotte

Midwood Smokehouse
1401 Central Avenue

"We sat around and I fed them barbecue and whiskey. And pretty soon everyone started to compete with each other on the guitars. It seemed the more everyone drank and ate, the more everyone got into it..."
Gary Allan

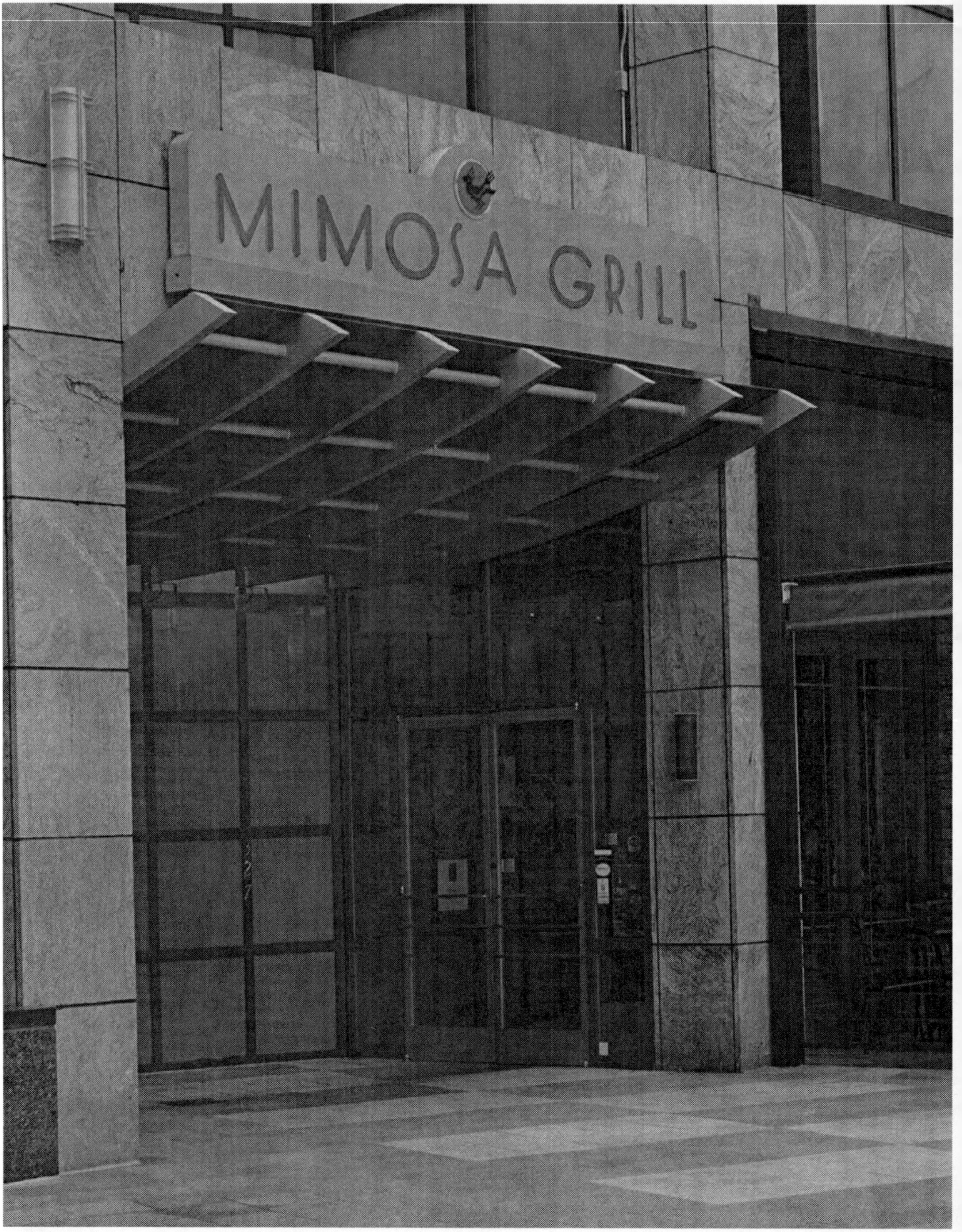
MIMOSA GRILL

Alaska Salmon with Potatoes, Dill, and Baby Fennel

Consistently named one of Charlotte' best restaurants since 1995, Mimosa Grill features globlal cuisine with a Southern twist. Dedicated to artisans, farmers and craftsmen whose passion for food creates the finest ingredients possible. Executive chef Jon Fortes creates Mimosa Grill's dishes using only the freshest natural ingredients that come straight from farm to fork. The cuisine, along with the stunning decor by renowned architect Bill Johnson, make Mimosa Grill one of Charlotte's most distinctive dining experiences.

White Asparagus Vinaigrette:
½ lb. white asparagus, blanched (this should be done in 1 C. milk and 1 C. salted water)
½ C. olive oil
¼ C. water
¼ C. red wine vinegar
1 Tbsp Dijon mustard
2 Tbsp tarragon, chopped
1 Tbsp honey

Potatoes:
2 lbs new dug potatoes (boiled in salted water until tender, and cooled)
3 Tbsp fresh dill, chopped
1 bulb. fennel
2 Tbsp olive oil
2 Tbsp butter
1 shallot, minced
Sea salt and pepper to taste
1 large piece of aluminum foil

Salmon:
4 5-oz. salmon
1 tsp dill
1 Tbsp olive oil
Salt and pepper to taste

White Asparagus Vinaigrette:
1. Place asparagus, water, red wine vinegar, honey and mustard in a food processor, and slowly drizzle in olive oil.
2. Season to taste with salt, white pepper, and tarragon.

New Dug Potatoes, Dill & Baby Fennel:
1. Split the fennel, and place in the foil with oil, shallot, sea salt and pepper.
2. Roast at 350°F for 1 hour, or until very tender.
3. Cool and cut into small strips. Reserve all liquid from the foil package.
4. In a sauce pot, add butter and potatoes. Cook for 4 minutes, or until heated through.
5. Add in fennel mixture and reserved liquid.

Grilled Alaskan Salmon:
1. Rub salmon with dill, oil, salt and pepper.
2. Preheat grill for 15 minutes, until grates are hot
3. Cook salmon for about 4 minutes per side.

Serve a portion on each plate, along with potatoes and fennel and drizzle with the asparagus vinaigrette.

Signature Tastes of CHARLOTTE

MIMOSA GRILL
Executive Chef Jon Fortes - 327 South Tryon Street

"I think we're going to the moon because it's in the nature of the human being to face challenges. It's by the nature of his deep inner soul... we're required to do these things just as salmon swim upstream."
Neil Armstrong

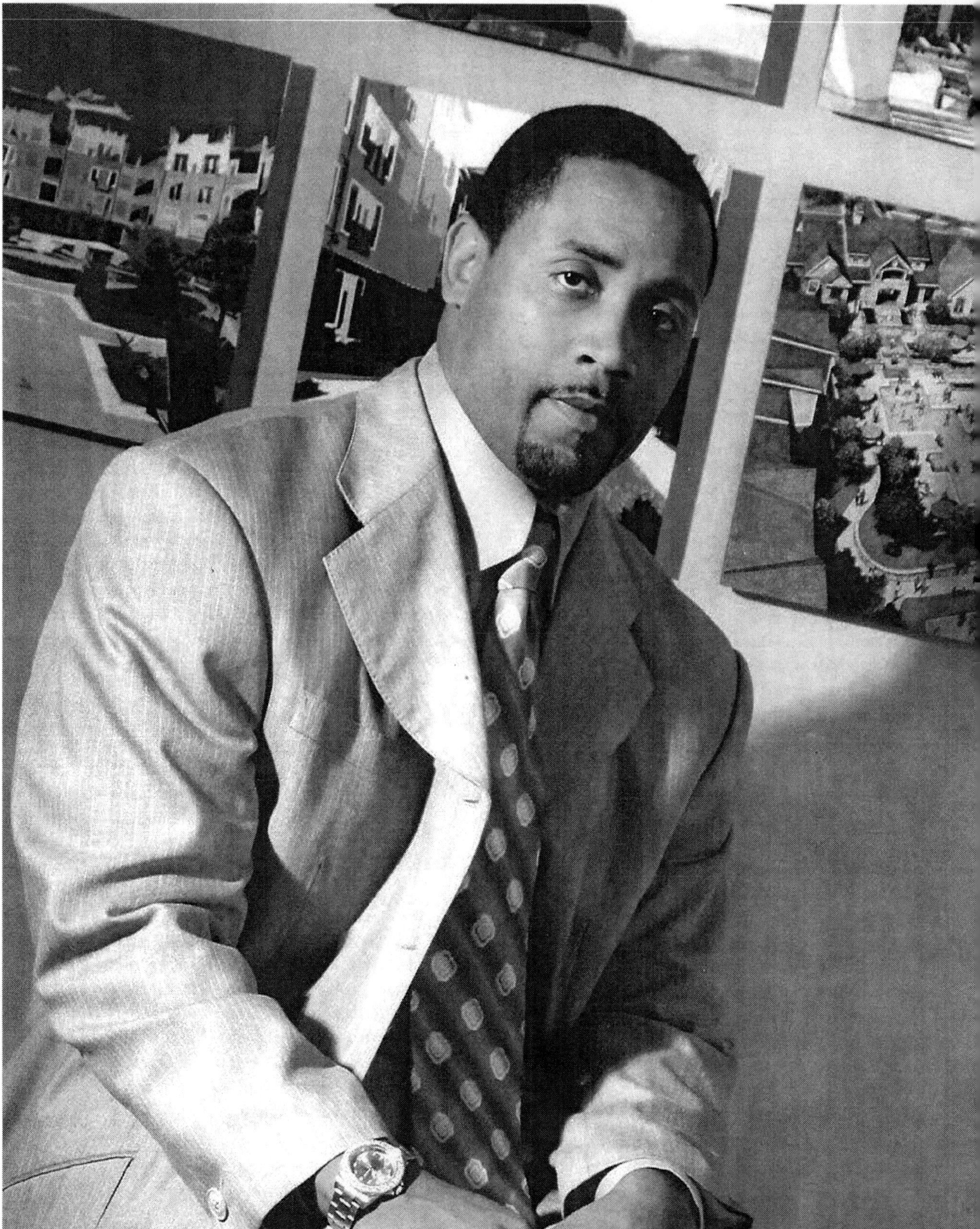

Layered Banana Pineapple Dessert

Having had the opportunity to speak and correspond with Mike several times for a previous undertaking in recent years, it should be noted that it was suggested by our AC repair guy to reach out to him in the first place. That's the kind of reputation he has - accessible, kind and thoughtful. My overall experience with him validates all the stories of good things with which he involves himself. He is a professional, a forward thinker, and a giver, all while keeping his feet firmly planted on the ground.

1½ C. vanilla wafer crumbs
¼ C. sugar
⅓ C. margarine or butter, melted
3 bananas, sliced
1 package (8 oz.) cream cheese, softened
3½ C. cold milk
2 packages (4-serving size) JELL-O Vanilla Flavor Instant Pudding
1 can (20 oz.) crushed pineapple, drained
1 tub (8 oz.) Cool Whip, thawed

1. Mix vanilla wafer crumbs, sugar and margarine in 13"x 9" inch pan.

2. Press evenly into bottom of pan.

3. Arrange bananas slices on crust.

4. Beat cream cheese in large bowl with wire whisk until smooth.

5. Gradually beat in milk. Add pudding mixes. Beat until well blended.

6. Spread evenly over banana slices.

7. Spoon pineapple evenly over pudding mixture.

8. Spread whipped topping over pineapple.

9. Refrigerate 3 hours, or until ready to serve.

Signature Tastes of CHARLOTTE

FORMER CAROLINA PANTHERS FREE SAFETY, MIKE MINTER ENTERPRISES

MIKE MINTER

"Football is like life - it requires perseverance, self-denial, hard work, sacrifice, dedication and respect for authority."
Vince Lombardi

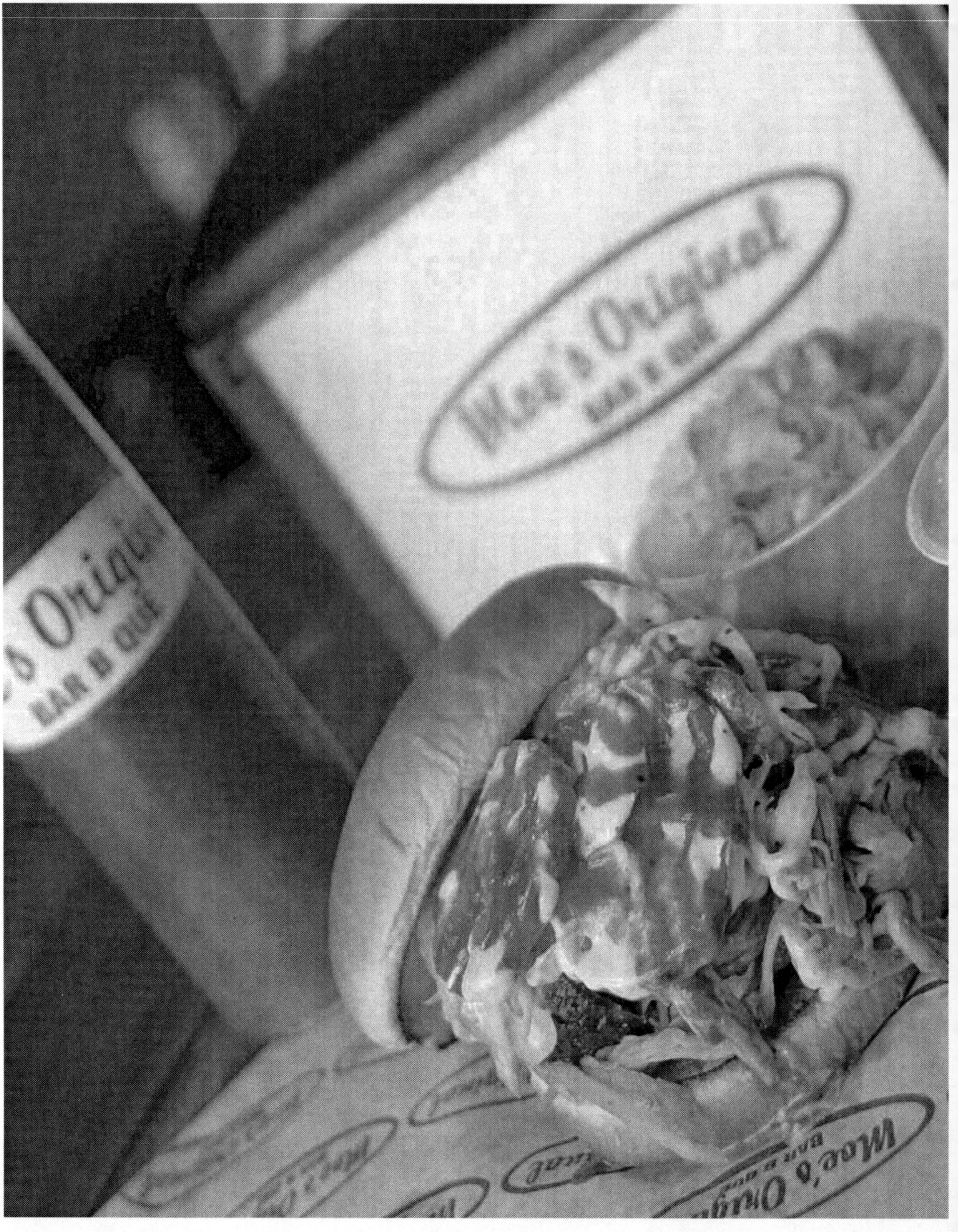
Moe's Original
BAR B QUE

Moe's Original Bar-B-Que Watermelon Salad

Moe's Original BBQ was founded by three Bama boys: Mike Fernandez from Tuscaloosa, Ben Gilbert from Athens, and Jeff Kennedy from Huntsville. After meeting at the University of Alabama in Tuscaloosa, they instantly became friends and had a mutual interest in all things Southern: BBQ, blues, college football, and whisky. And let's be honest...who can complain about those types of mutual interests?

½ seedless watermelon, large dice
4-5 tomatoes, large dice
½ C. yellow onion, chopped
1 Tbsp fresh mint, chopped
4 Tbsp salad oil
½ C. cider vinegar
1 C. sugar
1 dash salt

1. Combine all ingredients in a bowl.

2. Check for seasonings. (Remember you can always add salt, but you can never take it away.)

3. Cover and chill for a couple of hours.

4. Can be served right away, but it is best to let it sit for a while to let the flavors marry.

Signature Tastes of CHARLOTTE

Moe's Original Bar B Que
Greater Charlotte Area

"Dancing is my number one love. That was my first goal as a child. I would love to do stage, maybe do Chicago. I love being in front of an audience. It's so stimulating. I also love to barbecue."
Carmen Electra

145

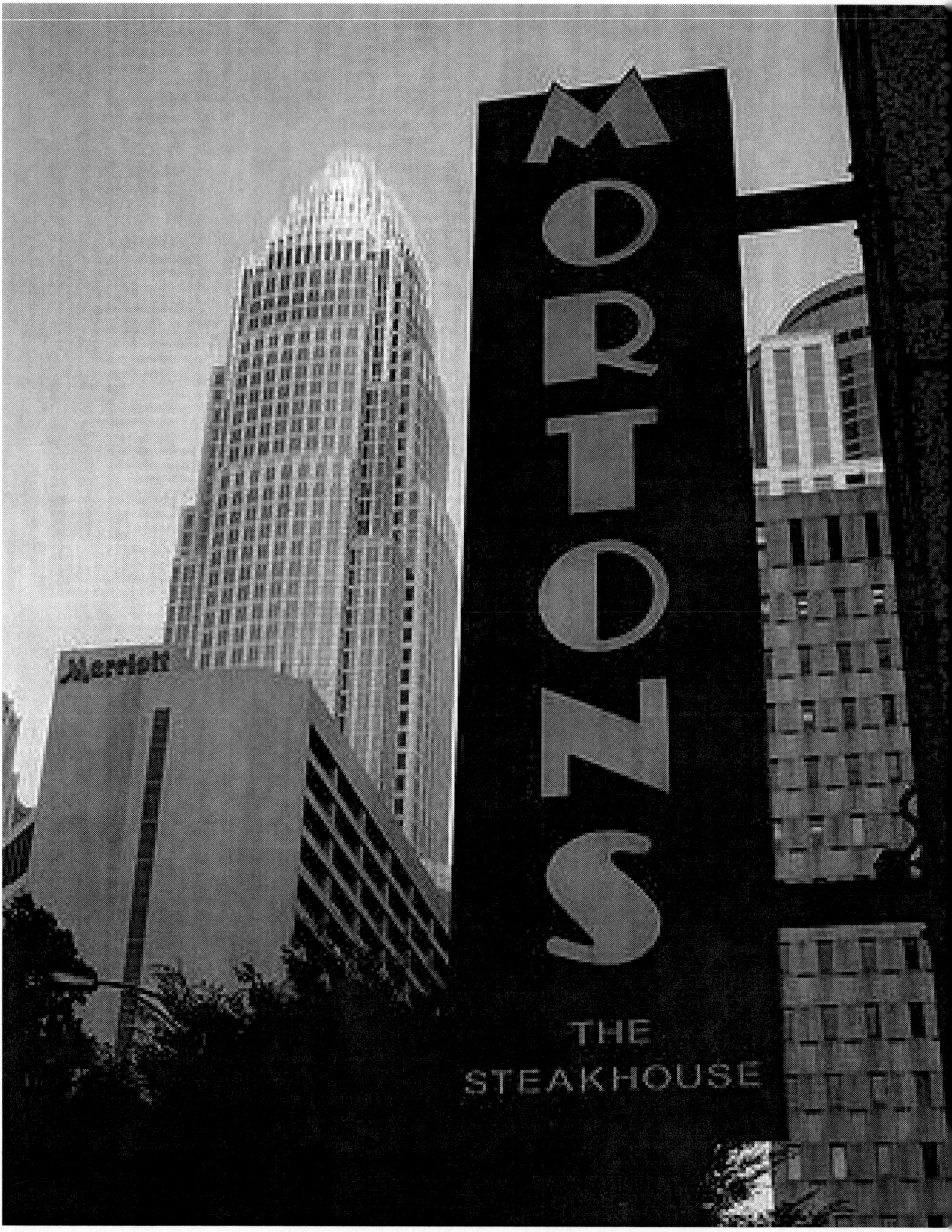
Marriott
MORTONS
THE
STEAKHOUSE

Baked Crab Cakes with Mustard Mayonnaise Sauce

Recognized for impeccable service, fabulous food and a comprehensive wine and spirits list, Morton's The Steakhouse is located in the center of Uptown Charlotte's business district. When Morton's opened there in 1994, it 'kicked off Charlotte's rise as a restaurant city,' according to Charlotte Magazine. Since then, Morton's has awed guests with its classic, hearty American fare, serving generous portions of its specialty, USDA grain-fed Prime-aged beef, fresh fish, lobsters, chicken entrees and spectacular desserts.

1 lb. fresh lump crabmeat (about 3 C. loosely packed)
1 C. Alex's Bread Crumbs
1 large egg
8 Tbsp mustard-mayonnaise sauce (see recipe)
1 Tbsp chopped parsley
1 tsp Dijon mustard
½ tsp Worcestershire sauce
¼ tsp Tabasco sauce
6 Tbsp clarified butter, melted, or olive oil

Alex's Bread crumbs:
8 oz. firm white bread (4-5 slices) Crusts removed
5 tsp fresh garlic, minced
2 tsp shallot, minced
2 tsp parsley, chopped
Salt and freshly ground white pepper

Mustard Mayonnaise Sauce:
1½ C. mayonnaise
3 Tbsp Dijon mustard
¾ tsp Worcestershire
1½ tsp prepared horseradish

1. Preheat oven to 450°F.
2. Add bread crumbs and gently toss until combined.
3. In a small bowl, whisk egg, 2 Tbsp of the mustard-mayonnaise sauce, parsley, mustard, Worcestershire and Tabasco sauces. Pour this mixture over the crabmeat.
4. Using a rubber spatula, gently fold the egg mixture into the crabmeat. Divide the mixture into (6) equal ½ C. portions.
5. Gently form each portion into a ball and flatten into 1" thick cakes.
6. Put the butter in a 7" x 11" ovenproof dish, and then put the crab cakes in the pan.
7. Bake for 7-8 minutes, or until golden brown.
8. Gently turn the crab cakes, and bake for 7-8 minutes longer, or until the cakes are golden brown on both sides, and cooked through.
9. Serve with the remaining 6 Tbsp of the Mustard-Mayonnaise sauce on the side.

Alex's Bread crumbs:
1. In a food processor fitted with a steel blade, process the bread to fine crumbs.
2. Pat the garlic and shallot dry with a paper towel. Add to the bread crumbs, and toss to mix.
3. Add the parsley, toss, and season to taste with salt and pepper. Mix well.

Mustard Mayonnaise Sauce:
1. In a mixing bowl, stir together the mayonnaise, mustard, Worcestershire sauce, and horseradish.
2. Whisk with a wire whisk until lightened and smooth.
3. Use immediately, or refrigerate for up to 5 days.

Signature Tastes of CHARLOTTE

Morton's The Steakhouse
Chef Greg Thompson—227 West Trade Street, #150

"For me the ideal date would be to drink wine in the backyard under the stars, listen to music and just talk. Then we'd eat steak and, later, dessert. If all went as planned, we'd save some of the dessert and play with it while making out."
Karen McDougal

New South

KITCHEN & BAR

Simple Roasted Chicken with Mushroom Risotto

Our food offerings are based on simple cooking techniques applied to the freshest, top quality, and when available, local ingredients. Typically, there are 20 entrée offerings nightly with an emphasis on seafood from the Carolinas. We also feature fresh vegetables, hand crafted cheeses, salads & pastas. Our breads and desserts are made in house daily. Dakotas' favorites, Fried Green Tomatoes, Shrimp & Grits and Crab Cakes, have returned as well as a few other Southern staples.

Chicken:
- (4) 8oz. boneless skin on chicken breasts- airliners or single lobe breasts work best
- ¼ C. fresh lemon juice
- ¼ C. j Lohr chardonnay
- ¼ C. olive oil
- 1 Tbsp kosher salt
- 1 Tbsp chopped garlic
- ¼ C. fresh herbs - parsley, thyme, oregano
- 2 Tbsp vegetable oil
- 1 C. dark chicken stock
- 4 Tbsp butter cut into chunks

Mushroom Risotto:
- ¾ lb. wild mushrooms- stems removed, washed and sliced
- 1 Tbsp fresh thyme leaves
- 7 Tbsp olive oil
- 1 C. aborio rice
- 1 C. J Lohr Chardonnay
- 2 C. chicken or vegetable stock
- ½ C. diced shallots or onion
- 2 Tbsp butter
- ¼ C. ground romano cheese
- 2 Tbsp snipped chives

1. Dissolve the salt into the lemon juice and J Lohr chardonnay. Stir in the olive oil, garlic and herbs.
2. Put the chicken in a large zip-lock bag with the marinade and refrigerate over night.
3. Preheat oven to 400°F.
4. Remove the chicken from the marinade and drain.
5. Heat the vegetable oil in a ovenproof sauté pan, large enough to hold all four breasts comfortably, over high heat until very hot. Add the breasts skin side down. Reduce the heat to med high and cook 2-3 minutes until the skin is well caramelized and crispy.
6. Turn the breasts over, cook 1 more minute then place the pan in the oven for 10-15 minutes to cook the chicken. Remove the pan from the oven. Place the chicken on a plate to rest.
7. Put the pan back on the stove over high heat. Add the chicken stock to the pan and reduce the stock to ¼ C. Reduce the heat to medium.
8. Return the chicken to the pan with the butter and swirl gently to incorporate the butter.

Mushroom Risotto:
1. Preheat oven to 400°F.
2. Toss the mushrooms with 3 Tbsp olive oil and thyme. Season with kosher salt and fresh ground pepper. Place the mushrooms on sheet pan and roast 10-12 minutes.
3. Heat the wine and stock together with the roasted mushrooms — reserve. (add any liquid the mushrooms released during the cooking too).
4. Sweat the diced shallots over medium heat in the remaining olive oil without browning.
5. Add the rice and stir well to coat the rice with the oil. Add ⅓ of the hot mushroom liquid to the rice. Stir the rice frequently as it cooks and absorbs the liquid.
6. When the liquid is almost completely absorbed add another ⅓ of the liquid. Repeat until all the liquid is absorbed.
7. Stir in the butter, romano cheese and chives. Serve immediately with roasted chicken and pan sauce spooned around.

Signature Tastes of CHARLOTTE

Owner Chris Edwards-8140 Providence Rd, 300 In the Arboretum

New South Kitchen

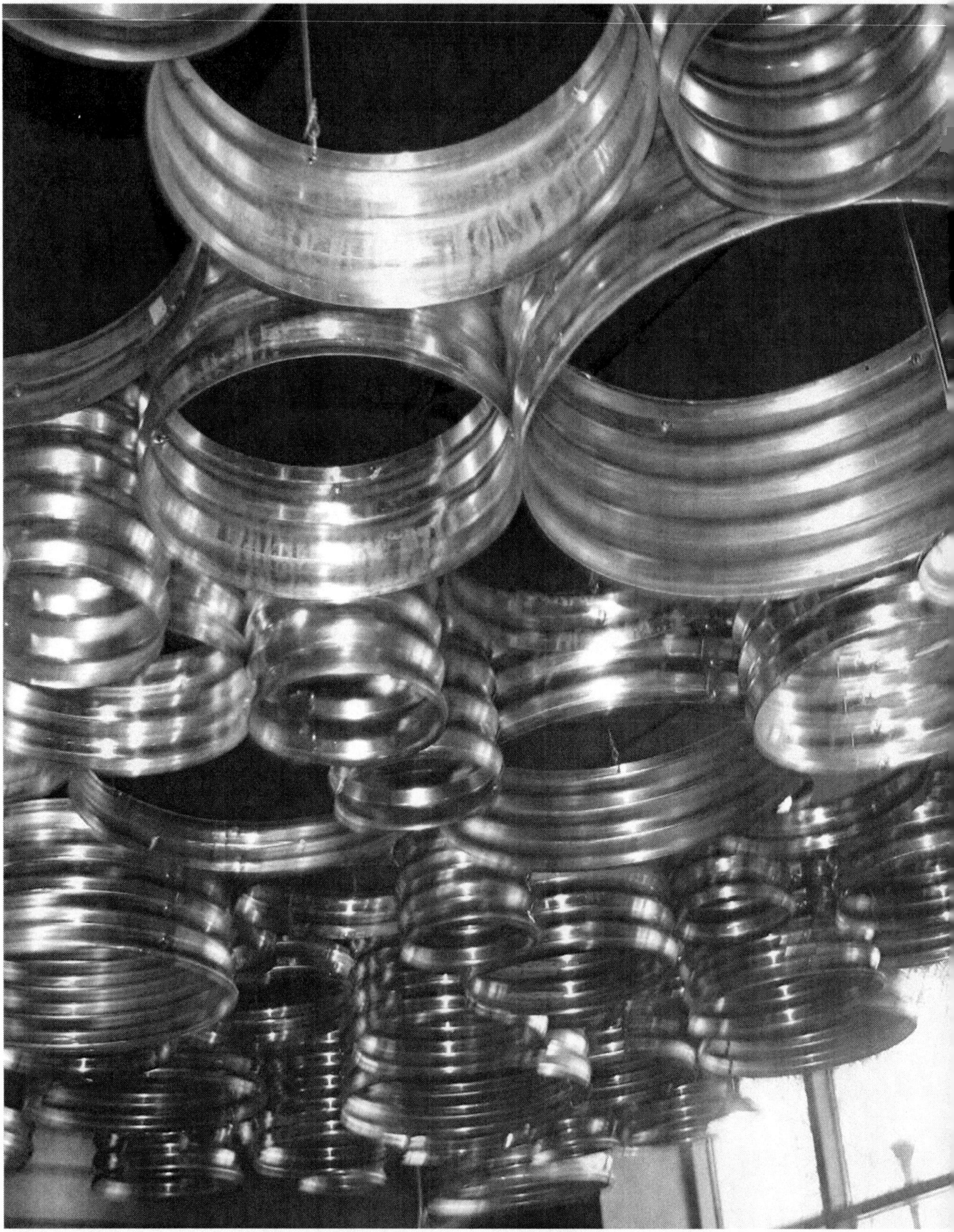

El Paso Me a Turkey Burger

Signature Tastes of CHARLOTTE

With twenty different half-pound burgers, there is no doubt that this small restaurant located in Uptown Charlotte celebrates chowing down on Beef but offers your choice on all of the burgers with Angus Beef, Bison, Chicken Breast, Turkey & Veggie Patties. This resturant features a fusion of biker décor and sleek modern uptown design — including parts of kegs hanging from the ceiling and images of flames throughout. Order a burger and cozy up to the bar or find a seat along the long booth lining the wall to watch the game on one of the restaurant's six plasma screens.

4 lb. ground turkey
1 8 oz. can green chilis, drained and minced
1 bunch fresh cilantro, stemmed and minced
1 C. Pico de gallo
1 C. pepper jack cheese, shredded
8 C. panko breadcrumbs, toasted with butter and herbs
2 C. iceberg lettuce, shredded

1. In a large mixing bowl, combine all ingredients and incorporate by hand, gently folding until all items are well incorporated.

2. Using a scale, weigh out the mixture to 8 oz. patties, and lightly form each one by hand until desired size. The restaurant uses a large ring mold that is 5" wide and 1" tall.

3. After forming all the patties, refrigerate and allow them to cool down before grilling to ensure a nice char on the outside, and to prevent sticking to the grill.

Assembly:
1. Toast the bun with light butter, and apply an herb mayonnaise to both sides.

2. Place grilled burger on bottom bun, and top with shredded pepper jack cheese, green chili salsa, and some shredded iceberg lettuce.

Corporate Chef Michael Rayfield—201 North Tryon Street

Nix Burger and Brew

"I would rather be having a burger and beers with my mates but I can't do that when I know I've got to dance."
Michael Flatley, founder of Riverdance

151

Photo by Carllisle Kellam

Mocha Latte

Signature Tastes of CHARLOTTE

Located just north of downtown, between Davidson and Caldwell, on 15th street, just inside the Area Fifteen artists' studios, Not Just Coffee is a community oriented coffee bar serving Charlotte's only pour over coffee. We proudly offer handcrafted espresso based drinks, and individually brewed cups of coffee, using a pour over method form Counter Culture Coffee. Teas and snacks are available as well. Coffee is our passion. Our pursuit of the perfect cup of coffee has led ut to open our own coffee bar, servicing the more discriminating coffee drinkers of Charlotte.

2 oz. of fine ground espresso coffee
1 oz. of Zuma chocolate sauce (scratch made)
7 oz. of perfectly steamed milk

1. Using your wonderfully functional espresso machine, pull two shots of espresso coffee into shot glasses.

2. Whilst the said espresso is doing its magic, use the steam attachment to steam a generous portion of milk. This action changes the sugar in the milk into creamy goodness.

3. Combine chocolate and espresso, pour in micro foamed milk and enjoy.

4. Thank whatever dieties you honour for the invention of both coffee and chocolate. Both come from South America, you know…

The Not Just Coffee Shop
Owner James Yoder, 512-A East 15th Street

"The morning cup of coffee has an exhilaration about it which the cheering influence of the afternoon or evening cup of tea cannot be expected to reproduce."
Oliver Wendell Holmes, Sr.

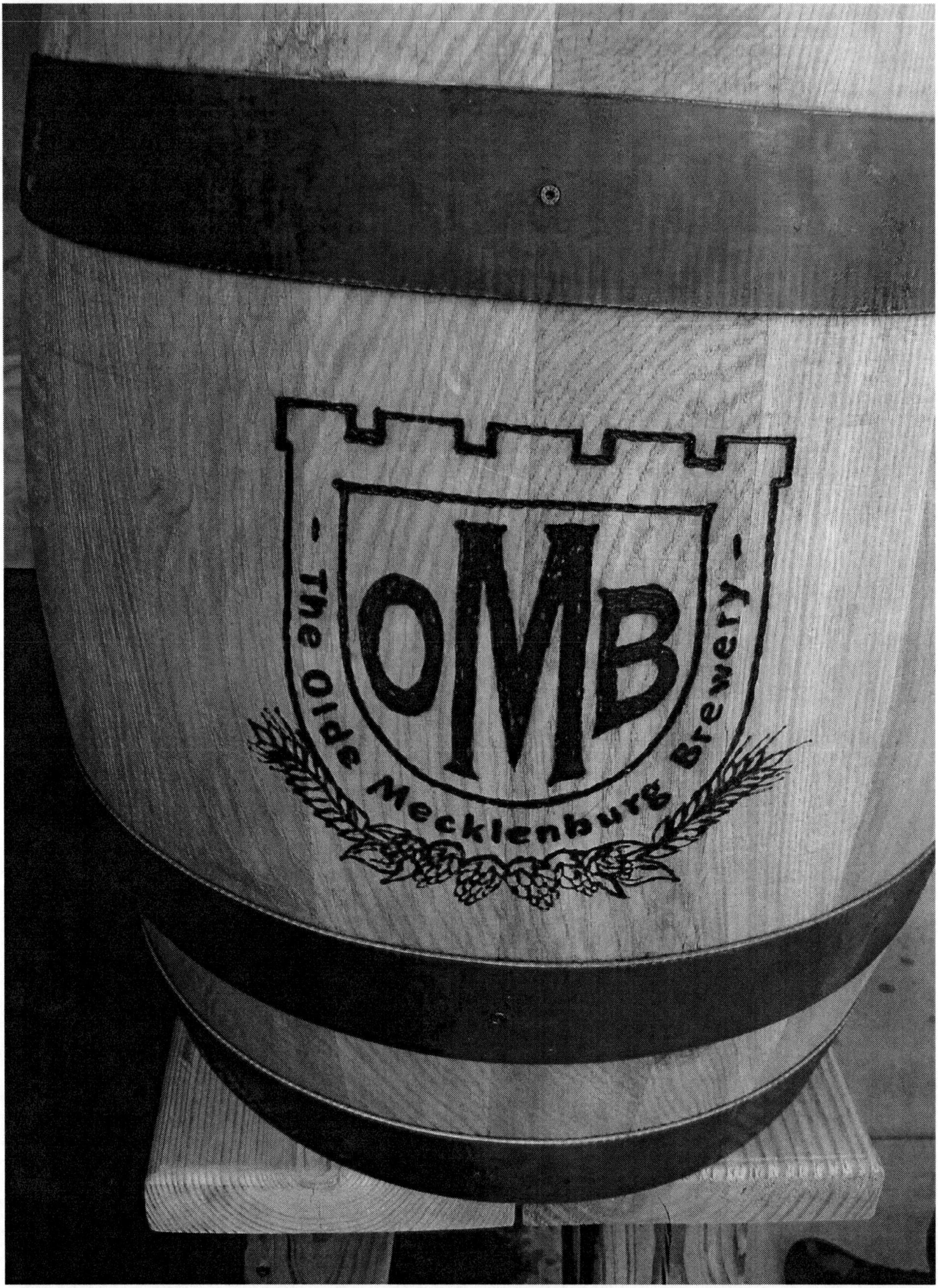
OMB
The Olde Mecklenburg Brewery

Bratwurst Panini

The Olde Mecklenburg Brewery (OMB), located in the heart of south Charlotte, produces premium, all natural beer and delivers it fresh weekly to bars, restaurants and retailers in the region. OMB uses only the finest ingredients available worldwide and employs traditional, intensive brewing methods to transform them into world class beer that's full-flavored yet amazingly refreshing. Although our methods are more costly, we think you'll agree the results are worth it.

Signature Tastes of CHARLOTTE

2 slices white bread (Italian country white)
1 bratwurst (sliced lengthwise)
3 Tbsp sauerkraut
2 slices of Provolone cheese
Spicy mustard
Olive oil

1. Grill the bratwurst on both sides until lightly browned and set aside.

2. Put mustard on the inside of the sliced bread.

3. Top the mustard with provolone cheese.

4. Put the bratwurst followed by sauerkraut on one of the slices.

5. Take the other piece of bread and top the sandwich.

6. Brush the outside of the Panini (both sides) with a small amount of olive oil and place in a Panini press until done.

THE OLDE MECKLENBURG BREWERY
EVENTS MANAGER LAURA KNOXX - 215 SOUTHSIDE DRIVE

"Beer is proof that God loves us and wants us to be happy..."
Benjamin Franklin

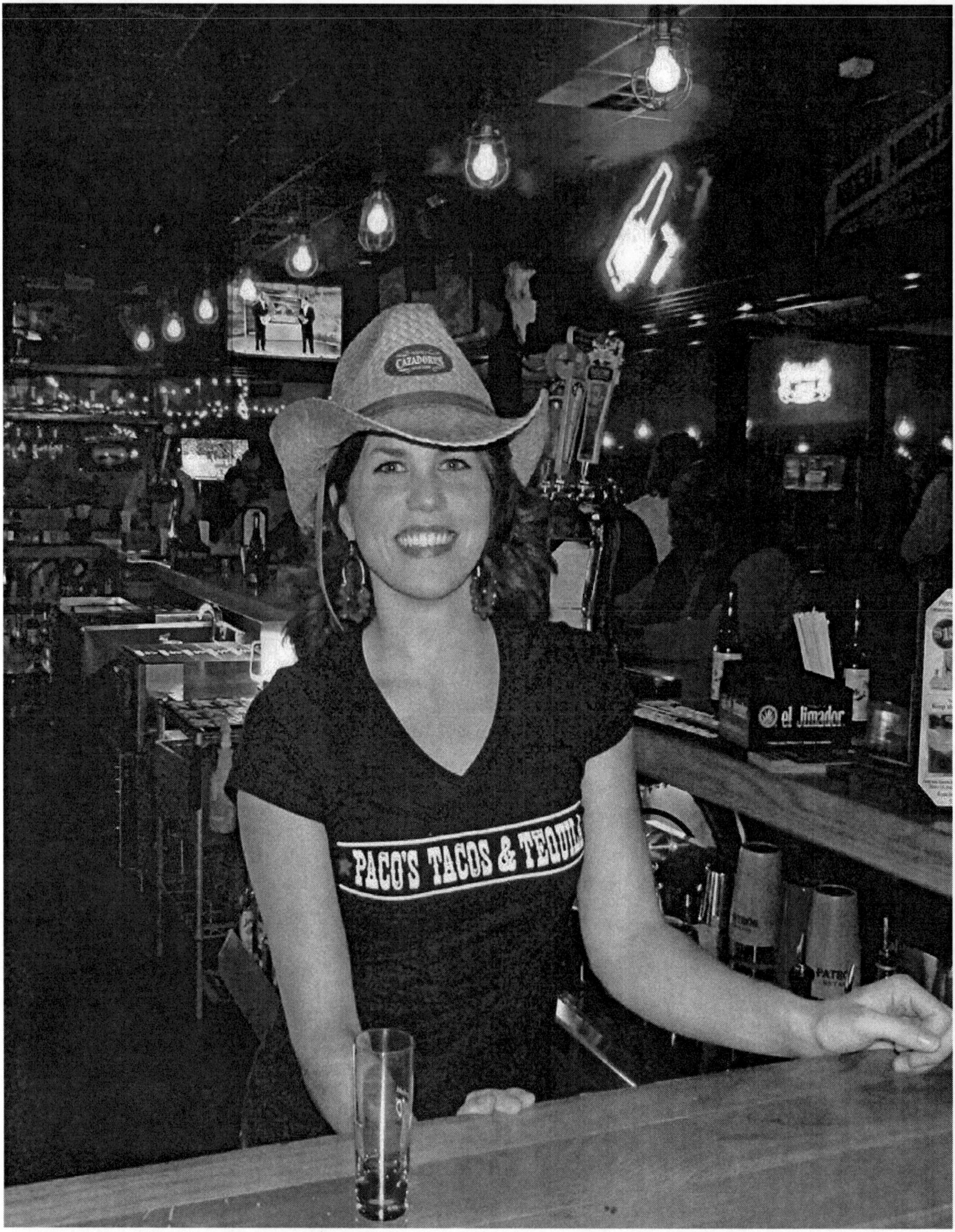
CAZADORES
PACO'S TACOS & TEQUILA
el Jimador

Tacos al Carbon
(Grilled Kobe Beef Ribeye Tacos)

Paco's Tacos & Tequila offers Big Texas flavor in The SouthPark neighborhood of Charlotte, N.C. Founded by restaurateurs Frank Scibelli and Dennis Thompson, the restaurant serves a menu of Tex-Mex favorites made with the freshest quality ingredients. Paco's Tacos has a really hip atmosphere and some of the best fish, shrimp and beef brisket soft tacos you've ever tasted...

Signature Tastes of CHARLOTTE

(12) 10" flour tortillas, steamed
24 oz. Grilled Kobe ribeye
3 C. green cabbage, shredded
3 Tbsp cilantro, chopped
2 limes, each cut into 8 wedges

Charred Tomato Salsa:
8 Roma tomatoes
4 cloves garlic, in their skin
½ white onion, skin on
2 Serrano peppers
½ bunch cilantro
Salt to taste
Juice of 1 lime

Oaxacan Pico de Gallo:
1 large ripe avocado, cut in half, pit removed, flesh scooped out and small dice.
6 radishes, small dice
5 Roma tomatoes, small dice
1 C. cilantro, chopped
½ white onion, small dice
Juice of 2 limes
Salt to taste

Steak:
1. Preheat a gas grill to medium high, or a light a charcoal fire and let it burn down until the goals are evenly white. Adjust the rack to 6 inches above the heat source.
2. Lay the ribeye on the rack and grill it, covered, turning the steak once, for a total of about 12 minutes for medium-rare, or done to your liking.
3. Transfer the steak to a cutting board, tent it with foil, and let rest for 10 minutes. Slice the ribeye at a slight angle into ½ inch thick slices. Set aside.

Charred Tomato Salsa:
1. On a griddle, roast tomatoes, serrano peppers, garlic and onion until softened, and lightly charred all over, about 10 minutes. Remove stems and seeds from peppers.
2. Remove skins from garlic and onion. Add all ingredients to a blender. Reserve one serrano. Puree until smooth.
3. Scrape the salsa into a bowl and taste for seasoning. Adjust with salt and reserved serrano.

Oaxacan Pico de Gallo
1. In a mixing bowl, combine all ingredients. Avocados should mash a little when mixing. Adjust season, lime and cilantro as needed.

Assembly:
1. Fill each 10" tortilla with 3 oz. Kobe ribeye, green cabbage, chopped cilantro and a squeeze of lime.
2. Garnish with Charred Tomato Salsa and Oaxacan Pico de Gallo.

Paco's Tacos and Tequila
1601 Morrison Blvd., #8A

"I'm a big taco fan."
Leslie Easterbrook, heroine of the "Police Academy" movie series

Park Lanes Restaurant

HOURS
BREAKFAST 9:00-11:00 AM
LUNCH & 11:00 - CLOSE
DINNER

Famous For Our Onion Rings!
-DAILY SPECIALS-

Summertime Brine Bone-In Pork Loin Chop

Signature Tastes of CHARLOTTE

Park Lane Bowling was established in 1982 under the management of Hall of Fame bowler George Pappas. Pappas came charging onto the Tour from the South to almost instant acclaim and success. He captured the Miller High Life Open and Buffalo Open on the 1970 Winter Tour and was one of the PBA's shining stars for years. A righthander with a classic swing and stroke, Pappas recorded the biggest triumph of his career when he captured the 1979 Firestone Tournament of Champions, leading the rich and prestigious event from the opening round to its conclusion.

4 thick, bone in loin chops

Brine:
½ C. peach nectar (orange juice is acceptable if peach nectar is unavailable)
2 C. apple cider
1 C. White House apple cider vinegar
1 Tbsp coarse salt
1 Tbsp crushed red pepper
1 tsp coarse ground black pepper
1 Tbsp herbs de Provence

1. Place all ingredients, except the 2 juices, into a small saucepan, and place on stovetop at medium heat until salt dissolves. This allows pepper and herbs to bloom. Then, add two juices, and let cool.

2. Place 4 chops in container large enough to hold, and fully submerge chops in the brine. Let stand overnight.

3. Heat grill to medium heat. Charcoal and wood chips are preferred for better smoke flavor.

4. To get those beautiful diamond grill marks, alternate sides at 2:00 and 10:00.

5. Baste with your favorite BBQ sauce, and put on grill for 4-5 minutes, depending upon the thickness. Repeat BBQ sauce application with every flip. Each side should get two 4-5 minute sessions, grill side down.

6. When you have achieved 155-160°F internal temperature, remove from grill and finish both sides with BBQ sauce.

7. Let rest for 5-8 minutes for a perfect glaze.

8. Serve with rosemary potatoes and seasonal veggies.

Park Lanes
1700 Montford Drive, #A

"Back then it was nothing like today. So you'd go to the bowling alley. We bowled and you could be in the back and you could make out, you know? And you know how hot it was to make out."
Steven Tyler, Aerosmith

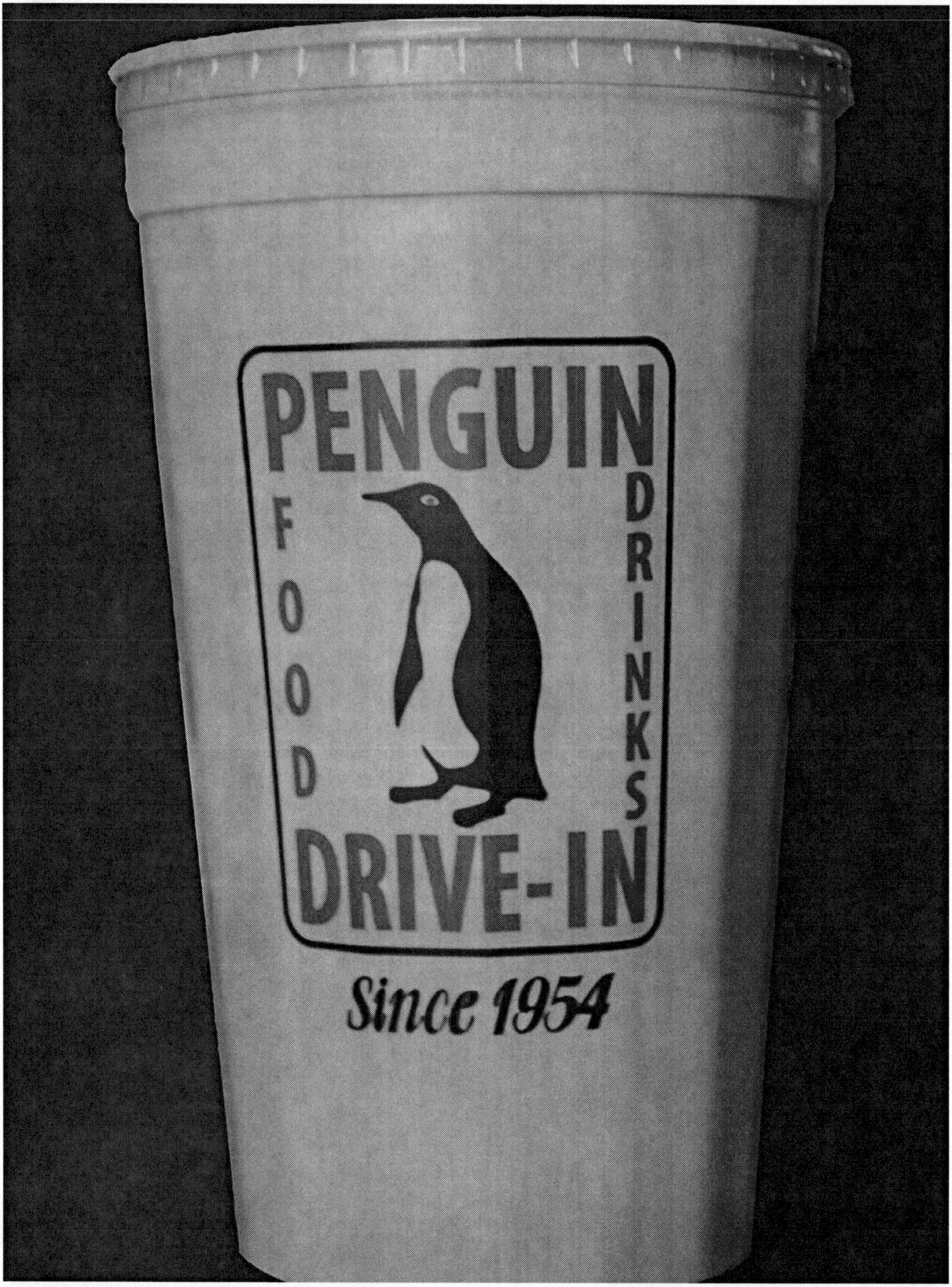
PENGUIN
FOOD
DRINKS
DRIVE-IN
Since 1954

The Penguin's Pimento Cheese

Signature Tastes of Charlotte

It all started with a man trying to feed his family. Now he's fed three generations of Charlotteans. Since 1954, The Penguin has been one of America's most legendary Drive-In Restaurants. Founded by Charlotte NC native Jim Ballentine, a World War II veteran and member of the US Army's renounced 101st Airborne Division, The Penguin Drive-In has received rave reviews by hundreds of food critics and has been featured on such programs as The Food Networks's "Diners, Drive-ins and Drives." After one bite, you'll know why customers have been saying "I'd Rather be at The Penguin" for over 50 years.

1 lb. shredded cheddar cheese 10 oz. shredded pepper jack 6 oz. diced pimentos and juice 1 C. Duke's Mayonnaise 1/8 tsp cayenne pepper 1 Tbsp granulated garlic 1 Tbsp ground black pepper	Mix all ingredients until well incorporated, working the cheese between your fingers.

Charlotte has been ranked as the capital of pimento cheese for a long time, according to Ed Simerly of Moody Dunbar, the nation's largest producer of pimento peppers. Dainty pimento cheese sandwiches were first introduced in the early 20th century and were regarded as a delicacy due to the high cost of cheese and imported pimiento peppers from Spain. Farmers began growing pimiento peppers in the South, reducing costs and James Lewis Kraft sold the first processed cheese in 1915. The cheese spread quickly reached the masses!

While the popularity of pimento cheese among the working class is what caused the spread to proliferate throughout the South, it remains an item on tearoom menus and as finger food suitable for formal weddings. Thus never losing its status as a product for the elite.

The Penguin Drive-In
1401 Central Avenue

Were you expecting their fried pickle recipe? Top secret stuff there. This pimento cheese is killer, and goes on several of their sandwiches. Hey, this is The Penguin ... what else is there to say?

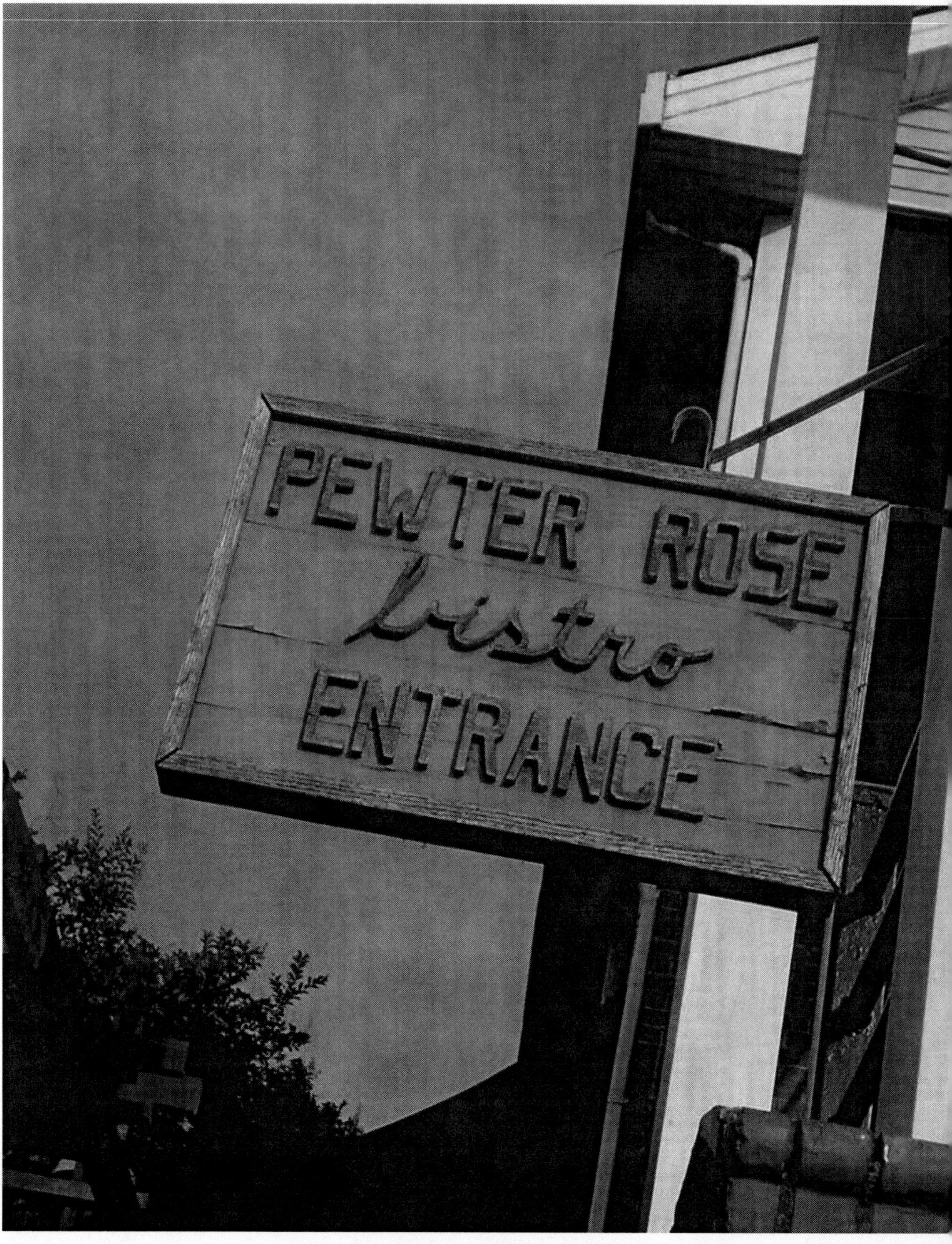
PEWTER ROSE
bistro
ENTRANCE

BAKED BRIE

Bring your date, family, or employees to have a fine meal in a relaxing casual dining atmosphere anytime for brunch, lunch or dinner. Pewter Rose is an eclectic casual bistro that offers internationally-American cuisine. Chef Brent Martin draws on the diverse, ethnic and cultural heritage of the United States, relating our menu to the palate of the region. Local produce, fresh seafood, poultry, beef, pork, game meats and vegetarian items are all interpreted in unique yet "comfortable" ways.

4 oz. butter
4 oz. sliced almonds
6 oz. brown sugar
¼ C. light rum
Small wheel of Brie

1. Blend the first four ingredients in mixer.

2. Form into a mound on top of Brie in an ovenproof dish and bake at 350°F for 10-12 minutes, or until bubbly.

3. Serve with sliced apples, grapes and crackers.

Signature Tastes of CHARLOTTE

PEWTER ROSE BISTRO
1820 SOUTH BLVD., SUITE 109

"Wine and cheese are ageless companions, like aspirin and aches, or June and moon, or good people and noble ventures..."
M.F.K. Fisher

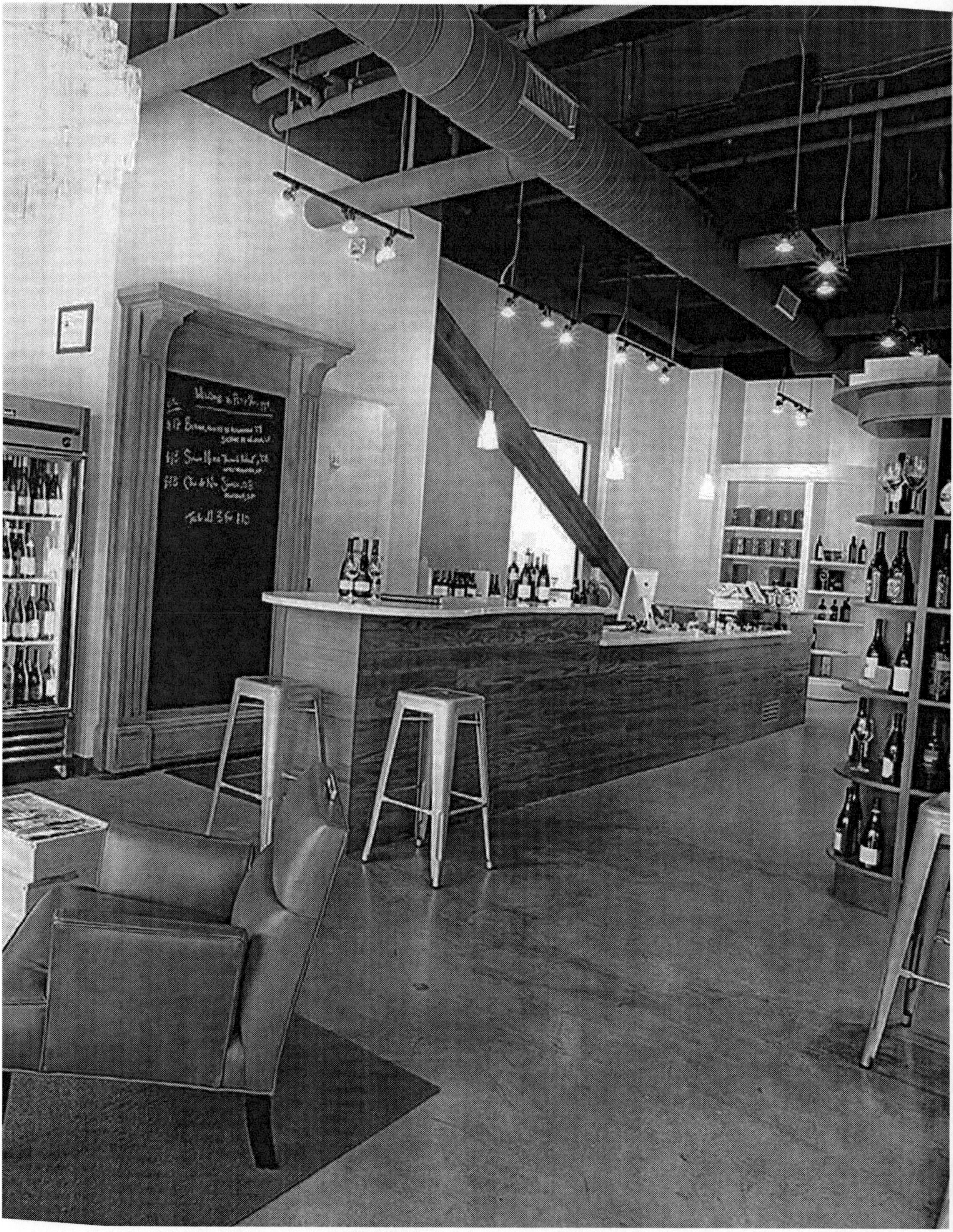

"Highlander" Pot de Creme

Petit Philippe is a wine and chocolate shop and tasting room in the Myer's Park neighborhood. We offer boutique and premium wines from California, the Pacific Northwest, France and other European wine regions. Whether you dash in for a quick bottle, linger over a tasting, or are looking for that perfect chocolate gift, we aim to provide you exactly what you need! Our goal is to provide swoon-worthy treats for your everyday indulgence. If we can bring a smile (or, better yet, a sigh!) to your lips, we've done our job.

Ingredients:
- 10 oz. heavy cream
- 5 oz. whole milk
- 2 oz. Glenmorangie "The Original" single malt Scotch*
- 2 oz. dark chocolate (60-65% cacao; E. Guittard 61% or Cacao Barry 64% work well,) chopped
- 7 oz. milk chocolate (Valrhona Jivara Lactee 40%,) chopped
- 5 large egg yolks
- 2 Tbsp sugar

1. Place the chocolates and Scotch in a medium sized heat-proof bowl and set aside.
2. In a heavy bottomed saucepan, heat cream and milk over moderate heat until bubbles form around edges.
3. While cream is heating, whisk sugar into eggs in heat-proof bowl.
4. Slowly stream about half of the scalded cream mixture into the eggs, whisking continuously.
5. Pour the tempered egg mixture back into the saucepan with the remaining cream and whisk.
6. Continue to cook over moderate heat, stirring continuously with a wooden spoon until it thickens enough to coat the back of the spoon. (You'll know it's ready when you can trace a line down the spoon, and the mixture holds the line.)
7. Pour the custard over the chocolates and allow mixture to sit for 2-3 minutes.
8. Using a spatula, start mixing in center of bowl, making small circles. As the emulsion forms, continue stirring in larger circles, working your way toward the outside of the bowl.
9. Once the mixture has completely combined and is smooth, strain it through a fine mesh sieve set over a pitcher or other container with a spout.
10. Pour into 8 3-oz. demitasse C., or 6 4-oz. ramekins placed in a larger baking dish.
11. Cover the entire dish with foil carefully, so as not to touch the tops of the custards.
12. Refrigerate at least 3 hours. Allow custards to come to room temperature before serving. Garnish with fresh whipped cream and our Spicy Nut Brittle.

Signature Tastes of Charlotte

Petit Philippe/Twenty Degrees Chocolate
Casey Hickey and Mark Meissner, co-owners - 2820 Selwyn Ave., Suite 120

"I was inspired to create a Pot de Crème recipe based on the most popular confections in our shop - The Highlander - which features Glenmorangie single malt Scotch and Valrhona Jivara Lactee milk chocolate. With so few ingredients, each one truly make an impact."
Casey Hickey, co-owner

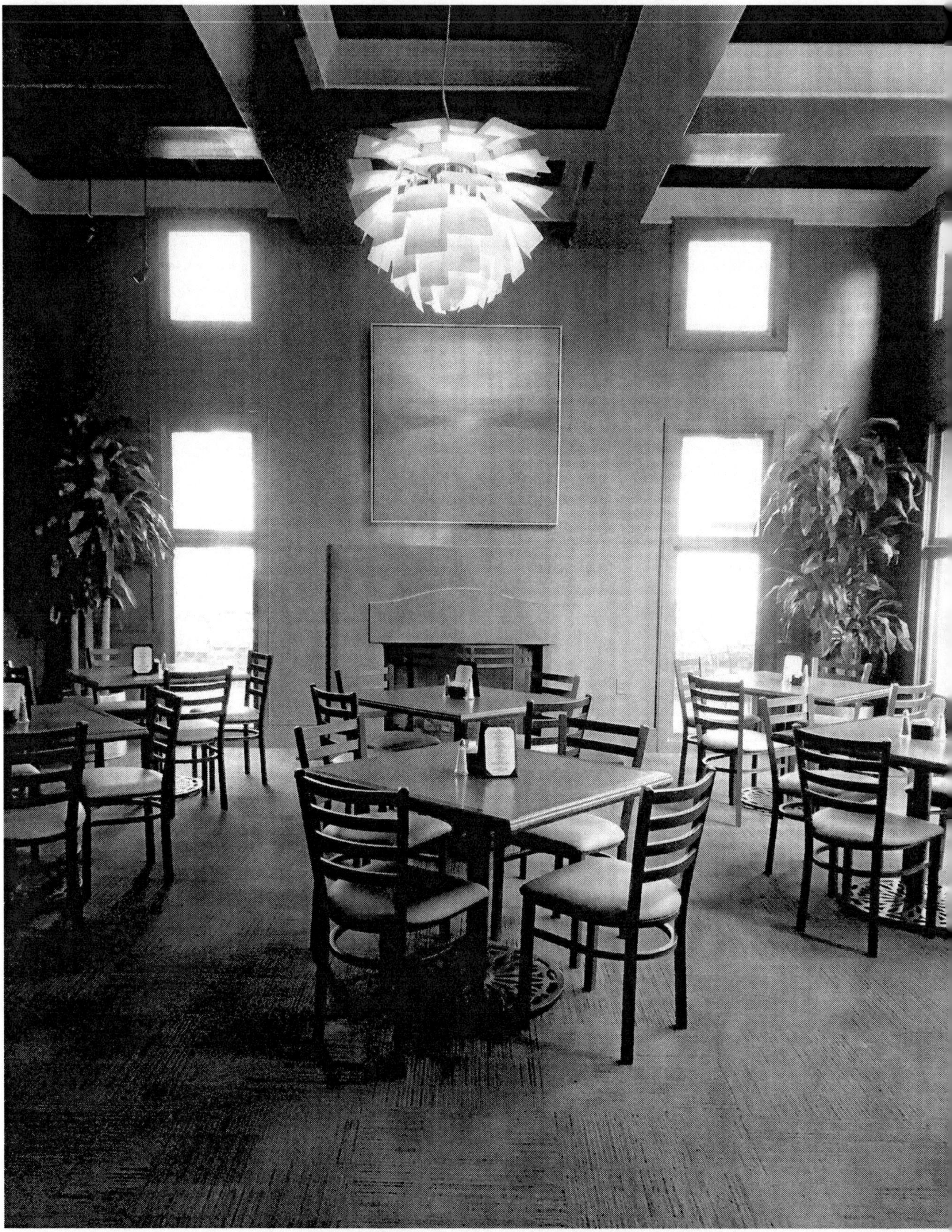

Bacon Wrapped Scallops with Blueberry Chili Sauce

Signature Tastes of Charlotte

As a Charlotte native, Eric grew up in the Dilworth neighborhood. His first cooking experience was at the side of his mother making pasta. He began working in a professional kitchen washing dishes for his uncle at the age of 14, and he's been immersed in restaurants ever since. School of hard knocks you might say ... from there he moved on to different cities and restaurants, learning every aspect of the kitchen.

4 jumbo scallops (U-10 preferred)
4 slices Jones' cherry wood bacon (or any smoked bacon)
(2) 6" skewers

Blueberry Chili Sauce:
1 C. fresh blueberries
½ C. sugar
½ C. water
½ tsp sambal oelek (found in Asian markets and most supermarkets)
¼ tsp fresh ginger, minced
¾ tsp cornstarch

1. Par cook the bacon, based upon your desired final crispness. Trim ¼" from each piece of bacon, lengthwise, and tightly wrap each scallop with one piece of bacon. Secure two scallops per 6" skewer, loose ends of bacon facing each other. Set aside.

2. In a 2 qt. saucepan, combine all the sauce ingredients. Bring to a boil and reduce heat. Simmer for 5-8 minutes.

3. While sauce is coming together, over medium high heat, bring 1 Tbsp butter to a simmer in a saute pan. Place scallops in pan, and cook on one side for 2½ minutes, until golden brown. Turn scallops over, and cook 1½ minutes more.

4. By now the sauce should have reached the proper consistency. Remove sauce from heat, place in a blender and puree. (Use caution when blending hot products, and hold the top in place with a hand towel.) Puree until smooth, and strain through a fine mesh sieve. Spoon sauce onto plate in any design you fashion. Place scallops on plate and enjoy!

Executive Chef Eric Litaker - **Providence Cafe** - 110 Perrin Place

"...I have always enjoyed food, be it simple or complicated, and remains passionate about creating dishes that will expose my guests to new and exciting flavors."
Chef Eric Litaker

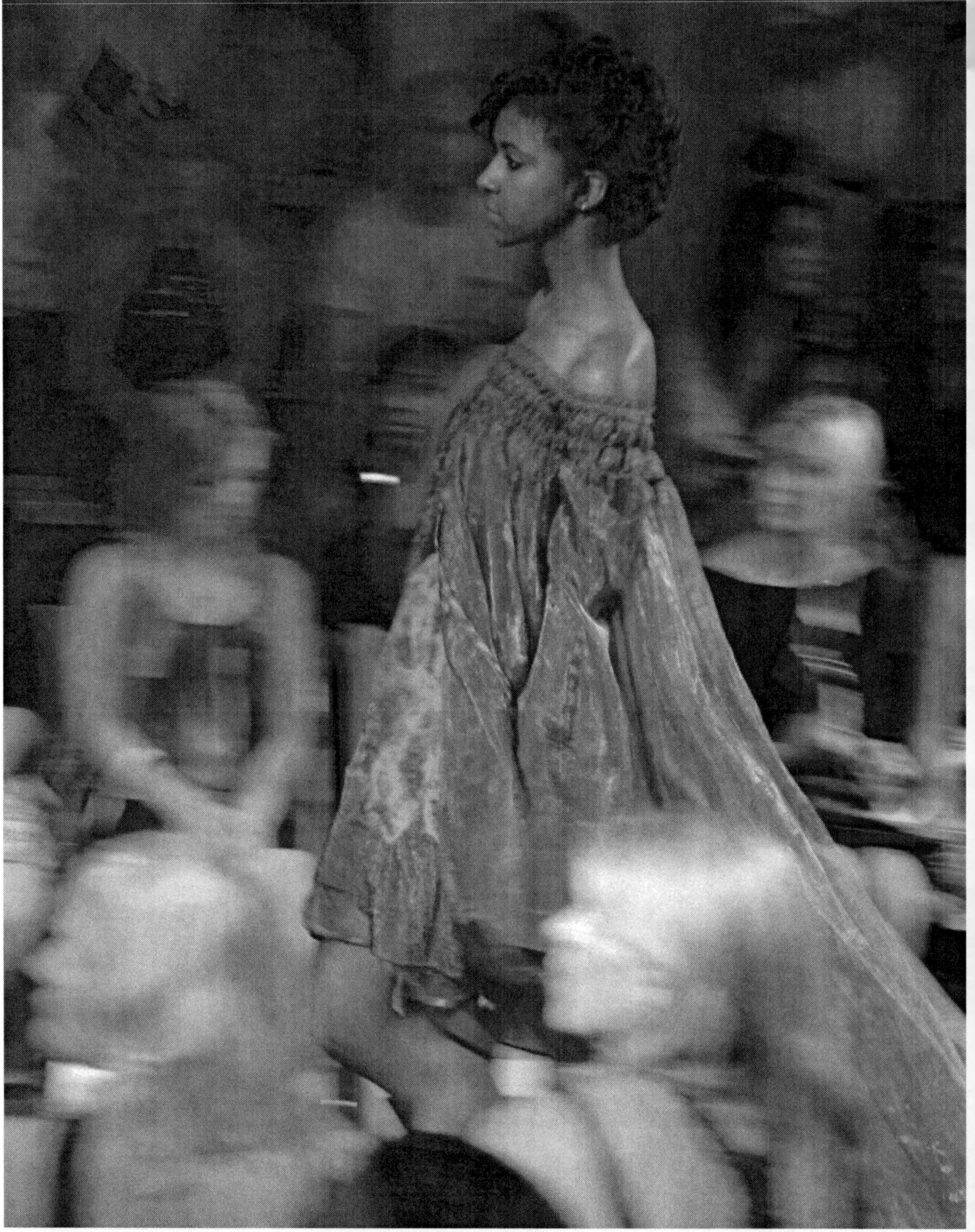

Melon Lime Meringue Pie

Terra Baltosiewich is the author of the food blog, CafeTerraBlog. A graduate of University of Arizona, with a degree in Nutritional Science, she works as a Food Safety/Quality Assurance Specialist for a third party auditor, and teaches culinary classes at a local gym. Her muffins and other sweet treats are a major attraction at a Charlotte cafe. Terra is developing 52 ways to use Greek yogurt, which will become an e-book. Terra enjoys developing healthy recipes that are both delicious and fun. She and her husband live in Charlotte, with their three cats, and a dog who is happy with leftovers.

2 C. honey dew melon, pureed
1 C. sugar
3 Tbsp cornstarch
3 egg yolks
4 Tbsp butter, melted and cooled
12 packets of True Lime, plus ⅓ C. water, or ⅓ C. lime juice
⅛ tsp salt

Crust:
One pack graham crackers (9 whole graham crackers)
½ C. pecans
½ C. butter, melted

Meringue:
3 egg whites
¼ C. sugar
2 tsp True Lime, or juice of one small lime

1. Preheat oven to 350°F.
2. Strain half the melon water off of pureed melon, and discard.
3. In a large bowl, whisk together sugar and cornstarch.
4. Add melon puree, yolks, melted butter, True Lime and salt. Mix with an electric mixer until homogeneous.
5. Blend graham crackers and pecans in a food process, and stir in melted butter.
6. Press into pie pan, and pour in melon mixture.
7. Place pie on a sheet pan (to catch any spills) and place on center rack of oven.
8. Bake for about 45-55 minutes, until center is set.
9. Set aside to cool before covering with meringue.
10. While cooling, set oven to 425°F.
11. In an electric mixer, whisk egg whites to soft peaks. Slowly add sugar and True Lime.
12. Spread over cooled pie, and place in oven to quickly toast the top. Alternately, this could be done with a kitchen torch.
13. Remove pie from oven and decorate with candied lime slices.

NOTES: Adding True Lime to your meringue will denature the protein strands in the egg whites, causing your meringue to deflate. You can avoid this by adding much less or using less lime zest.

Candied Lime Slices are thinly sliced limes coated with sugar, and baked at a low oven temperature on a silicone baking sheet to dehydrate.

"Men and Melons are hard to know."
Benjamin Franklin

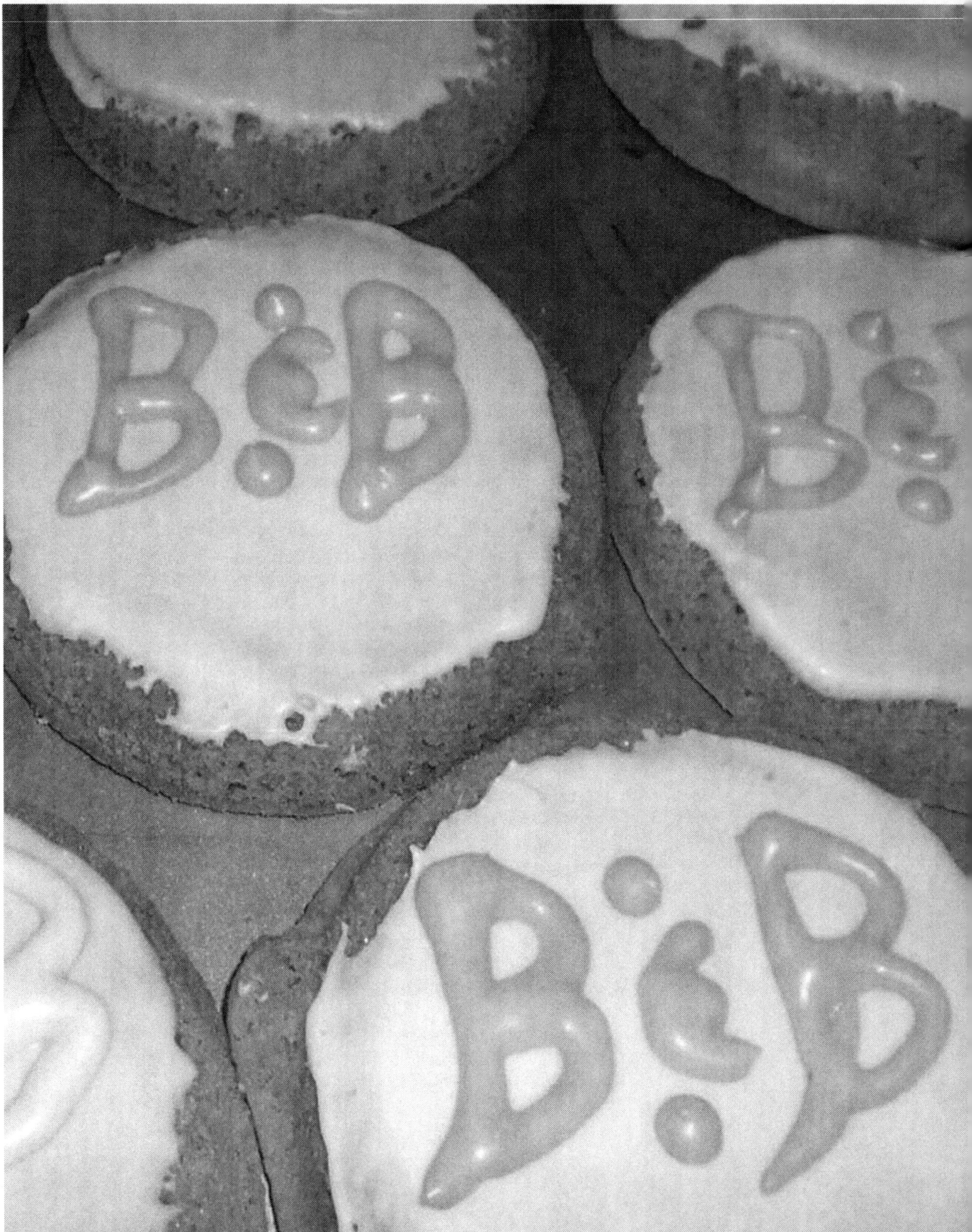
B&B
B&B
B&B

Aunt Evert's Sweet Potato Pie

Queen's Sweets is based out of Charlotte, NC, serving the surrounding communities including Huntersville, Lake Norman, Davidson, Concord, Matthews, Gastonia and Fort Mill, SC. All desserts are baked to order in a licensed kitchen in accordance with the state of North Carolina. We have desserts to fix your cravings. We offer desserts for any occasion whether big or small. If you are planning an event, corporate function, baby shower, bridal shower, office party or just craving something sweet we have a variety to choose from.

2½ C. mashed sweet potatoes
½ C. melted butter
1 C. milk
2 C. sugar
4 eggs
1 tsp cinnamon
1 Tbsp nutmeg
1 tsp vanilla
2 Tbsp fresh lemon juice
1 (9") unbaked pie crust
Whipped cream (optional...yeah right!)

2 Tbsp brown sugar w/1 Tbsp nutmeg for sprinkling on pie

1. Prepare filling by combining the mashed sweet potatoes with melted butter and mix well with hand mixer.

2. Add in sugar, milk, eggs, nutmeg, cinnamon, lemon and vanilla.

3. Beat on medium speed until mixture is smooth. Pour filling into unbaked pie crust.

4. Sprinkle brown sugar and nutmeg mixture over top, and bake at 350°F for 55-60 minutes, or until knife inserted in center comes out clean.

5. Serve pie with whipped cream, if desired.

Signature Tastes of CHARLOTTE

MEKEDA DEMPSEY - WWW.QUEENSWEETS.NET

QUEEN'S SWEETS

"Treats made by a Queen and fit for a Queen"

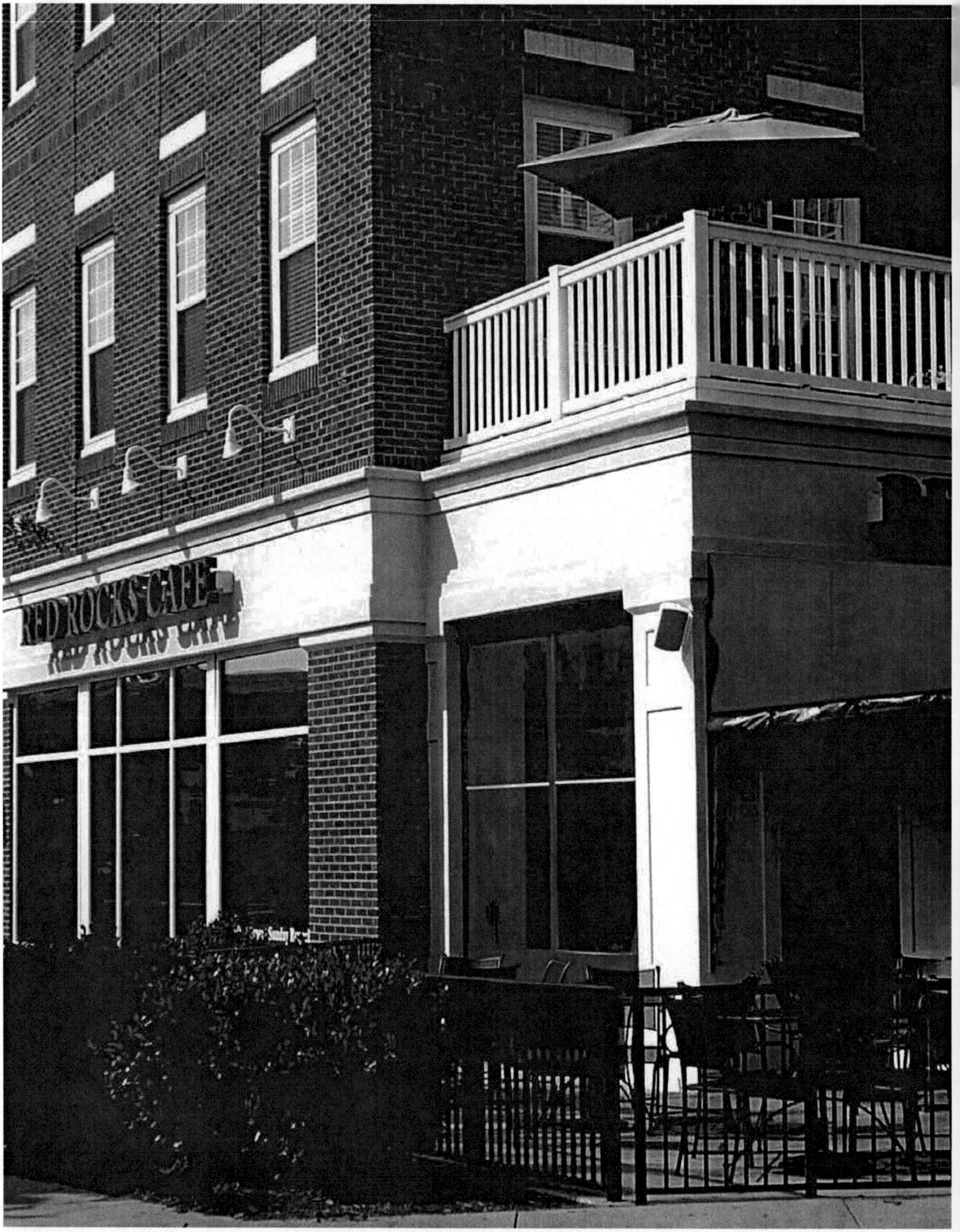
RED ROCKS CAFE

Honey Moon Cranberry Vinaigrette

Red Rocks is a guest experience. Hosted by local owners, catered with American cuisine, and served by a friendly and knowledgeable wait staff, Red Rocks is sure to please everyone. At Red Rocks the mission is to professionally and efficiently operate a clean, upscale, restaurant that consistently offers great food and beverage at a reasonable cost. Founded in 1992, together Ron Herbert and John Love developed Red Rocks Cafe into the now locally famous Red Rocks Cafe, Bar, and Bakery.

¼ C. minced shallots ¼ C. brown sugar 12 oz. Blue Moon Honey Moon ½ C. rice wine vinegar 18 oz. cranberry juice ½ C. red wine vinegar 3 C. extra virgin olive oil salt and pepper to taste	1. Combine shallots, Honey Moon and cranberry juice in an oversized sauce pot. 2. Simmer until the shallots are translucent. Reduce heat and allow mixture to reduce by over half, becoming almost sauce-like thick. 3. Remove from heat. Stir in brown sugar until it melts. 4. Stir in the 2 vinegars and olive oil. 5. Taste and add desired salt and pepper. Can now be used immediately, or put in air tight container and kept at room temperature for up to 2 weeks. (The citric acids and vinegars act as their own preservatives.) If using later, this will need aggressive stirring, as separation will occur. Use for dressing for any salad, or heated as a sauce to accompany fish, chicken, pork, or grilled veggies.

Signature Tastes of CHARLOTTE

Executive Chef Jamie Weatherly - 4223 Providence Road, Suite 8

Red Rocks Cafe

"In 1998 we decided to join forces to develop a great contemporary American Restaurant Concept."
John Love, co-owner

ROOTS
GOOD LOCAL FOOD
MENU

- Duck Confit Tacos with early spring slaw. $4/$7

- Grilled Cheese on Nova's Brioche with farmhouse cheese! $3

Visit Us on Facebook
ROOTS FARM

SEARED PORK BELLY WITH BLUEBERRY CHIPOTLE GLAZE AND CUCUMBER SALAD

Signature Tastes of CHARLOTTE

Roots is committed to working with local farmers to use the freshest local food possible. Our menus focus on using what is in season and available. Local food is far less traveled than its commercially distributed counterpart, which means it is allowed to ripen on the vine as opposed to the back of a tractor trailer. This imparts more flavor and nutrients into the food making the taste and quality far superior. We experience first hand the passion and care that goes into growing the ingredients we buy.

1 lb. block pork belly (available at farmer's market)
½ tsp red pepper flakes
Salt and pepper to taste
1 C. cider vinegar
1 large clove garlic, minced
12 oz. of your favorite beer
10" x 10" square of focaccia

½ pt blueberries
1 tsp canned chipotle peppers

2 medium cucumbers
1 Tbsp red wine vinegar
½ C. plain Greek yogurt
2 Tbsp fresh cilantro, chopped

1. Start cooking the pork belly while you're preparing the rest of the components. Score the fat of the belly by making small ¼ inch deep cross-hatched incisions.
2. Bring the beer, vinegar, and garlic to a boil.
3. In a medium, high sided pan, sear the pork on either side. Remove from the heat, and add the boiling liquid.
4. Cover and bake at 325°F for 2 hours. Once it is fork tender, remove the pork from the liquid, cover and let cool.
5. Once it is cooled completely, slice into ¼" thick planks. While the pork belly is cooking, place the blueberries in a medium saucepan, and add ¼ C. of the cooking liquid from the pork belly into the pot, as well.
6. Bring to a simmer, and simmer until all of the blueberries have popped and released their juices.
7. Add the juice from the canned chipotles to your desired level of spiciness.
8. Next, prepare the cucumber salad: wash the cucumbers. Julienne, and dress with red wine vinegar, yogurt, cilantro, and salt and pepper.

Assembly:
1. Salt and pepper the pork belly, and sear on either side until crispy.
2. Toast off the focaccia.
3. Place a few slices of the pork on each sandwich and top with some of the glaze.
4. Nestle some of the cucumber salad on top and place the other slice of focaccia to top the sandwich.
5. Slice in half and eat it up.

ROOTS FARM FOOD - GOOD LOCAL FOOD
CORNER OF 3RD AND TRYON, AND WHEREVER THE CART MAY TRAVEL...

"The fight to save family farms isn't just about farmers. It's about making sure that there is a safe and healthy food supply for all of us. It's about jobs, from Main Street to Wall Street. It's about a better America."
Willie Nelson

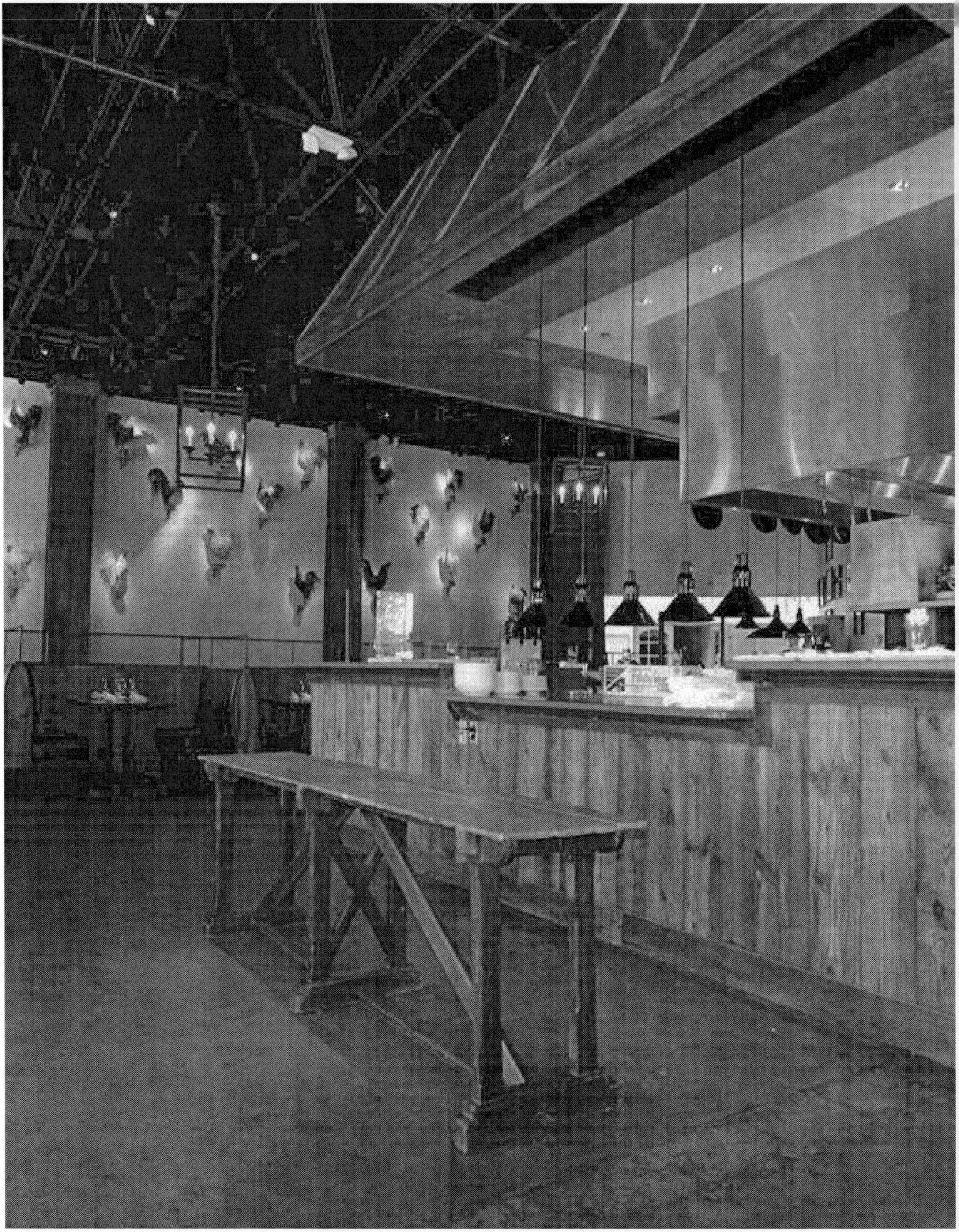

Tomato Basil Bisque

Joe Kindred was born and raised in Charlotte, and gained his culinary education all over the United States. A graduate of Johnson and Wales in Charleston, South Carolina, he started his career as an intern at Noble's Restaurant in Charlotte. Joe and his wife Katy went to San Francisco, where he furthered his skills and passion for European cooking at a James Beard Award-Winning restaurant, Delfina. In addition to his expertise in European cooking, Chef Kindred is a strong believer in the Farm to Table movement. His biggest influence is Chef Jim Noble, whom Chef Kindred calls his "mentor."

1 ½ lb. butter
2½ oz. garlic
24 oz. carrots, diced
10 oz. celery, diced
28 oz. onions, diced
(4) #10 cans tomatoes
½ oz. fresh basil
3 ½ qts. heavy cream
4 oz. kosher salt
1 oz. Tellichery pepper

1. Sweat butter and vegetables until they soften.

2. Add tomatoes and cream, and bring to a simmer. Let simmer for 45 minutes.

3. Add basil. Season with salt and pepper to taste.

Serve with NC Goat Lady Chevre and Tega Hills Farms micro basil as garnish.

"What's in my heart is on your plate"
Jim Noble, owner

Signature Tastes of CHARLOTTE

ROOSTERS WOOD-FIRED GRILL
6601 MORRISON BLVD.

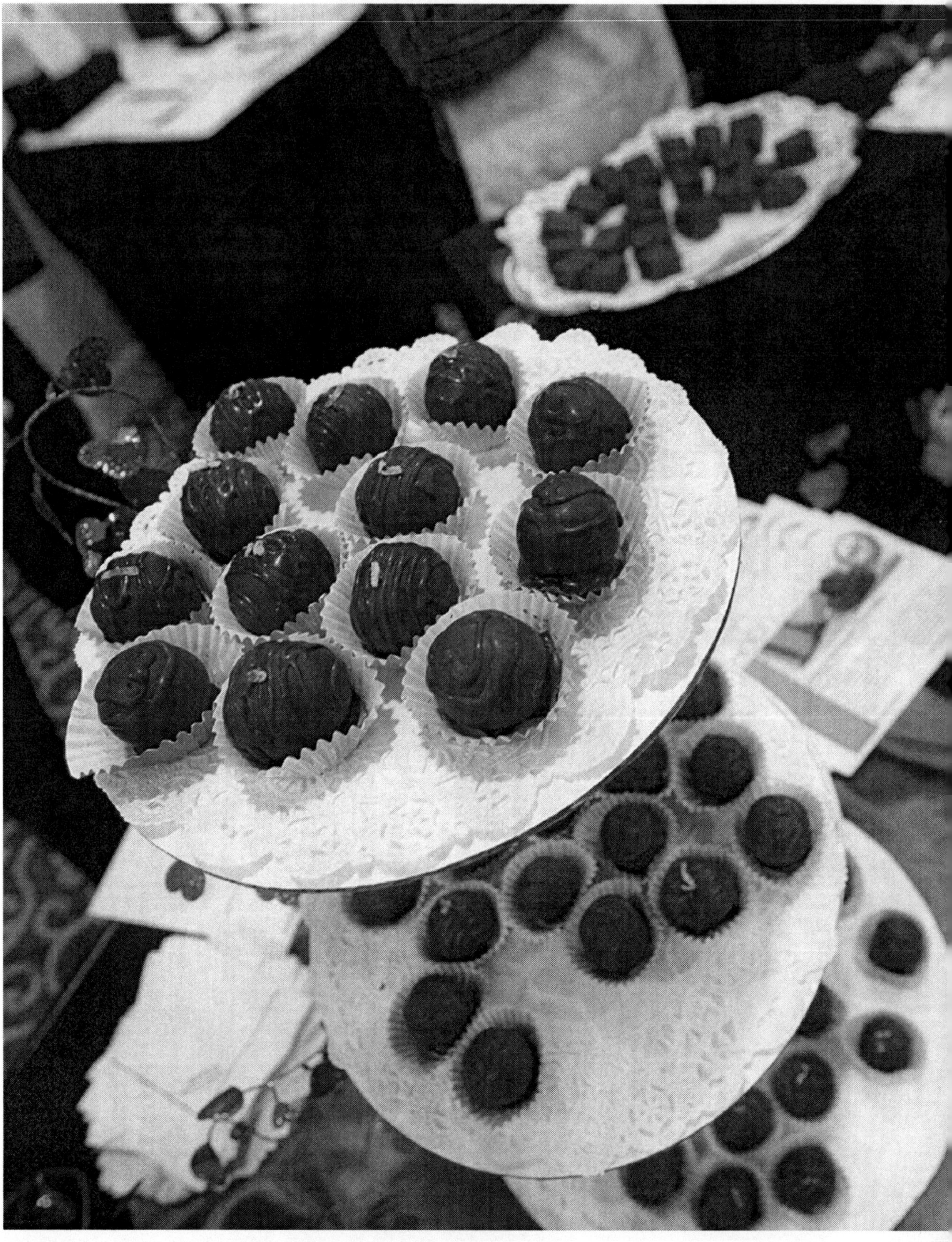

Fudge

Bill has a long pedigree of work from growing up in a family bakery. He serviced many of the resorts in the Myrtle Beach community for 12 years competing and winning many local awards. He has also owned his own bakery Mostly Muffins, in Columbia, SC where he was the hit of the town. He was also the lead pastry Chef for Taverna in Charlotte before it's untimely closure. Robin is an educator by profession but is quickly learning under her fathers tutelage.

6 oz. evaporated milk
1¾ C. sugar
½ tsp salt
1½ C. marshmallows
1 ½ C. semisweet chocolate chips
1 tsp vanilla extract
⅔ C. chopped walnuts (optional)

1. Combine evaporated milk with sugar and salt in a sauce pan. Bring to a boil.

2. Reduce heat, and simmer for 5 minutes.

3. Remove from the heat, and add remaining ingredients. Stir until marshmallows melt.

4. Pour mixture into buttered 9" x 9" inch pan. Cool.

Yield: 2 lb.

Simple, scalable and delicious. This chocolate fudge recipe comes from a time I can no longer recall, but I can the remember the recipe by heart. If 2 lb. of fudge is not enough, simply double the recipe, and you should have more than enough for yourself, family and friends.

The Secret Chocolatier
Bill Dietz, Owner - 2935 Providence Rd, Suite 104

"...There is chocolate, and then there is The Secret Chocolatiers chocolate"
Bill Dietz, owner

CHARLOTTE
MOTOR SPEEDWAY

NASCAR Banking

bankofamerica.com/RacePoints

GIFT SHOP TOURS DAILY

ON SALE

Coastal Shrimp & Goat Cheese Grits with Mild Cream Sauce

Signature Tastes of Charlotte

The Speedway Club Restaurant is widely regarded as the ultimate room with a view: delicious food, gracious hospitality, and a world famous panoramic look at Charlotte Motor Speedway. The Club prioritizes quality in everything from Certified Angus Beef to American coastal water seafood. If it's action and excitement that you are looking for, The Speedway Club overlooks more than 300 days of fun every year. From NASCAR to those famous driving schools to the Legends Summer Shootout, there is rarely a day when our view does not offer a bonus that will leave you excited about your next visit.

6601 Morrison Blvd. Executive Chef Michael Rosen - 5555 Concord Pkwy

The Speedway Club

Grits:
- 2 C. chicken stock
- 1 C. cut corn
- ½ C. peppers, diced
- ½ C. onions, diced
- 2 C. Adluh stone-ground white grits
- 1 C. heavy cream
- ½ lb. goat cheese
- 3 Tbsp unsalted butter
- Salt and pepper

Shrimp:
- 4 Tbsp olive oil
- 1 white onion, minced
- 1 clove garlic, minced
- 1 C. mixed peppers
- 1 lb. spicy sausage
- 1 tsp Creole Seasoning
- 1 tsp cayenne pepper
- 1 tsp cumin
- 1 tsp paprika
- ½ tsp ground thyme
- 2 Tbsp all purpose flour
- 4 C. chicken stock
- 1 bay leaf
- 2 lb. large shrimp, peeled, deveined, tails left on
- Kosher salt and freshly ground black pepper
- 2 Tbsp Italian parsley, chopped
- 1 green onion

Grits:
1. Place a 3 qt. pot over medium-high heat. Add half the butter and sauté the peppers, onions and corn.
2. Add the chicken stock and bring to a boil.
3. Slowly whisk in the grits. When the grits begin to bubble, turn the heat down to medium low and simmer, stirring frequently with a wooden spoon.
4. Allow to cool for 10-15 minutes, until the mixture is smooth and very thick.
5. Remove from heat and stir in the cream, goat cheese and butter.
6. Season with salt and pepper. Place in oversized, rimmed baking pan (hotel pan) and chill overnight.
7. Cut out with the cutter of your choice, lightly flour and deep fry until browned.

Shrimp:
1. Place a deep skillet over medium heat and coat with olive oil. Add the onion, mixed peppers, and garlic; sauté for 2 minutes to soften.
2. Add the sausage and cook, stirring until there is a fair amount of fat in the pan, and the sausage is brown.
3. Add all seasonings.
4. Sprinkle in the flour and stir with a wooden spoon to create a roux. Slowly pour in the chicken stock and continue to stir to avoid lumps. Toss in the bay leaf.
5. When the liquid comes to a simmer, add the shrimp. Poach the shrimp in the stock for 2-3 minutes, until they are firm and pink and the gravy is smooth and thick.
6. Season with salt and pepper. Stir in the parsley and green onion.

"I like racing but food and pictures are more thrilling. I can't give them up. In racing you can be certain, to the last thousandth of a second, that someone is the best, but with a film or a recipe, there is no way of knowing how all the ingredients will work out in the end. The best can turn out to be awful and the worst can be fantastic. Cooking is like performing and performing like cooking."
— Paul Newman

Friday October 30

CELEBRATING 200TH BIRTHDAY OF EDGAR ALLAN POE

POETRY IN A GLASS

AN EVENING OF *Absinthe & Atmosphere*

Classic Absinthe and Specialty Absinthe Cocktails with special ~ food ~ pairing features

Dramatic POE readings by Joe Rux of Actors Theatre Charlotte
Aural musings by Jah-Sun Rising

SOUL

1500 CENTRAL AVE - 704.348.1848 - UPSTAIRS @ PECAN

Soul Wings Asian Style

A gastro lounge is a new way of saying a gastro pub. Arriving stateside from London, this concept combines a restaurant with a pub (or bar, stateside lingo) that concentrates on the quality of food.. A hip lounge off the beaten path with sushi and Greek classics on the same menu, Soul Gastrolounge offers up innovative sushi, global tapas and crafted cocktails served with casual sophistication.

1 dozen jumbo party wings, disjointed
1 Tbsp vegetable oil
1 C. oyster sauce
¼ C. low sodium soy sauce
1 tsp honey
1 lime, juiced
1 tsp sesame seeds (preferably black & white mixed)
1 scallion, white and green parts chopped

1. Toss chicken wings with oil

2. Place on sheet pan and bake in 400°F oven for 45 minutes. Alternately wings can be pan or deep fried for 10 minutes.

3. Mix oyster sauce, soy sauce, honey, and lime juice in deep bowl.

4. When wings are done, toss hot wings in sauce and mix until well coated.

5. Serve sprinkled with sesame seeds and chopped scallions.

"I love tapas. They're like appetizers for a meal that never comes."
Marge Simpson

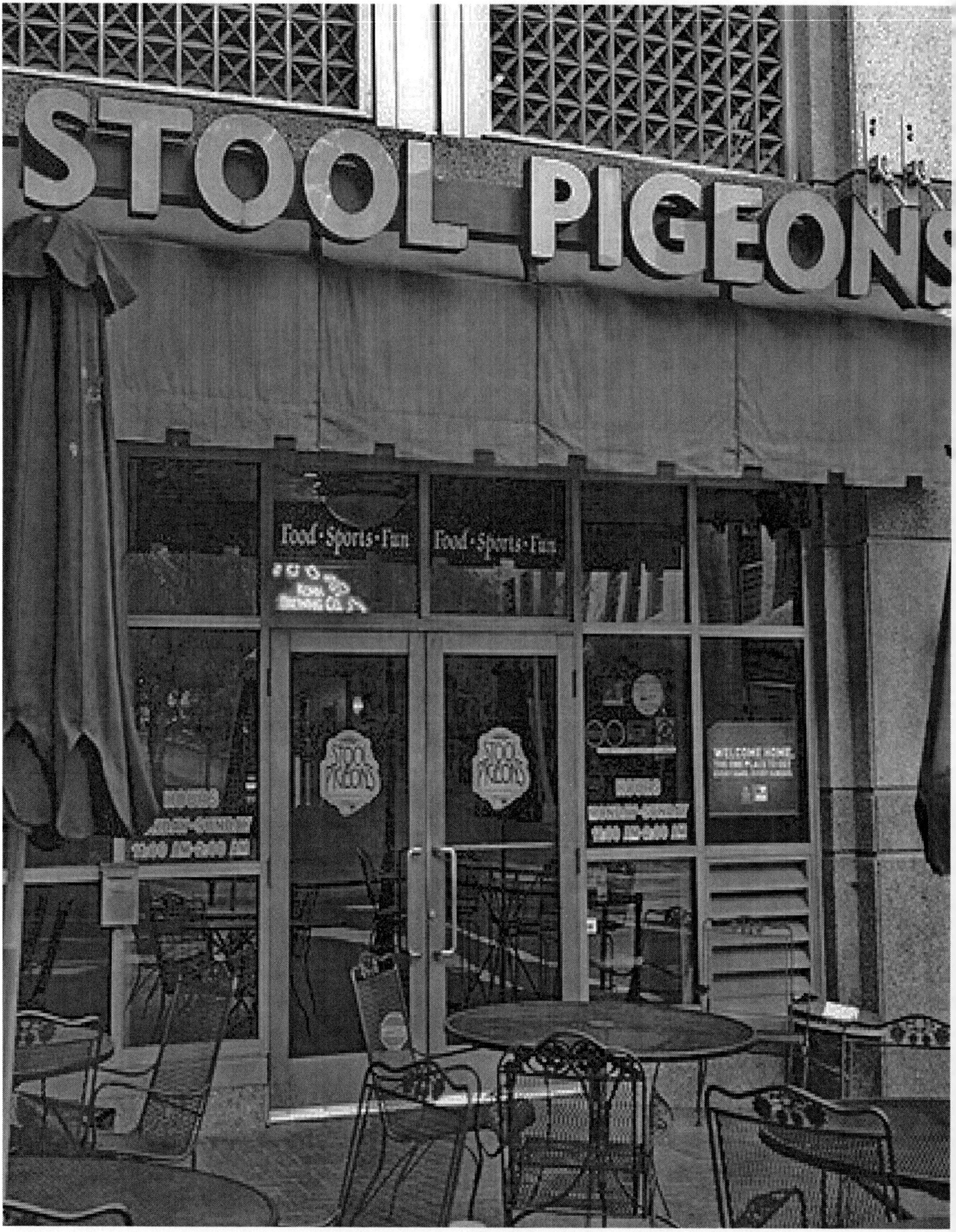
STOOL PIGEONS
Food · Sports · Fun
Food · Sports · Fun

Stool Pigeons' Chili

The only thing certain about the origins of chili is that it did not originate in Mexico. Charles Ramsdell wrote: "Chili, as we know it in the U.S., cannot be found in Mexico today except in a few spots which cater to tourists. If chili had come from Mexico, it would still be there. For Mexicans, especially those of Indian ancestry, do not change their culinary customs from one generation, or even from one century, to another."

10 lb. Angus beef
2 oz. Lawry's Seasoned Salt
½ #10 can kidney beans
½ #10 can black beans
1 can diced tomatoes
2 cans V-8
3 C. yellow onions, chopped
3 C. red bell pepper, chopped
3 Tbsp oregano
2 oz. crushed red pepper
2 Tbsp garlic powder
2 Tbsp cumin
1 C. chili powder
1 C. Frank's hot sauce

1. Season the beef and brown.

2. Drain grease.

3. Open can of diced tomatoes and chop into smaller pieces.

4. Mix ingredients together in large pot.

5. Simmer on low heat for 2 hours.

6. Serve, or store and refrigerate for a day or two and reheat to serve. (Flavor improves with time.)

Signature Taste of CHARLOTTE

Assistant General Manager, Drew Jenkins - 214 North Church Street

Stool Pigeons Restaurant

"The aroma of good chili should generate rapture akin to a lover's kiss."
Motto of the Chili Appreciation Society International

TABLE 274

Ricotta Gnocchi Ratatouille

All things at Table 274 are a labor of love. The farmers they collaborate with work hard to provide their great products. Their chefs prepare each meal without pretense. They support local agriculture and education through their culinary expertise while providing a casual and heart felt dining experience. This is central to our mission - enjoy the fruits of their labor with the ones you love. Table 274's menu features Carolina grown and produced products in an effort to support small, local farms, and they also make charitable donations from their Sunday dinner proceeds to a variety of foundations.

Ricotta Gnocchi:
- (1) 16 oz. container ricotta cheese
- 1 large egg
- ½ C. finely grated Parmesan
- ½ tsp salt
- ¾ -1 C. flour
- Juice and zest of 1 lemon

Ratatouille:
- ½ zucchini
- ½ yellow squash
- ½ yellow onion
- 2 cloves garlic
- ½ red bell pepper
- ½ Anaheim pepper
- 1 large heirloom tomato
- ½ C. tomato paste
- ½ C. white wine
- 4 large fresh basil leaves (chiffonade)
- Salt & pepper to taste

For Plating:
- 1 Tbsp butter
- 1 Tbsp vegetable oil
- Salt & pepper to taste
- ¼ C. chicken stock (or water)
- 1 leaf fresh basil (chiffonade)

Gnocchi:
1. Line a chinois with cheesecloth and strain the ricotta for 1 hour to remove moisture.
2. Move the ricotta to a food processor fitted with a steel blade, and add the egg, salt, lemon, and parmesan cheese. Process until smooth.
3. Move the ricotta to a mixer fitted with a hook attachment. Turn on low, and slowly add the flour in 3 different additions.
4. Let the flour become completely incorporated before the next addition. The dough should be slightly tacky, but not sticky.
5. Turn dough on a floured work surface. Make 2 oz. balls and sprinkle with flour. Roll each ball into a log about ¾" thick, and about 8-10 inches long.
6. Cut the logs into ¾" pieces. Roll each piece of gnocchi down the length of the gnocchi board. Do not press down too hard, keeping the piece from flattening out.
7. Bring a pot of lightly salted water to a boil, and prepare an ice bath of ice cubes and water.
8. In small batches, blanch the gnocchi for 2 minutes or until they begin to float. Stir gently with a wooden spoon.
9. Remove from the water and transfer to the ice bath. Let cool for 1 minute, drain and dry out for another 3 minutes.
10. Drizzle with a little olive oil, and set aside.

Ratatouille:
1. Cut all vegetables about ¾" x ¾". Add a little vegetable oil to a hot sauté pan.
2. Toast the garlic until fragrant and turning slightly brown. Add the remaining vegetables to the pan, except for the tomato.
3. Sauté on high for 2 minutes, or until they begin to caramelize. Add the tomato paste and cook for 1 minute.
4. Deglaze with half of the white wine and let reduce.
5. Add in the remaining wine and tomatoes, and cook for another minute. Season with salt and pepper fresh basil. Remove from heat.

Assembly:
1. In a sauté pan, add olive oil and butter. Let the butter become slightly brown and add in 1 C. of the gnocchi. Toast on all sides.
2. Add ½ C. of the ratatouille mixture into the pan, and season with salt and pepper.
3. Add the chicken stock and drizzle with olive oil.
4. Spoon into a bowl and garnish with fresh basil.

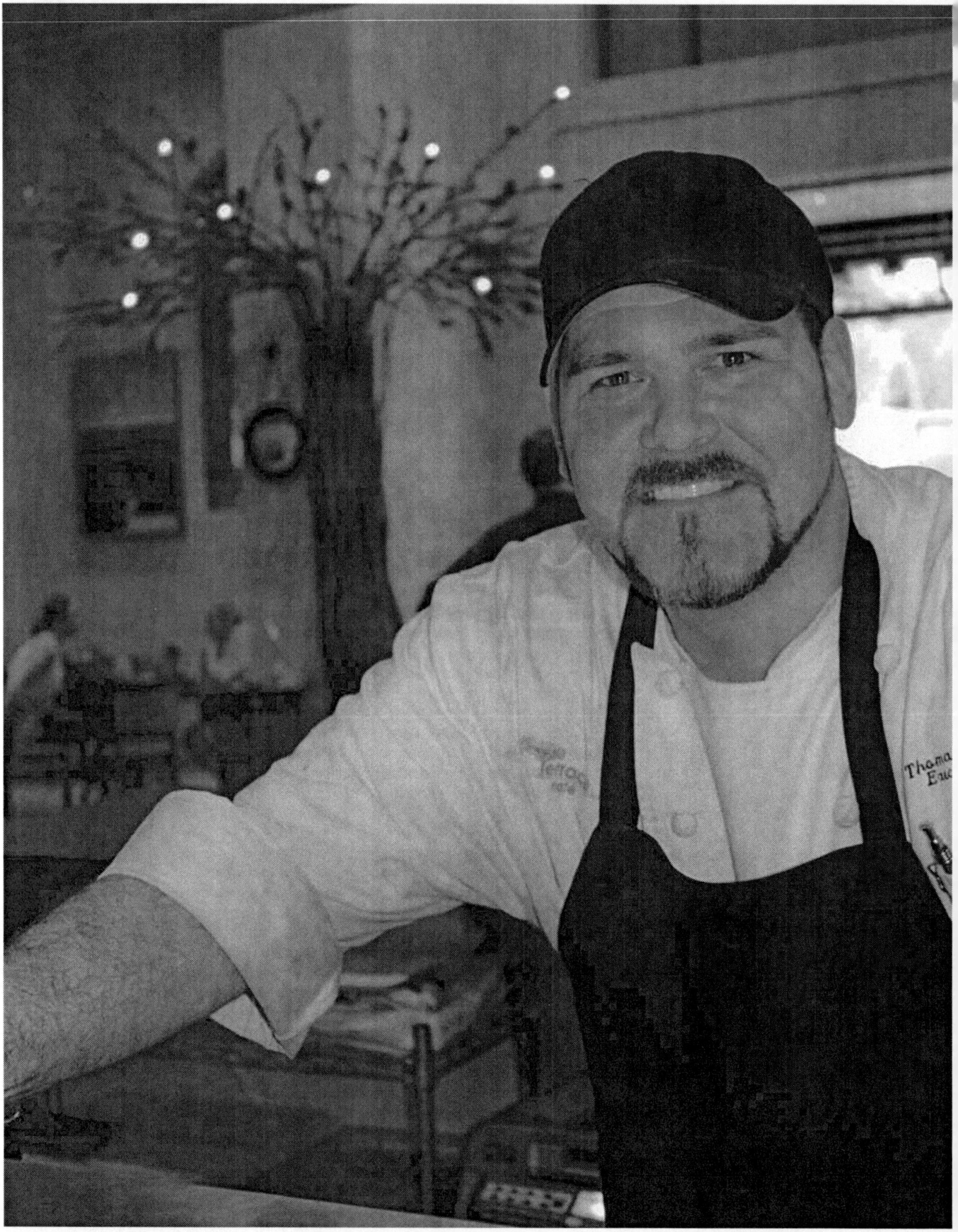

Jalapeno Jam

Signature Tastes of Charlotte

In a city already stuffed with dining choices, we realized we would have to do things quite differently to set us apart from other restaurants. And that's what drives us. Creating a place where friends and family can gather to savor eyebrow-raising meals always made from scratch with the finest ingredients. And, always with our own tempting little twists. Back in 2009, dishes like our Red Velvet Waffles and S'mores French Toast quickly made us the AM choice for those heading to work or to play. (And earned us "Best Breakfast Place" awards in magazines and online.)

6 medium jalapeno peppers
1 medium green bell pepper
1 medium red bell pepper
½ medium onion
1½ C. cider vinegar
1 Tbsp crushed red pepper
6½ C. sugar

1 pack Sure Jell

FOLLOW THESE DIRECTIONS EXACTLY!

1. Finely chop all the peppers and onion, and add to 6-8 qt. sauce pot.

2. Add cider vinegar, crushed red pepper, and sugar. Stir well, then bring to a rolling boil.

3. Stir in pectin quickly, then return to a rolling boil for exactly 1 minute, stirring constantly.

4. Remove from the heat and allow to cool to room temperature.

5. Then, let it sit in an ice bath until set.

At the cafe, we serve it over Berkshire Pork Tenderloin that has been brined and slow roasted.

Executive Chef Thomas A. Kerns - 4625 Piedmont Row Drive

Terrace Cafe

"There is no sincerer love than the love of food."
George Bernard Shaw

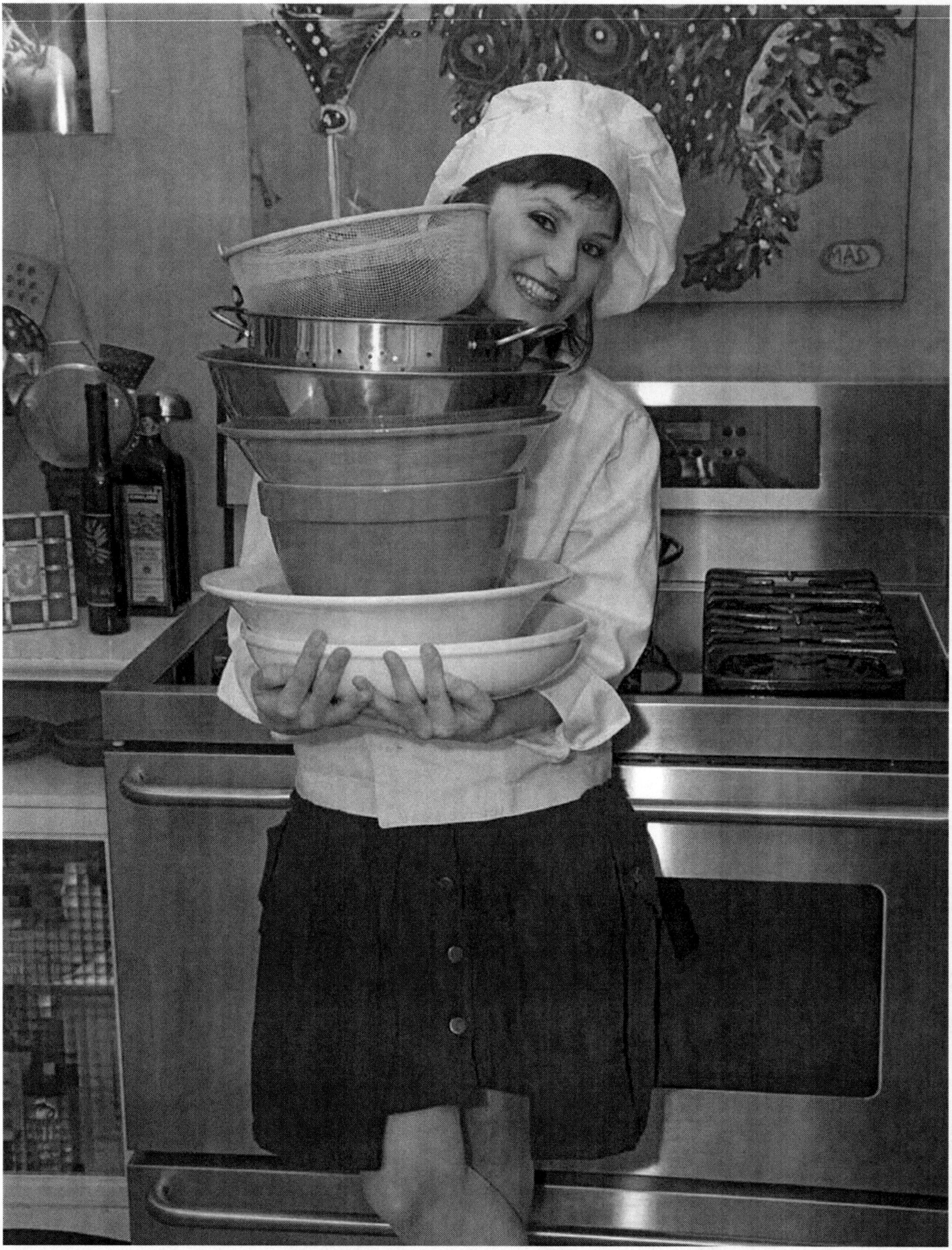

Polenta with Lamb and Pork Ragu

Buongiorno! My name is Susanne Dillingham and my business is called The Tiny Chef. I am indeed a tiny chef, with a tremendous passion for food, wine and farming. My business is dedicated to teaching those who have a passion for learning new, sustainable and practical ways to cook while supporting our local farmers in North Carolina. Whether you are a well-seasoned cook or a total beginner, it makes no difference to me! When we start cooking together we will have a blast! The Tiny Chef is an Italian trained Chef and Sommelier.

Polenta:
3½ C. polenta
3 C. milk
4½ C. vegetable stock

Lamb and Pork Ragu:
3 Tbsp olive oil
4 cloves garlic, chopped
1 white onion, chopped
1 carrot peeled and finely chopped
1 stalk celery, finely chopped
½ lb. ground lamb
½ lb. groud port
½ C. dry white wine
1 C. tomato puree
1 bay leaf
Parmigianino Reggiano cheese to serve
Salt and freshly ground black pepper to taste

1. Bring the liquids to a boil, and slowly whisk in the polenta.
2. Turn the heat down to a simmer and cook for 45 minutes, until done (if you don't have the instant polenta.)
3. Stir often. Serve with the ragu below.

Lamb and Pork Ragu:
1. Place a little olive oil in a sauté pan.
2. Add the carrot, celery, onion, and garlic, and sauté until soft.
3. Add the ground lamb and pork, and cook until browned.
4. Pour the wine in the pan, and cook until the wine has evaporated. Add the tomato puree, and bay leaf, and stir.
5. Reduce the heat to simmer, and cook for one hour. Season with salt and pepper.
6. Serve on tope of the cooked polenta on a large flat surface (like a wooden cutting board) and have guests cut their own pieces to serve themselves. Sprinkle with Parmigianino Regina cheese on top.

This recipe is so much fun!

This sauce may be prepared a day or tow in advance, and, in my opinion, the flavors improve significantly, making for a smoother taste.

"Ever consider what pets must think of us? I mean, here we come back from a grocery store with the most amazing haul - chicken, pork, half a cow. They must think we're the greatest hunters on earth..."
Anne Tyler

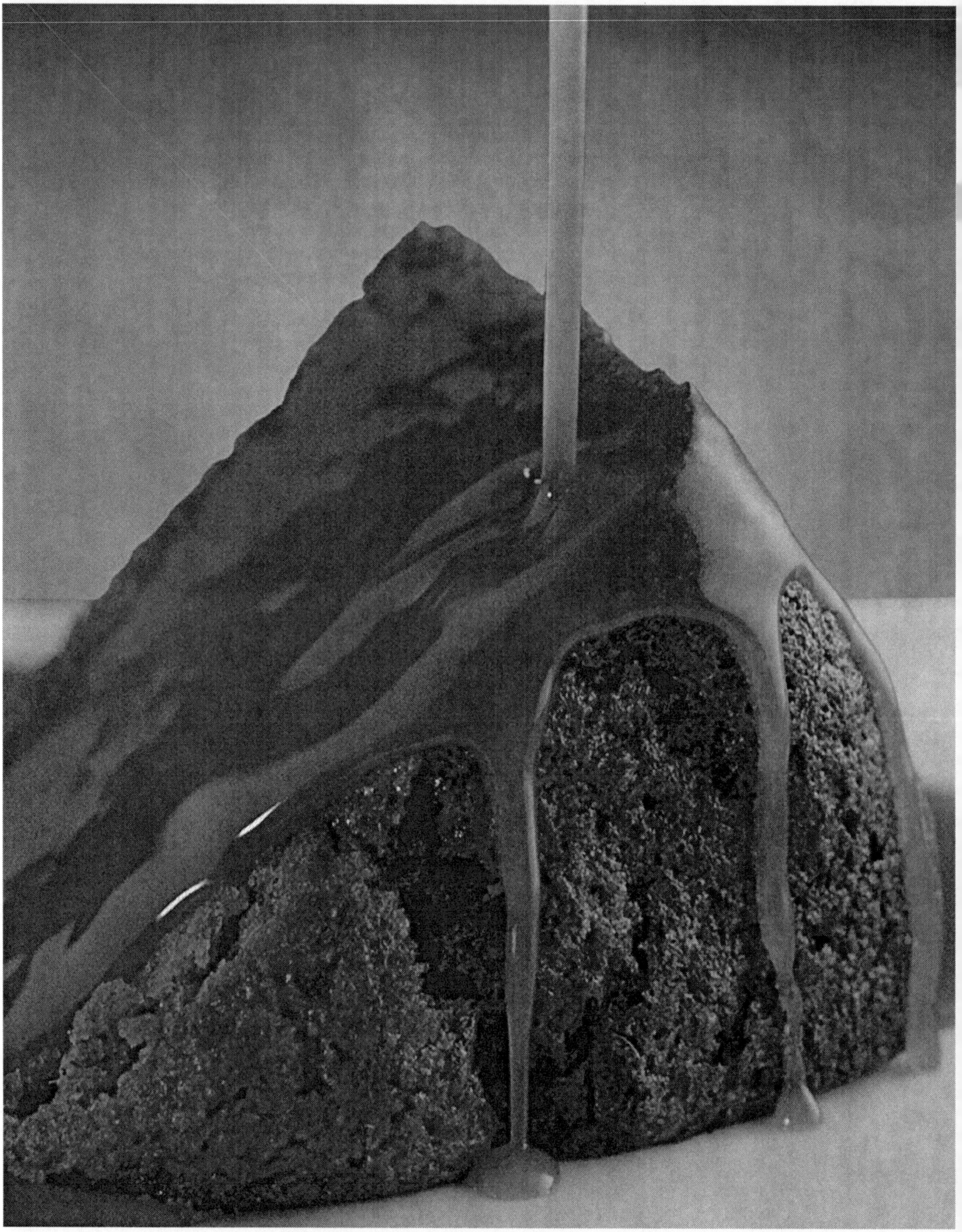

Cherry Sticky Toffee Pudding

This Sticky Toffee Pudding recipe is a great tasting recipe, and it is certainly a modern British 'classic', (alongside Jam Roly-Poly and Spotted Dick puddings) capturing for many the childhood memories of growing up in the 20th Century. Some say Sticky Toffee Pudding was developed in the Lake District in the 1960's while others claim it is from an earlier 1907 recipe, (never published) but whatever its true origin, getting the balance between the pudding being too sweet, and being just right, is essential.

1 lb. dates, pitted and chopped
1 C. dried currants, chopped
16 oz. port
3 C. water
3 C. dried cherries, chopped and poached in water
1¼ lbs butter
2 lbs dark brown sugar
12 large eggs
3 lb. all-purpose flour
2 Tbsp baking powder

Sauce:
24 oz. sugar
12 oz. butter
3 medium lemons, zested and juiced
12 oz. heavy cream
12 oz. milk
1 pt. brandied cherries, pitted
12 oz. sugar
3 oz. port

1. Place dates, dried cranberries, port and water in a saucepan and bring to a boil.
2. Cook 5 minutes and cool. Puree and reserve.
3. In a second saucepan, add the cherries and their liquid, and poach 5 minutes. Strain and reserve.
4. In a mixer, add the butter and sugar and mix until 'creamed.'
5. Add the eggs and date-cranberry puree.
6. Sift the flour and baking powder together and stir into the butter mix.
7. Fold in the diced cherries.
8. Preheat the oven to 325°F.
9. Butter and flour 12 molds.
10. Fill each ¾ full, and bake for 12 minutes, until done (toothpick inserted comes out almost clean.)

Sauce:
1. Caramelize butter and sugar in a saucepan until brown.
2. Remove from the heat and add lemon, zest and heavy cream.
3. In a second saucepan, add the remaining ingredients and bring to a boil (add a little water if needed.)
4. Remove from heat, cool, and puree in blender. Add a little of the caramel sauce in the process.

"Work is the meat of life, pleasure the dessert."
B. C. Forbes

Signature Tastes of CHARLOTTE

A GOOD CHERRY STICKY TOFFEE PUDDING, IN HOMAGE TO THE ENGLISH

TOM CONDRON

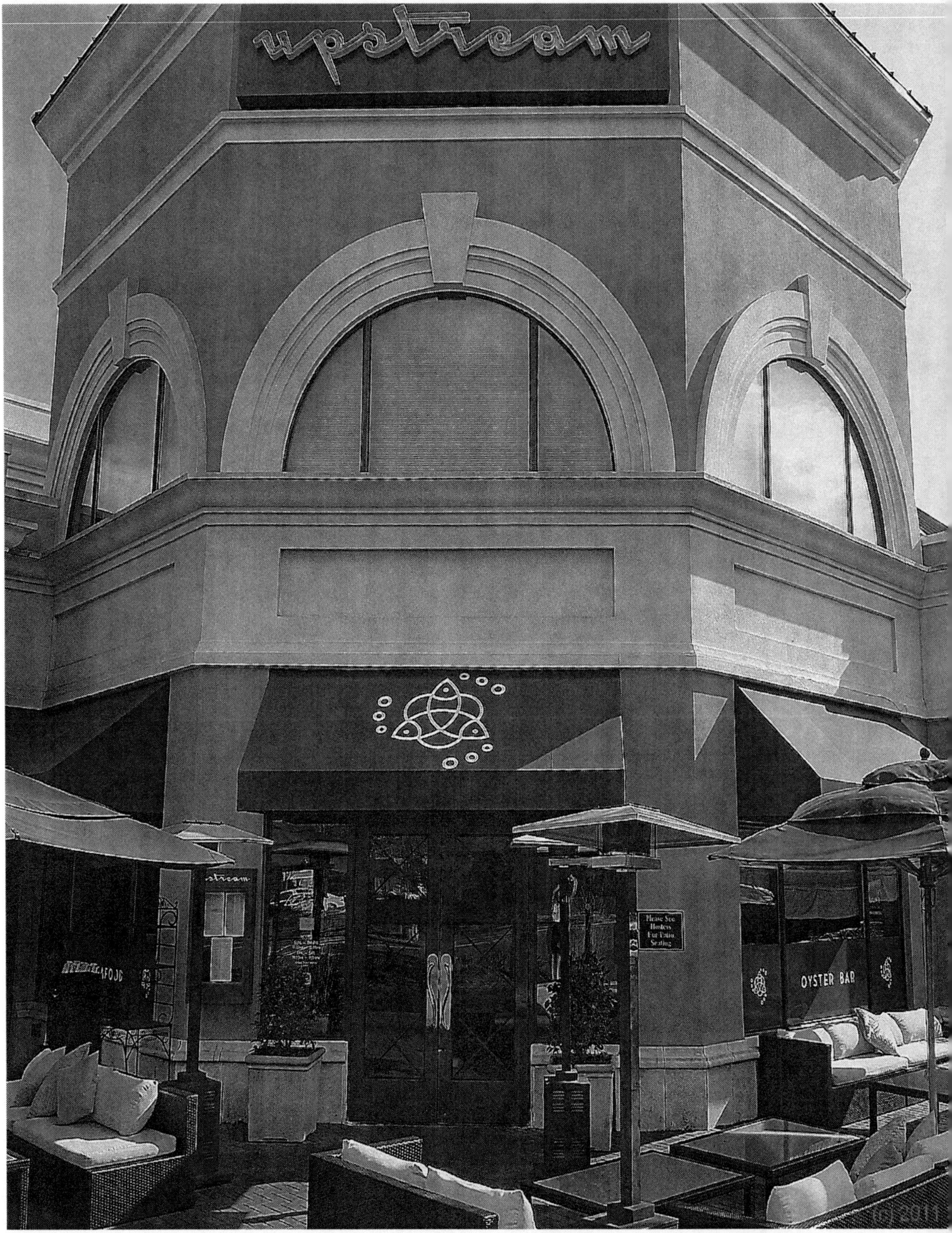
upstream
Please See Hostess For Patio Seating
OYSTER BAR

Sea Scallop with Shell Bean Salad, Fennel, and Aioli

The day's freshest catch is turned into innovative, spectacular cuisine each night at Upstream. Executive Chef Scott Wallen features only the freshest day boat seafood and the best sushi. And, the restaurant's award-winning Pacific Rim cuisine if matched only by it innovative wine list and cool, soothing ambiance. Esquire Magazine's John Mariani named Upstream one of the best new restaurants in the US, and Zagat subsequently named Upstream "Charlotte's most popular restaurant."

12 U-10 sea scallops
3 C. fresh shell beans, blanched and chilled
2 Roma tomatoes
2 Tbsp champagne vinegar
½ C. olive oil
2 Tbsp fresh basil
1 tsp chopped shallots
1 head fennel, sliced into ⅛" rounds
1 Tbsp fresh parsley
3 Tbsp lemon aioli

Citrus Marinade
¼ lemon peel
¼ orange peel
1 Tbsp lemongrass, chopped
1 Tbsp lemon juice
1 Tbsp orange juice
3 Tbsp olive oil
1 Tbsp shallots
1 Tbsp fresh thyme

Grilled Lemon Aioli:
2 lemons
1 Tbsp olive oil
1 tsp sea salt
1 tsp black pepper
1 C. olive oil
1 egg yolk
1 tsp white pepper
1 tsp fresh thyme

1. Mix all ingredients for marinade, and set aside.
2. Place sliced fennel in a shallow dish and pour the citrus marinade over the top, allowing them to marinate for 20 minutes, or up to 1 hour.
3. Place the fennel slices on the grill and allow them to cook over direct heat until slightly tender, 5-6 minutes. Remove, cool and do medium dice.
4. Place the fennel into a small mixing bowl, season with salt, pepper, chopped parsley and extra virgin olive oil.
5. Rub the surface of the tomatoes with salt, pepper and olive oil. Place on the grill over direct heat, and cook on all sides until the skins are slightly charred and the flesh begins to soften.
6. Remove from the heat, peel and discard the skins. Place the flesh into a small bowl, and smash gently with the back side of a fork.
7. Slowly whisk in the vinegar, chopped shallots, basil and olive oil.
8. Fold in the shell beans, season with salt, white pepper and set aside.
9. Prepare the scallops by removing the small tendon
10. Season the scallops with salt and pepper, and grill over direct heat for 3 minutes per side. Baste with the remaining citrus marinade.
11. Remove from the grill and keep warm.

Aioli:
1. Rub each lemon with pepper, salt, and olive oil, and grill over high heat, turning frequently until the lemons have charred slightly, the oils begin to release and they are slightly soft. Cool for 5-6 minutes.
2. Halve each lemon and juice through a fine holed strainer.
3. Whisk in the egg yolk and slowly emulsify in the olive oil, using a slow steady stream to create a smooth aioli.
4. Season with salt, white pepper, and fresh chopped thyme. Set aside.

Assembly:
1. Place a spoonful of the sautéed shell beans in the center of the warm entree plate.
2. Place a scallop on either side of the beans and garnish with the marinated grilled fennel.
3. Finish with a drizzle of lemon aioli, micro cress and sea salt.

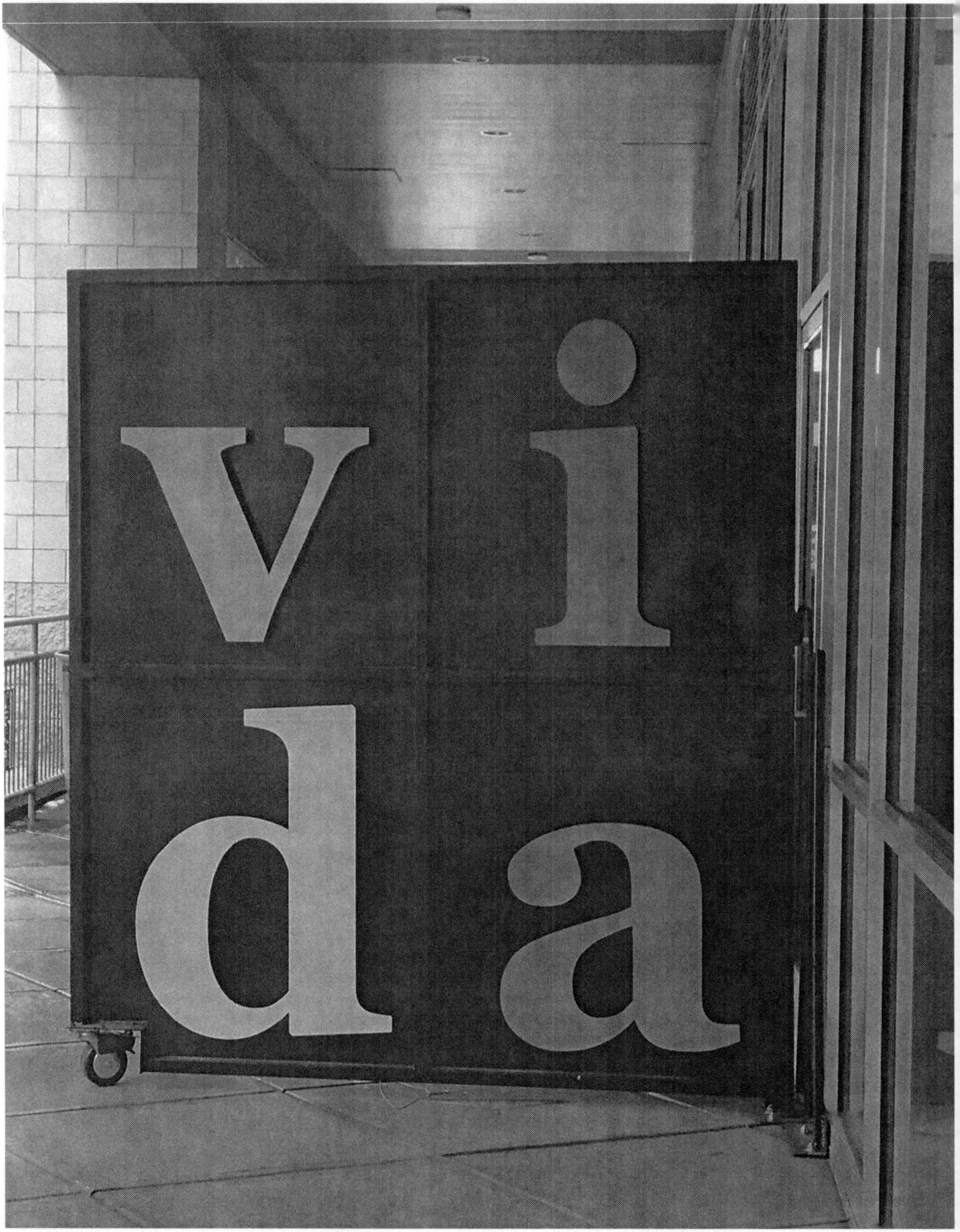
vi
da

Chipotle Braised Short Ribs

Vida Mexican Kitchen y Cantina serves traditional, old-world-style Mexican cuisine presented with refreshing style, alongside handcrafted cocktails, an extensive list of tequilas and our signature Skinny Margaritas. Located at uptown Charlotte's most vibrant corner – the intersection of Trade and College Streets – Vida's inviting atmosphere, specialty Mexican fare, hospitality and impeccable service offers a distinctive experience for its guests. Vida is evolved Mexican cuisine.

2 lb. beef short ribs

Spice rub:
⅛ C. kosher salt
2 Tbsp black pepper
1 Tbsp garlic powder
1 Tbsp onion powder
2 tsp cumin
2 tsp coriander

Braising liquid:
2 qt. beef broth
(1) 4-oz. can pureed chipotle peppers
2 C. tomato juice
5 cloves garlic, crushed
1 yellow onion, chopped
1 poblano pepper
½ bunch cilantro, chopped

Combine all ingredients and rub generously over short ribs, and allow to penetrate overnight in the refrigerator.

Braising liquid:
1. Combine all the braising ingredients, and bring to a boil. Allow to sit overnight.
2. Grill short ribs until browned.
3. Transfer to a braise pan, cover with hot liquid (add water/broth to cover if necessary.)
4. Remove short ribs, drain fat, return to stove.
5. Reduce by half, or until liquid is thickened (use as sauce.)

Serve with mashed potatoes and your favorite vegetable.

Signature Tastes of CHARLOTTE

VIDA MEXICAN KITCHEN Y CANTINA
EXECUTIVE CHEF RYAN BENTLEY - 210 EAST TRADE STREET

"Heaven sends us good meat, but the Devil sends cooks…"
David Garrick

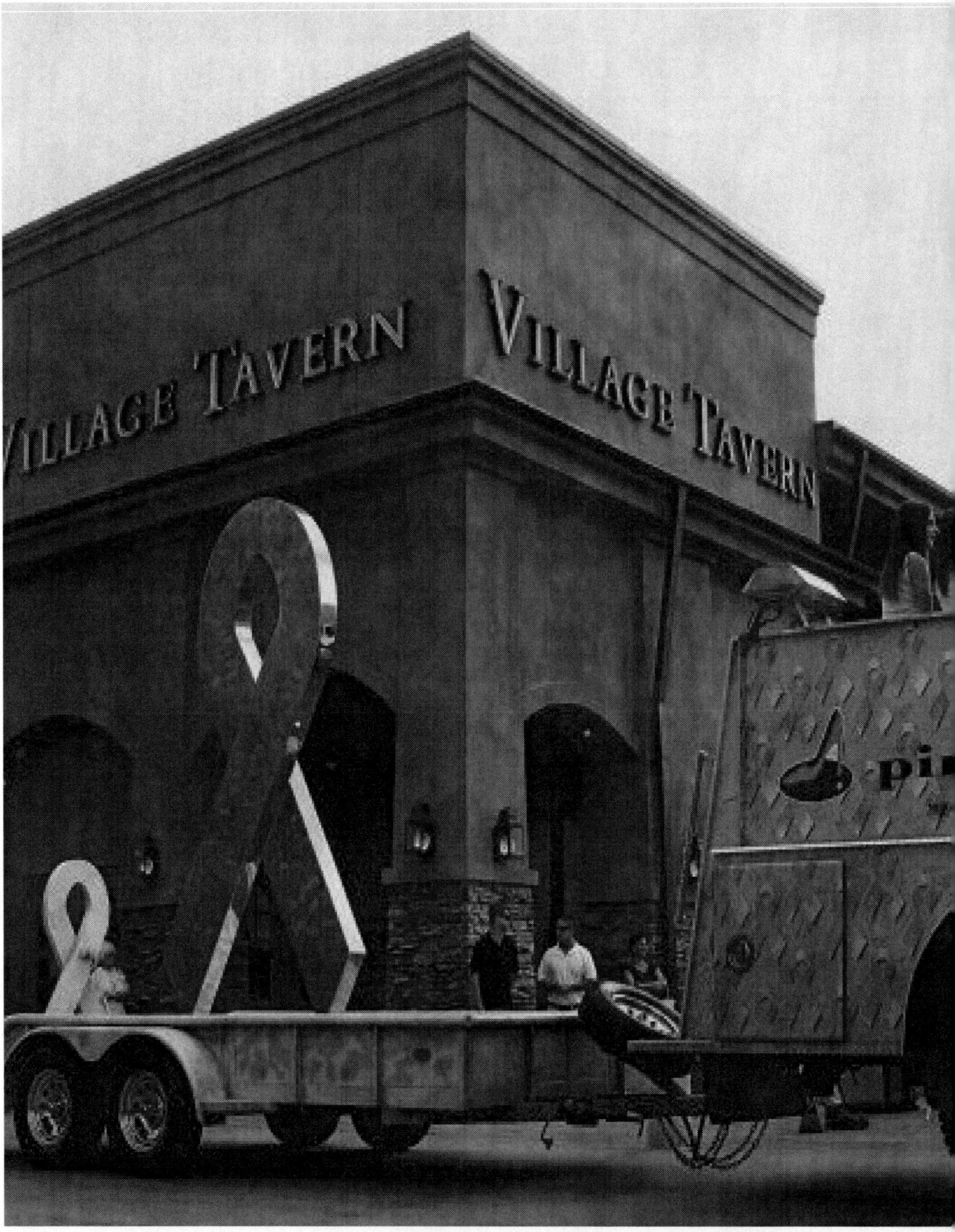
Village Tavern
Village Tavern

Grouper Hemingway

Signature Tastes of CHARLOTTE

Village Tavern was built on the tradition of the Old World tavern, viewed as the heart of the community and a place for information, entertainment and nourishment. Bringing people together, Village Tavern celebrates classic American food. At the Charlotte, NC Village Tavern, we have added a fresh spin to traditional foods as well as our classics. You'll find a wide variety of options all distinctly flavored using our own proprietary recipes, prepared with wood-fired ovens & grills.

2 Tbsp light olive oil
7 oz. grouper filet
1 tsp kosher salt
½ tsp ground black pepper

1 C. white wine
1 Tbsp capers
¼ tomatoes, diced ½"

1 stick unsalted butter, in 1 inch cubes
½ lemon
8 oz. angel pasta, cooked just before serving

1 Tbsp Parmesan, shredded
¼ tsp fresh parsley, chopped

1. Pre-heat sauté pan with oil.

2. Season fish with kosher salt and ground pepper. Carefully place filet in the sauté pan.

3. Sear for 1 minute. Flip the fish and continue to cook until medium-well.

4. Remove fish from a pan and keep warm. Add white wine, capers, and tomatoes.

5. Reduce by half. Add butter and squeeze half to sauté pan, and mix until melted.

6. Place pre-cooked angel hair pasta in the center of a serving bowl.

7. Place seared fish on top of pasta.

8. Pour sauce over the fish and pasta.

9. Garnish with Parmesan and parsley.

Village Tavern
4201 Congress Street

"As I ate the oysters with their strong taste of the sea and their faint metallic taste that the cold white wine washed away, leaving only the sea taste and the succulent texture, and as I drank their cold liquid from each shell and washed it down with the crisp taste of the wine, I lost the empty feeling and began to be happy, and to make plans."
Ernest Hemingway

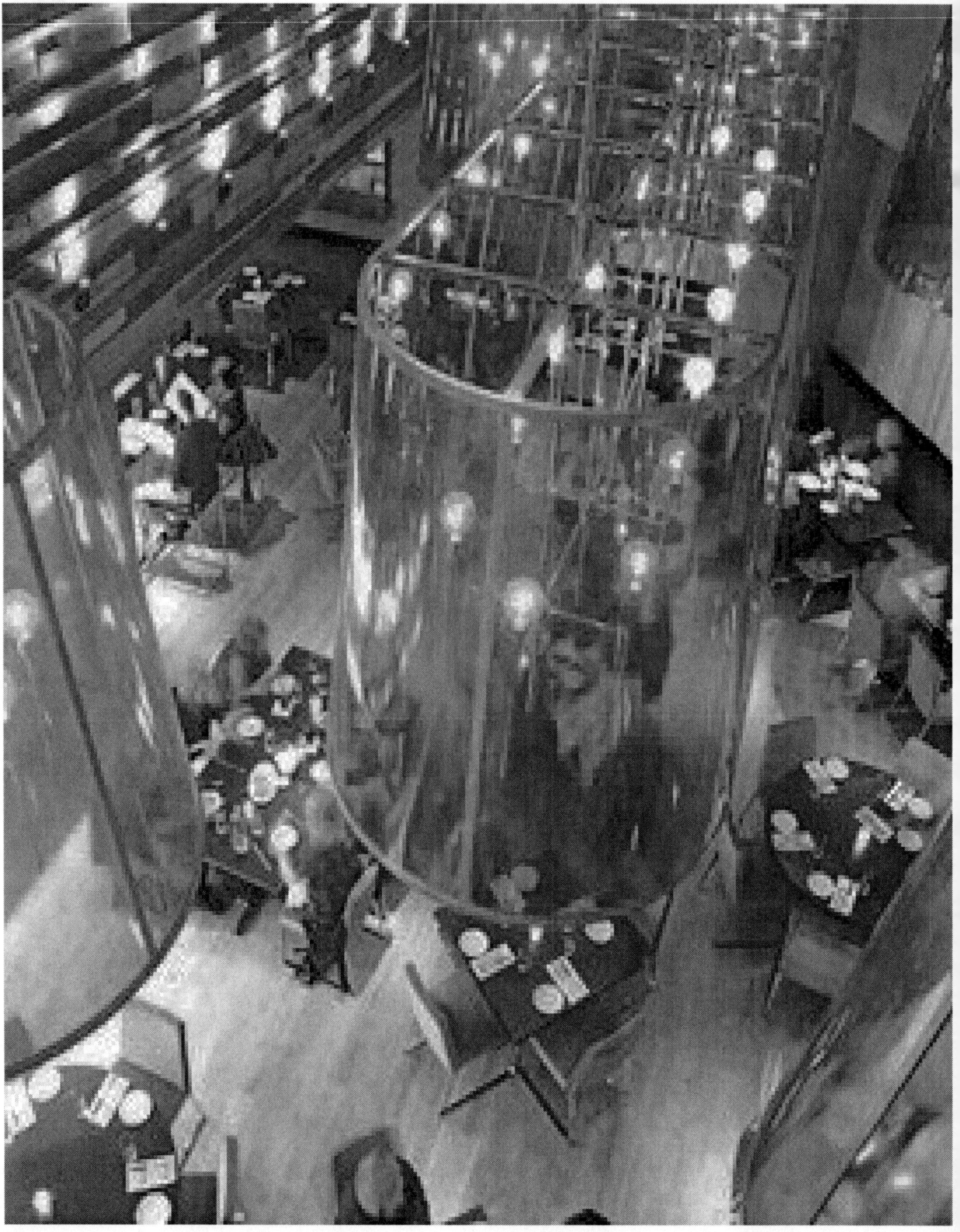

Bolognese with Papperdelle and Goat Cheese Crema

Part of Kevin and Stacey Jennings' Urban Restaurant Group, based out of Raleigh, Vivace establishes their concept restaurant here in Charlotte, offering contemporary Italian cuisine. Putting a modern slant on the traditional Italian Trattoria, Vivace offers a unique Bolognese sauce recipe. Bolognese is an Italian meat-based sauce for pasta which originates in Bologna, a city in Northern Italy. A thick, full-bodied meat sauce that's a staple of northern Italy's Bologna.

Bolognese:
- 8 oz. ground beef
- 8 oz. ground veal
- 8 oz. ground, boneless short ribs
- 1 medium Spanish onion, minced
- 2 carrots, minced
- 1 stalk celery, minced
- 2 cloves garlic, minced
- ¼ tomato paste
- 28 oz. can pureed plum tomatoes
- ½ C. dry white wine
- ½ C. whole milk
- ¼ C. fresh basil, torn
- Vegetable oil, as needed

Pasta Dough:
- 2 C. flour
- 6 egg yolks
- 1 whole egg
- 1½ tsp extra virgin olive oil
- 1 Tbsp milk

Goat Cheese Crema:
- 1 C. heavy cream
- 5 oz. chevre style goat cheese
- salt and pepper to taste

1. Heat a Dutch oven over medium heat.
2. Add a thin layer of oil to the pan, then add the ground beef, short ribs, and veal.
3. Cook until brown, then remove from the pot.
4. Add the vegetables to the pot with a little oil and cook until translucent. Add the tomato paste, and cook for 3-5 minutes.
5. Deglaze the pan with the wine, and reduce by half.
6. Add the milk, and reduce by a third.
7. Add the meat and tomatoes to the vegetables, and simmer for about 1½ hours.
8. Season with salt, pepper, and basil.
9. Toss cooked pasta in the sauce, adjust seasoning to taste.
10. To serve, place pasta and sauce in a bowl and top with the goat cheese creme.

Pasta Dough
1. Place the flour in a standing mixer, and add the we ingredients.
2. Mix on low speed with a dough hook until combined.
3. Turn up speed to 2 and knead for 5 minutes.
4. Remove the dough, cover with plastic wrap, and let rest 30 minutes before using.
5. Roll dough on a lightly floured surface into 12" sheets.
6. Cut sheets into ½" wide strips.
7. Cook in boiling salted water for 3 minutes.

Goat Cheese Crema
1. In a small saucepan, bring the cream to a simmer and add the goat cheese.
2. Cook on low heat until combined.
3. Season to taste and cool..

"A tavola non si invecchia (You don't age while seated for a meal.)"
Famous Italian phrase

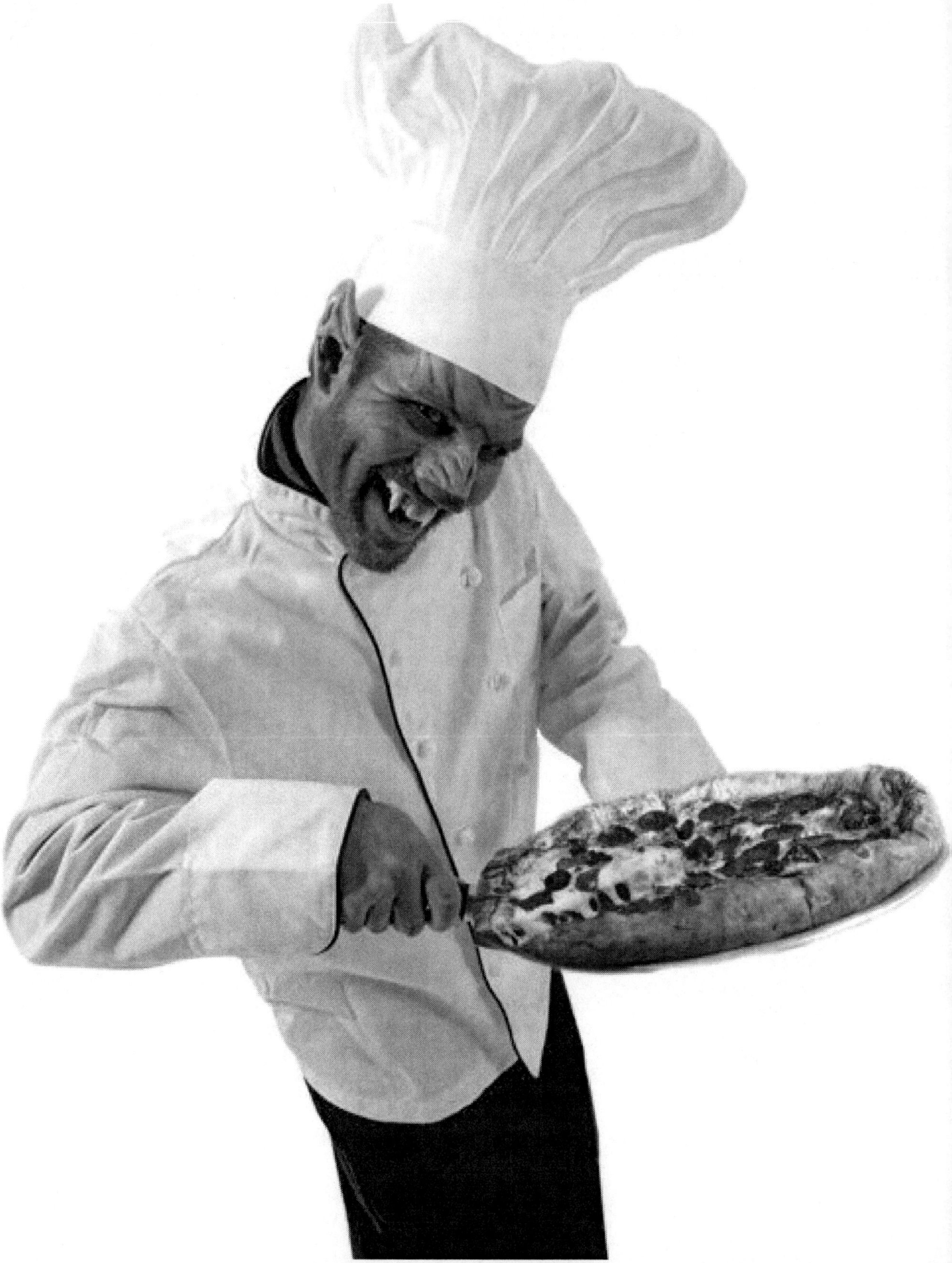

S'MORES PIZZA

The invention of the graham cracker is credited to the Reverend Sylvester Graham, an advocate of healthy living. Beleiving that physical lust was the cause of many ailments such as pulmonary consumption, spinal diseases , etc.- Graham looked for ways to suppress these carnal urges. Graham advocated a strict vegetarian diet rich in fiber as a way of fighting those desires, and as a result "Graham bread", fashioned from the coarsely ground wheat flour, was born. Today's graham crackers are made with bleached white flour; I suspect Mr. Graham is turning over in his grave today

1 8-inch uncooked pizza dough
1 oz. butter, melted
2-3 Tbsp cinnamon sugar
¼ brown sugar/graham cracker mixture (recipe below)
1 Tbsp chocolate chips
½ C. miniature marshmallows

Brown sugar/graham cracker mixture:
¼ C. granulated sugar
¼ light brown sugar
1 C. graham cracker crumbs
1 C. melted butter
(Plain Beyond Butter Substitute)

Graham Cracker Mixture:
1. Combine dry ingredients of brown sugar/graham cracker mixture in a bowl.
2. Pour in half of the butter and mix thoroughly. Pour in the remaining butter, and mix until thorough combined.
3. Set aside. (This makes enough for 7 pizzas)

Pizza:
1. Pour the melted butter or butter substitute on the dough. Spread evenly over the entire surface of the pizza with a gloved hand.
2. Sprinkle the entire surface with a thin layer of the cinnamon sugar.
3. Put ¼ C. of the brown sugar, graham cracker mixture in the center of the pizza, and spread evenly, leaving ½" for the crust.
4. Place pizza in pizza oven, or oven preheated to 450°F.
5. Watch carefully to make sure it doesn't burn.
6. Spray a 12" pan with cooking spray, and use as a cut tray. Cut the pizza into 6 slices.
7. Place marshmallows and chocolate chips on the pizza.
8. Put in the oven again just to melt the marshmallows and chocolate chips, and serve.

Signature Tastes of CHARLOTTE

LOCATIONS IN COTSWOLD, QUAIL CORNERS, PROVIDENCE ROAD, AND MYERS PARK

WOLFMAN PIZZA

"Stressed spelled backwards is desserts. Coincidence? I think not! "
Author Unknown

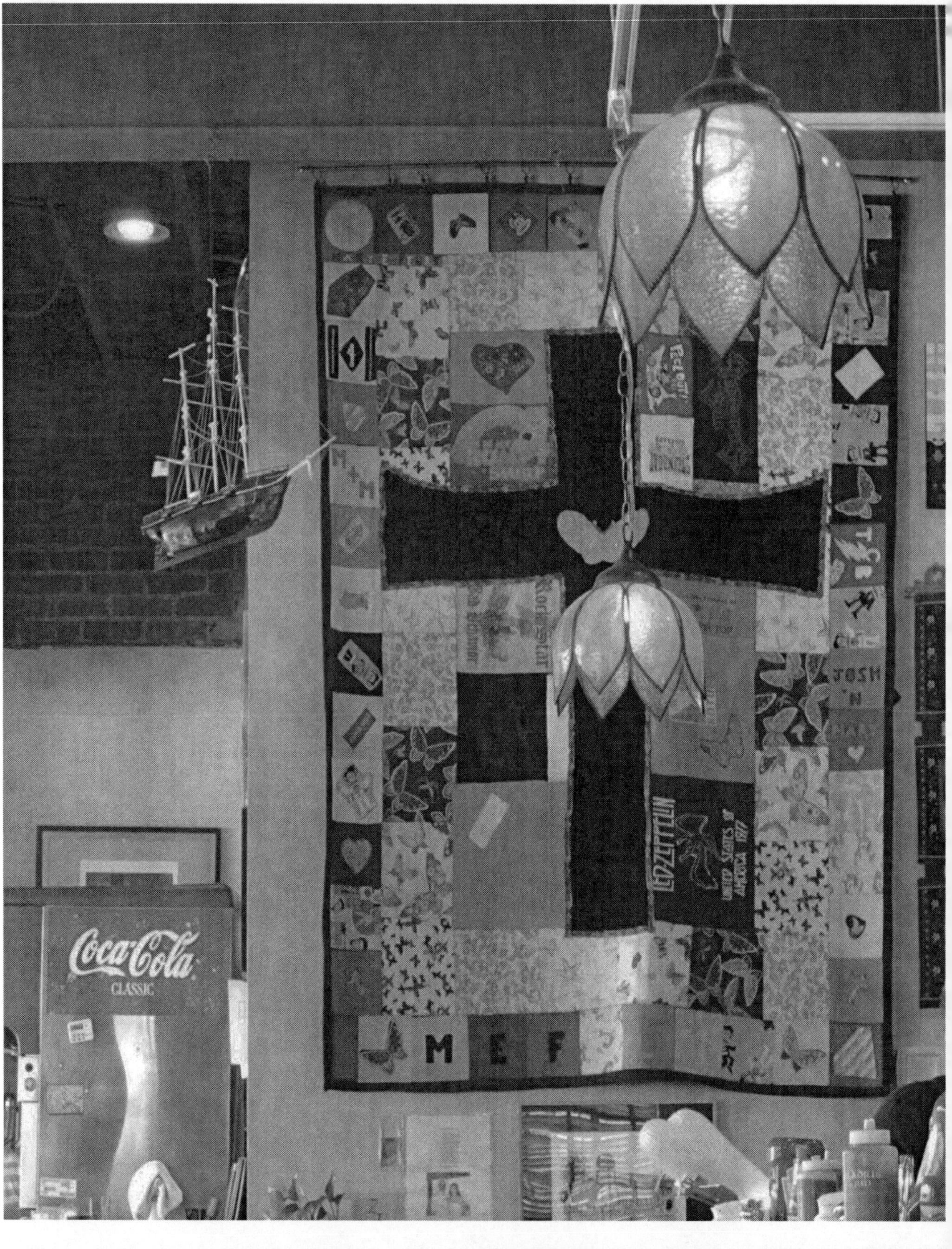
Coca-Cola
CLASSIC
M E F

Zucchini Cakes

We are a full service coffee joint with a rock star barista cranking out the goods bright and early. Also, tea drinkers are represented properly through Tea Rex, of Charlotte. There are also some danged awesome fresh baked goodies that words alone struggle to describe. Mmmmmmming and eye rolling will suffice. One of the greatest assets we will utilize is our local and regional farmers. This industry is booming and we want to bring ya'll their healthy produce and meats at a fair price. Zada Jane's is named after Roger's grandmothers. So, respect is not demanded...it is simply expected.

3 zucchini, shredded *3 yellow, shredded* *4 green onions, fine diced* *¾ C. Parmigianino Reggiano, shredded* *¾ C. Panko bread crumbs* *2 Tbsp semolina flour* *2 Tbsp chervil, chopped* *½ tsp fresh rosemary, minced* *1 clove roasted garlic, minced* *Juice of 1 lemon* *Pinch of nutmeg* *Splash of Tabasco* *3 eggs beaten* *Citrus Yogurt:* *2 C. Greek yogurt* *Juice and zest of 1 lemon and 1 lime* *¼ tsp sugar* *Tiny pinch of nutmeg* *Salt and White pepper to taste*	1. Grate whole zucchini and squash and mince the onion – 2. Mix and squeeze out as much of the liquid as possible – the more liquid removed the better. 3. Mince the parsley, rosemary and garlic and beat with the eggs. 4. Add the remaining ingredients and mix well. If mix is still too wet, add a bit more bread crumbs. 5. Form into cakes and pan sear in olive oil. 6. If you like you can bread the cakes lightly again in bread crumbs just before cooking for a crispy exterior. Serve with: Citrus Yogurt

Signature Tastes of CHARLOTTE

ZADA JANE'S CORNER CAFE
EXECUTIVE CHEF EDMUND BULLOCK - 1601 CENTRAL AVENUE

"It's all good, y'all"
The warm and fuzzy folks at Zada Jane's

ZEBRA
restaurant

Lobster Waldorf

Zebra Restaurant and Fine Catering boasts fine dining in the style of the French Laundry. Zebra offers a world class dining experience similar to the restaurants of New York, San Francisco and London. From our wine list of nine hundred bottles, to our four diamond award winning service staff, to our a la carte and nightly gastronomique grand tasting menu, Zebra consistently delivers the best Charlotte has to offer. Certified Executive Chef and owner Jim Alexander invites you to join us at Zebra to enjoy that special occasion or event, or, to just celebrate the good life.

1 live lobster (approximately 1½ lbs)
Salted water to boil lobster
¼ C. creme fraiche or sour cream
2 Tbsp mayonnaise
2 tsp star anise syrup or Sambuco
4 dried apricots, diced
1 stalk celery, diced
2 Tbsp dried cherries
8-12 pecan halves, toasted
1 large, ripe pear

1. Bring water to a boil, cook lobster for approximately 6 minutes.

2. Cool lobster in ice bath, remove meat, dice, and reserve.

3. Place lobster meat in medium bowl, and combine ingredients, accept for lobster claws, toasted pecans and pears.

4. Taste, and adjust seasoning with fresh squeeze of lemon, salt and pepper.

Assembly:
1. Using a mandolin, or other very sharp slicing tool, cut pear into paper thin slices.

2. Shingle approximately 6 slices for each portion.

3. Lay slices on work surface, top with lobster salad, roll up and serve cold with toasted pecan halves and lobster claw garnish.

Signature Tastes of CHARLOTTE

Zebra Restaurant and Fine Catering
Owner/Chef Jim Alexander - 4521 Sharon Road

So much to say about Zebra, and how it embodies Jim Alexander's vision and passion. Zebra's well deserved awards are plenty, and only rivaled by the chef's achievements. Then, I highly recommend taking the time to be entertained and enlightened by Zebra's very own Max Gilland, and his extensive knowledge about all things wine

The

End

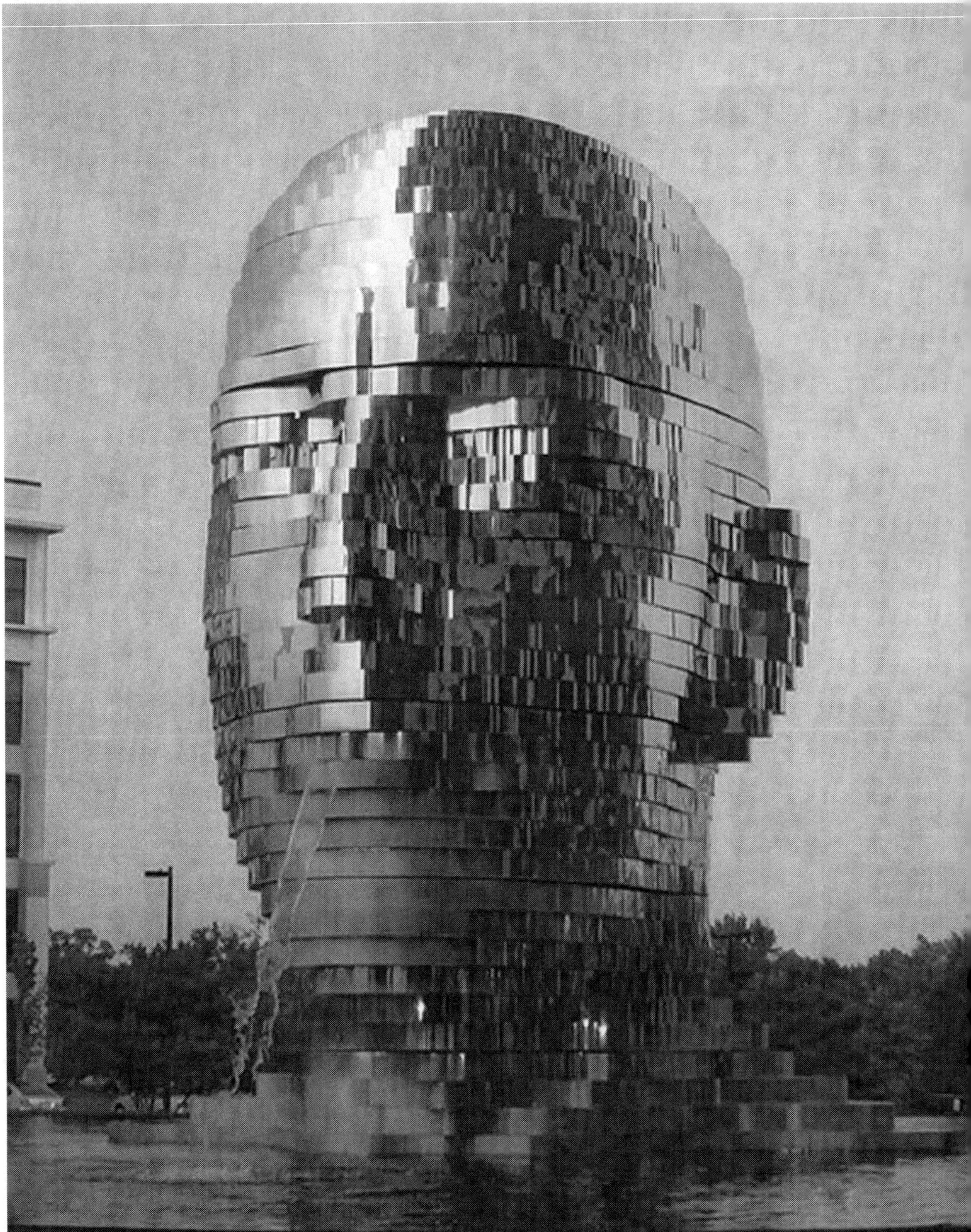

Index o' Recipes

"The Scarlett Letter" Red Velvet Cakes, 83
4th Ward Stroganoff, 21
Alaska Salmon with Potatoes, Dill, and Baby Fennel, 141
Apple Salad, 33
Asparagus Leek Soup, 23
Aunt Evert's Sweet Potato Pie, 169
Bacon Wrapped Scallops with Blueberry Chili Sauce, 165
Baked Brie, 161
Baked Crab Cakes with Mustard Mayonnaise Sauce, 147
Ballotine of Duck with Roasted Apples & Pecans, 55
BBQ Duck Spring Roll, 43
Bolognese with Papperdelle and Goat Cheese Crema, 199
Bratwurst Panini, 153
Bridget's Chicken-less Chicken Salad, 75
California Shrimp Tacos, 133
Canine Carob Chip Mutt-fins, 49
Caramel Chocolate Glazed Praline Tart, 71
Char Bar No. 7 Sauce and Signature Sandwiches, 65
Cherry Sticky Toffee Pudding, 191
Chicken and Arugula, 59
Chicken Salad, 109
Chicken with Savory Blueberry Sauce, 31
Chilled Spicy Cantaloupe and Minted Honeydew Melon Soup, 93
Chipotle Braised Short Ribs, 195
Chocolate Chip Cheesecake, 105
Chocolate Cream Cake with Vanilla Bean Sauce, 67
Coastal Shrimp & Goat Cheese Grits, 179
Collard Greens, 89
Crab Cakes, 119
Crab Salpicon (Tacos), 51
Creole BBQ Shrimp, 47
Customshop Mussels, Chorizo, Shishitos & Beer, 87
Diver Scallops Crudo with Mango Salsa & Arugula, 103
El Paso Me a Turkey Burger, 151
Explosion Pie, 63
Fab's Pate, 125
Firebirds Pecan Crusted Trout, 95
Fran's House Roast Chicken, 101
Frenchie, 29
Fresh Strawberry Cake, 79
Fudge, 177
Grilled Marinated Skirt Steak, 27
Grouper Hemingway, 197
Honey Moon Cranberry Vinaigrette, 171
Jalapeno Jam, 187
Kennedy's Shepherd's Pie, 115
Lamb Tagine, 41
Layered Banana Pineapple Dessert, 143
Lobster Waldorf, 205
Mac's Speed Shop Brisket, 127
Melon Lime Meringue Pie, 167
Moe's Original Bar-B-Que Watermelon Salad, 145
Mushroom Bolognese, 53
Old Fashioned Pound Cake, 123
Oysters Rockefeller, 37
Pan Roasted Grouper with Parley Horseradish Mojo, 73
Pan Seared Scallops with Shallot Jam & Roasted Tomato Vinaigrette, 91
Pecan Crusted Carolina Trout, 77
Pepper Crusted Tenderloin with Madeira Demi-Glaze, 61
Pimento Cheese, 117
Polenta with Lamb and Pork Ragu, 189
Pollo Carciofi, 129
Pork Belly with Sage, Garlic, Apple Sauce & Port Wine Reduction, 121
Pot de Creme, 163
Prince Edward Island Mussels, 39
Ricotta Gnocchi Ratatouille, 185
Ricotta Gnocchi with Sausage and Fennel, 25
Robin Marshall's Thanksgiving Feast, 131
S'mores Pizza, 201
Scallops over Butternut Squash Risotto with Fennel & Bacon, 35
Sea Scallop with Shell Bean Salad, Fennel, and Aioli, 193
Sea Scallops with Sweet Corn Risotto, Proscuitto and Basil, 135
Seared Ahi Tuna on Ginger Lemongrass French Toast, 137
Seared Pork Belly with Blueberry Chipotle Glaze and Cucumber Salad, 173
Shrimp and Artichoke Crepes, 45
Simple Roasted Chicken with Mushroom Risotto, 149
Smoked Stuffed Jalapenos, 139
Soul Wings Asian Style, 181
Sour Cream Fudge, 99
Station 39's Carolina BBQ, 57
Stool Pigeons' Chili, 183
Summertime Brine Bone-In Pork Loin Chop, 157
Tacos al Carbon, 155
Tangy Melon with Shrimp, 113
Thai Cucumbers, 81
Thai Lemon Grass Sauce, 85
The Penquin's Pimento Cheese, 159
Tomato Basil Bisque, 175
Tuna Tartare Trio, 97
Vanilla Braised Short Ribs, 19
Walnut Wonder Cake, 111
Zucchini Cakes, 203

"I should have no objection to go over the same life from its beginning to the end: requesting only the advantage authors have, of correcting in a second edition the faults of the first."
Benjamin Franklin

Signature Tastes of CHARLOTTE

Steven W. Siler is a firefighter-cum-chef serving in Bellingham, Washington. Long marinated in the epicurean heritage of the Deep South, Steven has spent over 20 years (dear God has it been that long?!) in the much-vaulted restaurant industry from BOH to FOH to chef. In addition, he has served as an editor and contributing writer for several food publications. When not trying to shove food down his fellow firefighters' gullets, he enjoys sailing and sampling the finest of scotches and wines, and has an irrational love affair with opera. He swears one day he will relive the above picture on the Gulf Coast with a good Will.

The Signature Tastes of Charlotte is the one of the first of a series of culinary celebrations from Smoke Alarm Media, based in the Pacific Northwest. Smoke Alarm Media is named for another series of unfortunate culinary accidents at an unnamed fire department, also in the Pacific Northwest. One of the founders was an active firefighter. Having been trained as a chef, he found himself in the position of cooking frequently at the fire station. Alas, his culinary skills were somewhat lacking in using the broiler and smoke would soon fill the kitchen and station. The incidents became so frequent that the 911 dispatch would call the station and ask if "Chef Smoke Alarm" would kindly refrain from cooking on his shift. Thus Smoke Alarm Media was born.

Find us online, if ya please : WWW.SIGNATURETASTES.COM

facebook SIGNATURE TASTES OF CHARLOTTE

CPSIA information can be obtained at www.ICGtesting.com
Printed in the USA
BVOW041457250413

319103BV00011B/14/P